Dear Swift & his Writings —

Swift   Moriarty,

        Ed. Norman Jeffares.

CASEBOOK SERIES

GENERAL EDITOR: A. E. Dyson

PUBLISHED

Jane Austen: *Emma* DAVID LODGE
William Blake: *Songs of Innocence and Experience* MARGARET BOTTRALL
Charlotte Brontë: '*Jane Eyre*' and '*Villette*' MIRIAM ALLOTT
Emily Brontë: *Wuthering Heights* MIRIAM ALLOTT
Byron: '*Childe Harold's Pilgrimage*' and '*Don Juan*' JOHN JUMP
Chaucer: *The Canterbury Tales* J. J. ANDERSON
Coleridge: '*The Ancient Mariner*' and *Other Poems* ALUN R. JONES AND
    WILLIAM TYDEMAN
Conrad: *The Secret Agent* IAN WATT
Dickens: *Bleak House* A. E. DYSON
Donne: *Songs and Sonets* JULIAN LOVELOCK
George Eliot: *Middlemarch* PATRICK SWINDEN
T. S. Eliot: *Four Quartets* BERNARD BERGONZI
T. S. Eliot: *The Waste Land* C. B. COX AND ARNOLD P. HINCHLIFFE
Henry Fielding: *Tom Jones* NEIL COMPTON
E. M. Forster: *A Passage to India* MALCOLM BRADBURY
Jonson: *Volpone* JONAS A. BARISH
James Joyce: '*Dubliners*' and '*A Portrait of the Artist as a Young Man*'
    MORRIS BEJA
John Keats: *Odes* G. S. FRASER
D. H. Lawrence: *Sons and Lovers* GĀMINI SALGĀDO
D. H. Lawrence: '*The Rainbow*' and '*Women in Love*' COLIN CLARKE
Marlowe: *Doctor Faustus* JOHN JUMP
Milton: *Paradise Lost* A. E. DYSON AND JULIAN LOVELOCK
John Osborne: *Look Back in Anger* J. RUSSELL TAYLOR
Pope: *The Rape of the Lock* JOHN DIXON HUNT
Shakespeare: *Antony and Cleopatra* JOHN RUSSELL BROWN
Shakespeare: *Hamlet* JOHN JUMP
Shakespeare: *Henry IV Parts I and II* G. K. HUNTER
Shakespeare: *Henry V* MICHAEL QUINN
Shakespeare: *Julius Caesar* PETER URE
Shakespeare: *King Lear* FRANK KERMODE
Shakespeare: *Macbeth* JOHN WAIN
Shakespeare: *Measure for Measure* C. K. STEAD
Shakespeare: *The Merchant of Venice* JOHN WILDERS
Shakespeare: *Othello* JOHN WAIN
Shakespeare: *Richard II* NICHOLAS BROOKE
Shakespeare: *The Tempest* D. J. PALMER
Shakespeare: *Twelfth Night* D. J. PALMER
Shakespeare: *The Winter's Tale* KENNETH MUIR
Swift: *Gulliver's Travels* RICHARD GRAVIL
Tennyson: *In Memoriam* JOHN DIXON HUNT
Virginia Woolf: *To the Lighthouse* MORRIS BEJA
Wordsworth: *Lyrical Ballads* ALUN R. JONES AND WILLIAM TYDEMAN
Wordsworth: *The Prelude* W. J. HARVEY AND RICHARD GRAVIL
Yeats: *Last Poems* JON STALLWORTHY

TITLES IN PREPARATION INCLUDE

Jane Austen: *'Sense and Sensibility'*, *'Pride and Prejudice'*, and *'Mansfield Park'*
  BRIAN SOUTHAM
Browning: *'Men and Women' and Other Poems* J. R. WATSON
Bunyan: *Pilgrim's Progress* ROGER SHARROCK
Hardy: *The Tragic Novels* RONALD DRAPER
Hopkins: *'The Wreck of the Deutschland' and Other Poems* MARGARET
  BOTTRALL
The Metaphysical Poets G. HAMMOND
Milton: *'Comus' and 'Samson Agonistes'* JULIAN LOVELOCK
Webster: *'The White Devil' and 'The Duchess of Malfi'*
  R. V. HOLDSWORTH

Swift

Gulliver's Travels

A CASEBOOK

EDITED BY

RICHARD GRAVIL

MACMILLAN

First published 1974 by
THE MACMILLAN PRESS LTD
London and Basingstoke
Associated companies in New York Dublin
Melbourne Johannesburg and Madras

SBN 333 14521 6 (hard cover)
      333 14522 4 (paper cover)

Printed in Great Britain by
THE ANCHOR PRESS LTD
Tiptree, Essex

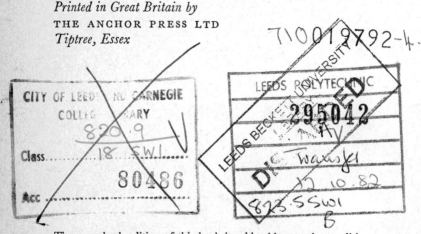

CONTENTS

ACKNOWLEDGEMENTS

The editor thanks Miss Etsuko Nishiyama, Professor Osamu Takayama, and the British Council Home Librarian, for supplying copies of many Swift studies and making this compilation possible. The editor and publishers wish to thank the following, who have kindly given permission for the use of copyright material: Ronald S. Crane, 'The Rationale of the Fourth Voyage' from *Gulliver's Travels* ed. by R. A. Greenberg published by W. W. Norton, reprinted by permission of Mrs Julia Crane; Herbert Davis, 'Moral Satire' from *Jonathan Swift: Essays on His Satire and Other Studies* by permission of Mrs Davis; A. E. Dyson, 'Swift: The Metamorphosis of Irony' from *The Crazy Fabric*; C. H. Firth, 'The Political Significance of Gulliver's Travels' from *Proceedings of the British Academy*, IX (1919–20); M. M. Kelsall, '*Iterum* Houyhnhnm: Swift's Sextumvirate and the Horses' from *Essays in Criticism*, XIX, no. 1 (1969); Philip Pinkus, 'Sin and Satire in Swift' from *Bucknell Review*, XIII (1965); C. J. Rawson, 'Order and Cruelty: A Reading of Swift (with some Comments on Pope and Johnson)' from *Essays in Criticism*, vol. XX (1970); John F. Ross, 'The Final Comedy of Lemuel Gulliver' from *Studies in the Comic*, University of California Press Publications in English, vol. 8:2 (1941), originally published by the University of California Press, reprinted by permission of The Regents of the University of California; T. O. Wedel, 'On the Philosophical Background of Gulliver's Travels' from *Studies in Philology*, XXIII (1926) by permission of The University of North Carolina Press; Kathleen Williams, 'Gulliver's Voyage to the Houyhnhnm's from *English Literary History*, vol. 18 (1951) pp. 275–86, © The Johns Hopkins University Press; Kathleen Williams, 'Gulliver in Laputa' from *Jonathan Swift in the Age of Compromise* by permission of The University Press of Kansas; W. E. Yeomans, 'The Houyhnhnm as Menippean Horse' from *College English*, © March 1966 by the National Council of Teachers of English, reprinted by permission of the publisher and the author.

GENERAL EDITOR'S PREFACE

Each of this series of Casebooks concerns either one well-known and influential work of literature or two or three closely linked works. The main section consists of critical readings, mostly modern, brought together from journals and books. A selection of reviews and comments by the author's contemporaries is also included, and sometimes comments from the author himself. The Editor's Introduction charts the reputation of the work from its first appearance until the present time.

The critical forum is a place of vigorous conflict and disagreement, but there is nothing in this to cause dismay. What is attested is the complexity of human experience and the richness of literature, not any chaos or relativity of taste. A critic is better seen, no doubt, as an explorer than as an 'authority', but explorers ought to be, and usually are, well equipped. The effect of good criticism is to convince us of what C. S. Lewis called 'the enormous extension of our being which we owe to authors'. A Casebook will be justified only if it helps to promote the same end.

A single volume can represent no more than a small selection of critical opinions. Some critics have been excluded for reasons of space, and it is hoped that readers will follow up the further suggestions in the Select Bibliography. Other contributions have been severed from their original context, to which some readers may wish to return. Indeed, if they take a hint from the critics represented here, they certainly will.

A. E. Dyson

INTRODUCTION

In August 1726, Pope reported, Benjamin Motte received the manuscript of *Gulliver's Travels* 'he knew not from whence, nor from whom, dropped at his house in the dark, from a hackney coach'. On 28 October he proved himself to be a printer 'brave enough to venture his ears', as Swift had hoped, by bringing out the first edition in two octavo volumes. Within weeks the plaudits of a delighted London were reaching Swift, now back in Ireland, by similarly devious and hilarious means. In such high spirits did Swift, this 'monster gibbering shrieks and gnashing imprecations against mankind – tearing down all shreds of modesty, past all sense of manliness and shame; filthy in word, filthy in thought, furious, raging, obscene' (as Thackeray was to caution his Victorian audience) launch a work which succeeded in hugely diverting both enemies and friends. Such success may, of course, be merely a sign of the moral pollution of the times: it may be that Pope and Gay and Dr Arbuthnot were merely corrupted by too long an acquaintance with the arch-blasphemer and the high misanthropist. Arbuthnot is surely too impressionable: 'I will make over all my profits to you, for the property of *Gulliver's Travels*, which I believe, will have as great a run as John Bunyan. Gulliver is a happy man that at his age can write such a merry work.' Praise from one's inseparable friends is a form of self-flattery, but as Swift learned from Pope and Gay – who, with Arbuthnot and others, had been in on the secret – not merely his friends but 'the whole town, men, women, and children, are quite full of it' and 'all agree in liking it extremely'. Of greater note is Gay's report that 'The Duchess Dowager of Marlborough is in raptures at it; she says she can dream of noth-

ing else since she read it; she declares, that she hath now found
out, that her whole life hath been lost in caressing the worst part
of mankind, and treating the best as her foes' and though the
author 'had been the worst enemy she ever had, she would give
up all her present acquaintance for his friendship'. Nor was
this a passing whim of Sarah Churchill (or just Gay's gift for
reported speech), for ten years later she is writing as much in her
Memoirs.

What spark could bridge the enmity of half an era? It is, I
suspect, the savage iconoclasm of Swift that appeals so directly
to his oldest enemy – and appeals to Whigs of every age. Sarah,
above all people, could relish Swift the boat-rocker, the cant-
detector. For though a sober assessment of Dr Swift finds him
intolerant and austerely Tory, it is far from obvious that strict
sobriety is the proper approach to the most agile satirist in an age
of satire. Crusty and prejudiced though Swift was, he was the
vessel of an animus which brought him into brilliant and illumin-
ating conflict with the eighteenth-century clerical mind, the
schools of the logicians, the projectors of the Royal Society, the
Whig Establishment, and indeed the whole current of anthropo-
centric pride which connects Lockean Whiggery, Deism and the
late Victorians. Nor can it have appeared to any but the most
jaundiced reader that in the eye of a Brobdingnagian monarch
a little odious Tory was more likely to 'scape whipping than a
little verminous Whig. It is the democratic inclusiveness of Swift's
ironic gaze, not Motte's suppression of the more overt political
barbs, that saved the printer's 'ears'. While Swift often allied
himself with intolerant reaction, his genius is rather a radical
scepticism, brought to bear, without favouritism, on religious
trivia as on the delusions of astrology, on Tory pomp as much as
Whiggish theories, on the pretensions of wealth and the inequities
of class no less than the facile optimisms of science and reform.
Swift combined a few vigorous and respectable principles with
a restless and corrosive scepticism. Such a formula is a question-
mark in any age : and readers of Swift, at any age in any age, have
found in him the questions to set against their own.

The book Motte published in 1726 was not entirely as Swift

had intended. He complained to Pope of passages introduced, suppressed or amended, and spurred by Charles Ford (possibly the man in the hackney-coach) the printer produced a somewhat corrected version when the fourth octavo edition came out in 1727. Even this edition retained most of the major 'emendations' made by Motte the previous year, and it was not until Faulkner's Dublin edition of 1735 that a published text approximated to the manuscript. By a curious injustice of scholarship Motte's version prevailed as the popular one until 1926 when Sir Harold Williams edited a *Gulliver* based on Faulkner's text. An eminent Swiftian, A. E. Case, made the last important attempt to prove the legitimacy of a text based on Motte,[1] but Williams refuted Case point by point in his 1950 Sandars Lectures on Bibliography (*The Text of Gulliver's Travels*, Cambridge, 1952) and the standard edition by Herbert Davis in 1941 is the monument to Sir Harold's advocacy. Even Faulkner's nerve failed in some instances, but this apart, Williams argued, the Faulkner edition 'restored the "sting" to most of the passages which, as altered by Motte, formed the chief ground of Swift's complaints'.

What the later legend of Swift the misanthropic recluse kept most fully hidden was that *Gulliver's Travels* is the product of a mind and personality deeply and practically concerned with political matters. Its author was not the peevish and forgotten man of legend but a famous man of letters, with many close and celebrated friends, now in his late fifties and just reaching his best campaigning stride. It is now generally agreed that the *Travels* were written mainly between 1721 and 1725. His first great Irish pamphlet, the *Proposal for the Universal Use of Irish Manufacture*, was written in 1720. *The Drapier's Letters*, including the fourth climactic instalment *A Letter to the Whole People of Ireland*, unified the opposition to Walpole's administration in 1724, and £300 was now offered by the Irish Privy Council for the identity of this reluctant champion of Irish patriotism. As the decade ended he was producing *A Short View of the State of Ireland* (1728) and *A Modest Proposal* (1729). Swift's impact on public affairs extends over thirty years, but it was never more immediate, more exuberant, or more passionate, than in the years which produced *Gulliver's Travels*.

With so great and controversial a character (real or legendary) to contend with, neither his own nor the following century produced much in the way of genuine criticism of the *Travels*. As Kathleen Williams' *Swift: the Critical Heritage* (1970) shows, Lord Orrery, Patrick Delaney and Deane Swift are largely – not exclusively – concerned to vindicate their conceptions of Swift's character. Only in incidental comments by Voltaire and Fielding, and in Desfontaines' introduction to his 1727 translation, is Swift treated as a comic writer in a literary tradition. But for a slighting reference to 'big men and little men' Dr Johnson is silent. Without Scott's genuine and thorough appreciation of Swift's talents, even when 'unworthily employed', and Hazlitt's spirited empathy, criticism in the nineteenth century would present a simple crescendo of execration. By the middle of the century Lord Macaulay's deprecation of a mind so 'richly stored with images from the dunghill and the lazar house' is representative. Between Orrery's *Remarks* (1752) and Thackeray's 1851 lectures there are but a few, unavailing, attempts to turn aside the lash from Swift the atheist, the calumniator of mankind, the embittered misanthrope hurling his obscenities at church, state and the human form divine. 'Great and Giant as this Dean is,' and not only Thackeray admitted this much, 'I say we should hoot him' : and Huxley, Leavis and Orwell have successively echoed some of that ambivalence.

The reputation of Swift was stabilised, temporarily, by Leslie Stephen's *Swift* (1882) and Henry Craik's *Life of Jonathan Swift*, a more balanced study first published in the same year. But the modern reader looking for a general introduction to Swift will prefer Ricardo Quintana's *The Mind and Art of Jonathan Swift* (1936; 1953) which sees Swift whole and in his age, or his still better *Swift: An Introduction* (1955). Complemented by Kathleen Williams' *Jonathan Swift and the Age of Compromise* (1958) and Irvin Ehrenpreis's *The Personality of Jonathan Swift* (1958), Quintana's studies will remain the best introduction to Swift until Ehrenpreis's biography *Swift: The Man, His*

Works and the Age reaches the Gulliver years.[2] Herbert Davis's
Jonathan Swift: Essays on his Satire and Other Studies (1964)
is a collection of modest and perceptive essays by Swift's editor,
covering much ground and grinding no axes.

But axes and old saws abound. The scholarship of Quintana,
Ehrenpreis and others has cleared away most of the obfuscation
surrounding Swift's personality. In consequence critical debate
has been more clearly focused on real problems, and no less heated
than when prejudice and conjecture were the sole fuel of debate.
Three celebrated essays have kept alive the 'problem' of Swift:
Huxley's on Swift's scatology, Leavis's on his moral nihilism, and
Orwell's on his politics.

Aldous Huxley's savage essay in *Do What You Will* (1929)
lends the authority of a brilliant and sometimes scientific mind
to something like the Thackeray position. 'Swift's greatness lies
in the intensity, the almost insane violence of that "hatred of
bowels" which is the essence of his misanthropy, and which underlies the whole of his work.' Though begging three questions
in one sentence, Huxley recognises the fact that what Murry later
called Swift's 'excremental vision'[3] is, in its intensity, unique in
literature. Most readers, however, are likely to feel after reading
Norman O. Brown's chapter 'The Excremental Vision' in *Life
Against Death* (1959) that Huxley's valuation of this fact may
be the wrong one. Brown shifts from the argument *ad hominem*
to an important Freudian discussion of the meaning of Swift's
vision. In a brilliant inversion of the argument he tosses and gores
several persons, those who seek to 'domesticate and housebreak
this tiger of English literature' as well as those, both critics and
psychoanalysts, who 'issue certificates of lunacy'. Brown's thesis,
that Swift developed in *A Tale of a Tub* an original analysis of
sublimation, may not convince entirely, but his refutation of Huxley and the analysts does: 'Only Swift could do justice to the
irony of Huxley condemning Swift for misanthropic distortion
in a volume of essays devoted to destroying the integrity not only
of Swift but also of St Francis and Pascal . . . or the irony of
psychoanalysts, whose capacity for finding the anus in the most
unlikely places is notorious, condemning Swift for obsessive pre-

occupation with anality.'⁴ Swift may be sick, but in the excremental aggression of the Yahoos he has diagnosed a 'universal neuro-
sis of mankind'.

The physicality of *Gulliver's Travels*, and what G. Wilson
Knight called its 'symbolic, sensory-physical structure',⁵ have been
noticed from other angles in this century. Early critics often noted
the inventiveness and circumstantial air of the narrative: modern critics have been interested in the symbolical method implied
in Swift's use of scale as a moral device, and in how the 'clothes
philosophy' of the *Tale* is used in the *Travels* both for traditional
sartorist satire and to characterise Gulliver in terms of physical
frailty and moral and psychological instability.⁶ Even apart
from their symbolic uses, Swift's exuberant irruptions of imagery
have struck many readers as procreative, and his manipulation
of a world of tangible and delightful effects is part, I think, of
the answer to Dr Leavis. F. R. Leavis argued in 'The Irony of
Swift' (*Determination*, 1934)⁷ that what is important in Swift
is an 'emotional intensity' which is 'purely destructive'. Leavis
finds this restless energy in negation highly disturbing – more, for
example, than the irony of Gibbon. And he finds in the *Travels*
nothing substantially realised in the way of the Augustan
positives, such as Pope achieves. It may be that one would claim
Swift's intense scepticism – a self-directed scepticism – as in itself
a positive. But one can also approach the matter historically,
as T. O. Wedel does, and see Swift combating a shift away from
seriousness and faith. Canon Wedel's 1926 essay, reprinted here,
claims Swift as a protagonist in the eighteenth century for the
traditional Christian view of man. John Wesley, whose faith is
admittedly a much more convincing matter than Jonathan
Swift's, clearly saw the *Travels* in this way,⁸ and Wedel's view
has found support in important essays by Kathleen Williams
and S. H. Monk and among all those who take Swift to be opposing the stream of sentimental optimism.

Whether or not the Houyhnhnms are intended as a satire on
Bolingbroke and Shaftesbury and their conception of a progressive moral rationality, the Yahoos are certainly Swift's statement
of one side of the human fact which comfortable Augustan and

Victorian benevolence ignored. Swift's counterstatement is perhaps as one-sided as the view he is contesting, but satire does not
claim to show the whole truth : only to give the lie to untruth.
To project the negative passionately in an age of too complacent
positives may be the most necessary task of truth, and may, despite the charges of irreligiousness laid at Swift's door, be the task
of a religious mind. *A Tale of a Tub*, which was central to Leavis's
argument, is a peevishly sectarian and therefore irreligious work.
Gulliver's Travels is fundamentalist and universal and therefore
– though not a religious work – arguably the product of a religious mind at the end of its tether. For all its gaiety, it is a work
of painful awareness, impelled by a sense of sin and folly. But to
an age devoted to a pervasive, and irreligious, sense of man's
self-sufficiency, or to Huxley's modish humanism of the twenties,
Swift's war upon the idols of the tribe will appear as criminal
perversity.

A conception of irony founded on Gibbon or Pope may find
Swift close to nihilism, but to Søren Kierkegaard, in *The Concept
of Irony*, what the true ironist posits in the last resort is in fact
nothingness. If he takes this nothingness personally, says Kierkegaard, the ironist will arrive at 'something' : that something being
despair. Otherwise irony is 'sheer form'. If he is serious about it,
the ironist, in religious resignation, refuses to exempt himself from
his conclusion that 'all is vanity'. In quite different terms, C. J.
Rawson appears to have reached a similar valuation. Rawson's
'Order and Cruelty' (*Essays in Criticism,* xx, 1970, pp. 24–56)
elucidates – as Leavis's pioneer essay did not quite do – the ni-
hilistic effect of Swift's art : the 'haze of extra hostility' which
overspills the logic of Swift's specific onslaughts. 'The images,
which begin as specific tokens of guilt aimed at certain human
types, teasingly turn into general signs of the human condition.
The images' strong charge of undifferentiated blame is thus
left to play over undefined turpitudes attributable to the whole
of mankind.' And Rawson finds Swift deeply self-implicated in
the anarchy of which he is the scourge. The satire devolves
upon reader and satirist, for perhaps Swift was 'and sensed that
he was, in all rebellious recalcitrance, himself Yahoo'.

This is a long step from Sir Charles Firth deciding in 1919
that by the Yahoos Swift meant merely the 'savage old Irish'.
The moral implications of the *Travels* have always seemed darker
than the surface play of political satire, though the surface itself,
where it speaks of tyranny, war and famine, is often nasty enough,
and there is a valid fascination in discovering that Swift's satire
is concerned with contemporary 'facts' as much as general 'truths'.
A. E. Case and Irvin Ehrenpreis have refined some of Firth's
generally definitive conclusions about who and what were the
immediate referents of the satire.[9] The arguments of Firth and
Case are based on different assumptions about when some of
the passages they interpret were written, whether in 1714 or 1724,
and their almost equal convincingness is one reason for feeling
that a similarly detailed transference could be made to 1824 or
1924 – or 1974, as every reader knows very well.

More fundamental valuations of Swift's politics appeared in
Zera Fink's 'Political Theory in *Gulliver's Travels*' (*E.L.H.*, XIV,
1947), which sees Swift in the tradition of 'the classical Repub-
licans of the Puritan era and their Renaissance predecessors
[Machiavelli, Harrington, Milton, Sidney]', and in George
Orwell's 1946 essay 'Politics vs Literature : an Examination of
Gulliver's Travels'. Orwell's comprehensive liberal critique dubs
Swift 'a Tory anarchist, despising authority while disbelieving
in liberty' and sees him as both a brilliantly prophetic castigator
of the totalitarian state (in Laputa) and the proponent of in-
cipient anarcho-fascism (in Houyhnhnmland). This interpretation is far from a simple identification of Swift with blinkered
Toryism. Swift was indeed dedicated, as Basil Willey says, 'to
reason and good sense, to the Anglican church as their embodiment, and to settled and orderly government',[10] but he was
mostly unable to see reason or good sense, or orderly and settled
government, in any direction he looked. The ideal was within :
and it is partly expressed in the political recalcitrance approved by
Ehrenpreis, Barzun and others,[11] partly in the utopianism which
has led the *Travels* to be considered alongside Plato's *Republic*
and More's *Utopia*.[12] In *The Shape of Utopia* (1970) Robert C.
Elliott's brilliant chapter on Swift stresses not so much the pre-

ternaturally ideal society of the horses as that of Brobdingnag, where Swift presents 'an ideal to be aimed at, a utopia with a practical meaning for man'. But this view of Swift as more pragmatic than utopian is disputed by M. M. Kelsall whose cogent 'Iterum Houyhnhnm: Swift's Sextumvirate and the Horses' (*Essays in Criticism,* xix, 1969) claims that there is a basic inflexibility of mind in Swift and his six heroes, and reinstates some derided facets of Houyhnhnm society as close to Renaissance ideals.

What complicates the quest for Swift's 'real' utopia, indeed the quest for any positives at all, is the presence in the book of a protean and prismatic sensibility called Gulliver, whose literary status is somewhere between Defoe's prosaic castaway and Lewis Carroll's Cheshire Cat. Some critics have found Gulliver a fully realised character. Others have thought him a fairly autonomous *persona* who is sometimes more, sometimes less, identified with Swift. Still others have found him an optical device or a verbal will-o'-the-wisp whose status changes with the current of the satire. Gulliver is all and none of these. He is a mobile mask for Swift's changing mood : a mask which Swift raises and drops at will, but whose appearance in any case is never quite the same, both because he develops and because he is at one moment the experiencing voyager, and in the next a writer of his edifying memoirs. It is true that Gulliver is whatever Swift wants him to be at the time, in this game of intellectual relativity, but it is also true that a lot of the time Swift wants him to be real enough to inspire again with the sense of his veracity, if for no other purpose than to deepen the void which opens up when Swift next subverts his compact with the reader.

Modern critics have not questioned the veracity which early readers found in Gulliver, but they have doubted his grasp upon reality : he is no longer the reliable observer, but rather a figure in a myth, or in a maze. John M. Bullitt sees Gulliver on an Oedipan journey 'from the ignorant complacency of the typical Englishman towards an undeceived, though intensely bitter, knowledge of reality' (*Jonathan Swift and the Anatomy of Satire,* Harvard, 1953, p. 9). A. E. Case and R. S. Crane think Gulli-

ver's final state shows what would happen to 'an intelligent man
who spent a long period in the company of creatures who were
perfect in every way'.[13] Other critics, notably John F. Ross, S. H.
Monk and Joseph Horrell,[14] have denied Gulliver this stature or
this intelligence, preferring an essentially comic vision of Gulliver
as naïve, deluded, and finally deranged, and equally comic in
his original naïveté and his terminal pride. Such narrative pro-
gression as the book possesses supports this view. Horrell and
Monk noticed how the events which deposit Gulliver in his various lands – shipwreck, desertion, piracy, and, finally, mutiny –
leave him progressively alienated from mankind (and perhaps
the mutiny which opens Book IV is a consequence of this aliena-
tion). The merit of this interpretation is that it recognises the
structural and thematic importance of the much derided third
book. The sixties produced many useful discussions of the Voyage
to Laputa,[15] but Kathleen Williams saw most clearly the atmosphere of decay, death and purposelessness which pervades the
third voyage and prepares Gulliver – by now an invisible man –
for his role in the final book.

Only those who take Gulliver at face value – his perennial
childhood audience – will find the fourth book easy. For those
who think he is over the edge, and for those who think that Gulliver is an abstraction manipulated in the service of the satire, the
reader is on his own, to come to terms as he may with a philo-
sopher-horse. It is too simplistic to claim, with the 'hard' school,
that if Gulliver is mad, the satire is muted.

It is the demented ferocity of Gulliver's attack in the fifth chapter of Book IV, his frenzied indictment of princes, soldiers and
the bench – relieved only by the gentle socratic interventions of
his Houyhnhnm master – that prepares us to adopt, with very
little resistance I think, the same interlocutor's dispassionate account of the Yahoos as a just account of ourselves: and if Swift
risks our repudiation of Gulliver's undiscriminating, unquestion-
ing and irascible onslaught on certain classes of men, he does so
in order to have us recognise ourselves, in more fundamental
moral categories, as kin to the Yahoo. The only sleight of hand is
that it is now not Gulliver but his master who persuades by re-

lating 'plain Matter of Fact in the simplest Manner and Style'. And the Socratic lesson comes direct to the reader. Gulliver, immediate victim of invidious comparisons, merely learns to hate his wife, to rail against mankind, and even, in that extreme dislocation which permits him to identify his *kind* with Yahoos but to make for *himself* shoes and a vessel of Yahoo-skins, to turn cannibal. We, I think, interiorise the question : we see ourselves as all that Gulliver's master says we are, without supposing that if so it is all the fault of the others. We know that unlike the Houyhnhnms we have within us an evil principle as well as a good. Unlike Gulliver we know that Houyhnhnmland is irrelevant to us as long as man is man. Few readers will follow Gulliver in his comi-tragic devotion, both because we know we cannot be horses, and because, on the other hand, we cannot help feeling that Gulliver's master learns more than Gulliver from their bizarre discussions : about good and evil, and that the heart has its reasons. This wonderful horse even takes a step towards a moral existence : he acquires, as Gulliver surrenders, the faculty of doubt.

For fifty years, since Wedel threw down his challenge to the hardliners, the debate about the meaning of the fourth book has been conducted with brilliance on both sides. According to Halewood and Levich 'Swift fully approved of the Houyhnhnm life of reason and conceived of it as fully possible for man – as, indeed, the only realistic standard by which to judge the adequacy of human conduct.' Seeing the ideal and knowing it unattainable, says Sherburn, Gulliver is 'the victim of a misanthropic author'.[16] Yet Kathleen Williams, in the essay reprinted here, argues that 'the inadequacy of the life of reason' is Swift's comic message in the fourth book. The recurrence of the tough school of criticism in the sixties, after the Wedel/Williams view had almost passed from controversy into orthodoxy, has shown that it is wrong to suppose that if the Houyhnhnms are less potent an ideal than we could wish, they are therefore meant ironically. The horses clearly represent an ideal if not an imaginatively compelling one. But the case put forward in their defence by Sherburn, Crane and others has too often neutralised *Gulliver's* primary component, comedy.

It is a simple test, but a fair one, to return from criticism to the
text itself : and most readers will find that they turn with relief
from learned articles about Swift's relations to schools of logic,
Hobbes' *Leviathan*, Berkeley's *A New Theory of Vision*, or
Locke's *Essay on the Human Understanding*, to the text itself,
which shrugs off such attributions.[17] And one gleans from Kathleen Williams, S. H. Monk or John F. Ross a sense of heightened
observation and a fresh realisation of how impossible it is to pin
Swift down. For *Gulliver's Travels*, while the product of a philosophically lettered mind, is not a philosophical treatise or a
utopian handbook. If one concludes that Swift is a positive and
deliberative writer it is in the sense that Kathleen Williams has
it : 'his most typical satire is built upon an elaborate system of
checks and counterweights, by means of which we may guess at
his positive intentions and so by indirections find directions out'.

For a full appreciation of modern criticism Milton Voigt's
Swift and the Twentieth Century (1964) is an invaluable guide.
A briefer survey is given in W. B. Carnochan's 'The Complexity
of Swift'.[18] There is not, and this is the proof of true irony, a
standard interpretation of *Gulliver's Travels*. The debate will continue between those who view Swift's quadruped commonwealth
with Gulliver's solemnity – that this is a well-based view is shown
by Kelsall and others – and those who regard the Houyhnhnms'
shortcomings and Gulliver's pride as fracturing that ideal so that
Swift is cautioning us against the ideal itself. Gulliver, as Horrell
wryly concludes in 'What Gulliver Knew', supports his final
claim to veracity by quoting from the *Aeneid* 'a similar protesta-
tion by Sinon, who has just told the Trojans a lie about a horse'.
The debate has by now included every gradation on the axis
from solemn vision to pure burlesque, and these disagreements
betoken Swift's real and deliberate complexity.

The complexity is never greater than in the last two chapters
where comedy, character, burlesque and passionate irony take
their turn in Swift's representative manner at its most accomplished. From the moment when Gulliver is picked up by Don
Pedro's crew the author discredits him utterly. The eleventh chapter has the consistency of lunacy, for Gulliver, under Houyhn-

hnm tuition, has lost any capacity to draw a rational conclusion from the simplest evidence. Like the inhabitants of a later utopia his reason stops at the unproblematical dictum 'four legs good, two legs bad', and while Gulliver tells us the truth about his treatment, for he could not say the thing that is not, he turns his back on the sailors' 'great humanity' (though not Don Pedro's excellent wine), and ends up talking to horses.

But with the 'story' over, Swift spins his satiric wheel with more virtuosity than ever. Each turn of the final chapter requires the reader to modify his response, and there are few more exhilarating rides in literature than this ironic merry-go-round provides. The comic figure of page 290 is addressing us two pages later in what the most tender of the tender critics will admit to be the authentic voice of Swift: 'For who can read of the Virtues I have mentioned in the glorious Houyhnhnms, without feeling ashamed of his own Vices, when he considers himself as the reasoning, governing Animal of his Country?' Yet only a reader who has skipped much of the book will fail to smile at the amnesia which lets Gulliver claim a moment later that he never wrote with 'Passion, Prejudice or Ill-will against any Man or Number of Men whatsoever' [p. 293]. A paragraph later, Gulliver's former self is debating with prudence and pedantry the probable outcome of battle between Houyhnhnms and a European army, but Swift himself ventriloquises through his hero the deteriorationist motif with which the paragraph concludes. And it is a Swift we have not heard with such passion before who moves straight into a diatribe against colonial arrogance and butchery, on a plane altogether higher than Gulliver has yet been permitted to attain: at once a terminal critique of Euro-'Christian' pride, and a diversitarian manifesto in favour of the cultural integrity of indigenous peoples – in short a credo of political philosophy which has at its centre not ideology but a giant moral passion.

Thence to the disillusioned Gulliver who hopes to reconcile himself to mankind by the bizarre remedy of beholding 'my Figure often in a Glass', and who speaks with unconscious irony (given so recent a revolution in his sensibility) of how difficult it is for a man late in life to remove 'old habits'. Next a tolerant Gulliver –

so much more tolerant than his creator – who, with his customary sangfroid and placid unconcern, can view 'a Lawyer, a Pickpocket . . . an Evidence, a Suborner, an Attorney, a Traytor, or the like' (and is it Swift or Gulliver who accommodates the 'Whoremunger' to the 'Physician' in this passage?) as 'all according to the due Course of Things'. Finally a Gulliver who rises to merge with his creator as he flails such a creature as man 'smitten with Pride', only to fall, in the longest fall that ever befell one so sage, into the realms of everlasting burlesque in the very last sentence of all : 'I here intreat those who have any Tincture of this absurd Vice, that they will not presume to appear in my sight'.

This statuesque posture of pride finds Swift subjecting to burlesque a character who has grown through experience to encompass all the bile of the satirist, and who therefore embodies an important part of Swift himself; but who has not the strength Swift possessed to feel as he did the folly of the world without losing his humanity. The close of the *Travels*, Dr Leavis notwithstanding, is the product of a mind in possession of its experience; a mind scrutinising itself; telling itself as it contemplates its surrogate reflection in Gulliver's looking-glass, to 'bring your own Guts to a reasonable compass'.[19] Swift knew that misanthropy is the end a satirist risks. Many writers with a comparable animus have sublimated it, as Wordsworth did, out of a healthy respect for the tenor of their own lives. *Gulliver's Travels* is a coming to terms with the ironic vocation, a farewell to spleen and a further honing of the satiric edge. Swift draws a conclusion exactly opposite to Gulliver's, as we are surely aware when we turn back to the beginning and read, in Gulliver's letter to Sympson, that '. . . some corruptions of my Yahoo Nature have revived in me . . . else I should never have attempted so absurd a Project as that of reforming the Yahoo Race in this Kingdom : but, I have now done with all such visionary Schemes for ever'.

RICHARD GRAVIL

NOTES

1. A. E. Case, *Four Essays on 'Gulliver's Travels'* (Princeton, 1945).
2. Two volumes are so far published : *Mr Swift and his Contemporaries* (Harvard University Press, 1962), and *Dr Swift* (1967).
3. J. M. Murry, *Jonathan Swift: A Critical Biography* (Jonathan Cape, 1954).
4. Norman O. Brown, *Life Against Death: The Psychoanalytical Meaning of History* (Routledge & Kegan Paul, 1959), cited from the Sphere edition (1968) p. 167.
5. G. Wilson Knight, 'Swift and the Symbolism of Irony', in *The Burning Oracle* (Oxford University Press, 1939).
6. See for example, Paul Fussell, 'The Frailty of Lemuel Gulliver', in *Essays in Literary History*, ed. Rudolf Kirk and C. F. Main (Rutgers University Press, 1960) pp. 113–25; and Ellen Douglass Leyburn, 'Gulliver's Clothes', *Satire Newsletter*, I (1964) pp. 35–40.
7. Reprinted in *The Common Pursuit* (Chatto & Windus, 1953) pp. 73–87.
8. Wesley's citations from Swift are mentioned by Wedel and by R. M. Frye in 'Swift's Yahoo and the Christian Symbols for Sin', *Journal of the History of Ideas*, xv (1954) pp. 201–17.
9. C. H. Firth, 'The Political Significance of *Gulliver's Travels*', *Proceedings of the British Academy*, IX (1919–20) pp. 237–59; A. E. Case, 'Personal and Political Satire in *Gulliver's Travels*', op. cit.; Irvin Ehrenpreis. 'The Origins of *Gulliver's Travels*', *PMLA*, LXXII (1957) pp. 880–99 (reprinted in *The Personality of Jonathan Swift*, 1958).
10. Basil Willey, *The Eighteenth-Century Background* (Chatto & Windus, 1940), cited from the Peregrine edition (1962) p. 102.
11. Irvin Ehrenpreis, 'Jonathan Swift', *Proceedings of the British Academy*, LIV (1968) pp. 149–64; Jacques Barzun, 'Swift, or Man's Capacity for Reason', in *The Energy of Art: Studies of Authors Classic and Modern* (Harper & Bros, 1956) pp. 81–100.
12. See John F. Reichert 'Plato, Swift and the Houyhnhnms', *Philological Quarterly*, XLVII (1968) pp. 179–92; William H. Halewood, '*Gulliver's Travels* I, vi', *Journal of English Literary History*, XXXIII (1966) pp. 422–33; Brian Vickers, 'The Satiric Structure of *Gulliver's Travels* and More's *Utopia*' in *The World of Jonathan Swift*, ed Vickers (Basil Blackwell, 1968) pp. 233–57.
13. A. E. Case, op. cit.

14. Samuel H. Monk, 'The Pride of Lemuel Gulliver', *Sewanee Review*, LXIII (1955) pp. 48–71, reprinted in *Eighteenth-Century English Literature*, ed. James Clifford (Oxford University Press, 1959) pp. 112–29, and elsewhere; Joseph Horrell, 'What Gulliver Knew', *Sewanee Review*, LI (1943) pp. 476–504.

15. Maurice Johnson, 'Remote Regions of Man's Mind', *University of Kansas City Review*, 27 (1960–1) pp. 299–303; Edmund Reiss, 'The Importance of Swift's Glubbdubdrib Episode', *Journal of English and Germanic Philology*, LIX (1960) pp. 223–8. See also Robert P. Fitzgerald, 'The Allegory of Luggnagg and the Struldbruggs in *Gulliver's Travels*', *Studies in Philology*, 65 (1968) pp. 656–76 for a suggestion that Swift balanced against his satire of the Royal Society an allegory of the French Academy.

16. George Sherburn, 'Errors Concerning the Houyhnhnms', *Modern Philology*, LVI (1958) pp. 92–7; William H. Halewood and Martin Levich, 'Houyhnhnm *est* Animal Rationale', *Journal of the History of Ideas*, XXVI (1965) pp. 273–81.

17. See John D. Seelye, 'Hobbes' *Leviathan* and the Giantism Complex in the First Book of *Gulliver's Travels*', *Journal of English and Germanic Philology*, LX (1961) pp. 228–39; Edward Wasiolek, 'Relativity in *Gulliver's Travels*', *Philological Quarterly*, XXXVII (1958) pp. 110–16; and W. B. Carnochan, '*Gulliver's Travels* : An Essay on the Human Understanding', *Modern Language Quarterly*, XXV (1964) pp. 5–21.

18. W. B. Carnochan, 'The Complexity of Swift : Gulliver's Fourth Voyage', *Studies in Philology*, LX (1963) pp. 23–44, see also W. E. Yeomans, 'The Houyhnhnm as Menippean Horse, *College English*, XXVII (1966) pp. 449–54.

19. *A Tale of a Tub*, Works, I, 28, also cited by Carnochan.

PART ONE

Swift and his Contemporaries,
1721—1784

CORRESPONDENCE OF SWIFT AND HIS CIRCLE

I am now writing a History of my Travells, which will be a large Volume, and gives Account of Countryes hitherto unknown; but they go on slowly for want of Health and Humor.

> SOURCE: This and the subsequent letters are extracted from *The Correspondence of Jonathan Swift*, ed. Harold Williams (1963).

19 JANUARY 1723-4

My greatest want here is of somebody qualifyed to censure and correct what I write, I know not above two or three whose Judgement I would value, and they are lazy, negligent, and without any Opinion of my Abilityes. I have left the Country of Horses, and am in the flying Island, where I shall not stay long, and my two last Journeys will be soon over. . . .

14 AUGUST 1725

I have finished my Travells, and am now transcribing them: they are admirable Things, and will wonderfully mend the World.

SWIFT TO ALEXANDER POPE   29 SEPTEMBER 1725

. . . I have employd my time (besides ditching) in finishing correcting, amending, and Transcribing my Travells, in four parts

Compleat newly Augmented, and intended for the press when the world shall deserve them, or rather when a Printer shall be found brave enough to venture his Eares, I like your Schemes of our meeting after Distresses and dispertions but the chief end I propose to my self in all my labors is to vex the world rather then divert it, and if I could compass that designe without hurting my own person or Fortune I would be the most Indefatigable writer you have ever seen without reading I am exceedingly pleased that you have done with Translations Lord Treasurer Oxford often lamented that a rascaly World should lay you under a Necessity of Misemploying your Genius for so long a time. But since you will now be so much better employd when you think of the World give it one lash the more at my Request. I have ever hated all Nations professions and Communityes and all my love is towards individualls for instance I hate the tribe of Lawyers, but I love Councellor such a one, Judge such a one for so with Physicians (I will not Speak of my own Trade) Soldiers, English, Scotch, French; and the rest but principally I hate and detest that animal called man, although I hartily love John, Peter, Thomas and so forth. this is the system upon which I have governed my self many years (but do not tell) and so I shall go on till I have done with them I have got Materials Towards a Treatis proving the falsity of that Definition *animal rationale*; and to show it should be only *rationis capax*. Upon this great foundation of Misanthropy (though not Timons manner) The whole building of my Travells is erected : And I never will have peace of mind till all honest men are of my Opinion : by Consequence you are to embrace it immediatly and procure that all who deserve my Esteem may do so too. The matter is so clear that it will admit little dispute. nay I will hold a hundred pounds that you and I agree in the Point. . . .

Mr Lewis sent me an Account of Dr Arbuthnett's Illness which is a very sensible Affliction to me, who by living so long out of the World have lost that hardness of Heart contracted by years and generall Conversation. I am daily loosing Friends, and neither seeking nor getting others. O, if the World had but a dozen Arbuthnetts in it I would burn my Travells but however

he is not without Fault. There is a passage in Bede highly com-
mending the Piety and learning of the Irish in that Age, where
after abundance of praises he overthrows them all by lamenting
that, Alas, they kept Easter at a wrong time of the Year. So our
Doctor has every Quality and virtue that can make a man amiable or usefull, but alas he hath a sort of Slouch in his Walk. I
pray god protect him for he is an excellent Christian tho not a
Catholick and as fit a man either to dy or Live as ever I knew.

SWIFT TO ALEXANDER POPE   26 NOVEMBER 1725

. . . Drown the World, I am not content with despising it, but I
would anger it if I could with safety. I wish there were an Hos-
pital built for it's despisers, where one might act with safety and
it need not be a large Building, only I would have it well endowed.
. . . I desire you and all my Friends will take a special care that
my Affection to the World may not be imputed to my Age, for
I have Credible witnesses ready to depose that it hath never
varyed from the Twenty First to the f—ty eighth year of my
Life, (pray fill that Blank Charitably) I tell you after all that I
do not hate Mankind, it is vous autres who hate them because
you would have them reasonable Animals, and are Angry for
being disappointed. I have always rejected that Definition and
made another of my own. I am no more angry with [Walpole?]
Then I was with the Kite that last week flew away with one of
my Chickins and yet I was pleas'd when one of my Servants Shot
him two days after, This I say, because you are so hardy as to tell
me of your Intentions to write Maxims in Opposition to Roch-
foucault who is my Favorite because I found my whole character
in him, however I will read him again because it is possible I may
have since undergone some alterations.

JOHN GAY TO SWIFT   17 NOVEMBER 1726

About ten days ago a Book was publish'd here of the Travels of
one Gulliver, which hath been the conversation of the whole town

ever since : The whole impression sold in a week; and nothing is more diverting than to hear the different opinions people give of it, though all agree in liking it extreamly. 'Tis generally said that you are the Author, but I am told, the Bookseller declares he knows not from what hand it came. From the highest to the lowest it is universally read, from the Cabinet-council to the Nursery. The Politicians to a man agree, that it is free from particular reflections, but that the Satire on general societies of men is too severe. Not but we now and then meet with people of greater perspicuity, who are in search for particular applications in every leaf; and it is highly probable we shall have keys published to give light into Gulliver's design. Your Lord [Bolingbroke] is the person who least approves it, blaming it as a design of evil consequence to depreciate human nature, at which it cannot be wondered that he takes most offence, being himself the most accomplish'd of his species, and so losing more than any other of that praise which is due both to the dignity and virtue of a man. Your friend, my Lord Harcourt, commends it very much, though he thinks in some places the matter too far carried. The Duchess Dowager of Marlborough is in raptures at it; she says she can dream of nothing else since she read it; she declares, that she hath now found out, that her whole life hath been lost in caressing the worst part of mankind, and treating the best as her foes; and that if she knew Gulliver, tho' he had been the worst enemy she ever had, she would give up all her present acquaintance for his friendship. You may see by this, that you are not much injur'd by being suppos'd the Author of this piece. If you are, you have disoblig'd us, and two or three of your best friends, in not giving us the least hint of it while you were with us; and in particular Dr. Arbuthnot, who says it is ten thousand pitys he had not known it, he could have added such abundance of things upon every subject. Among Lady-critics, some have found out that Mr. Gulliver had a particular malice to maids of honour.[1] Those of them who frequent the Church, say, his design is impious, and that it is an insult on Providence, by depreciating the works of the Creator. Notwithstanding I am told the Princess hath read it with great pleasure. As to other Critics, they think the flying island is the least entertaining; and so great an opinion the town have of the impossibility of Gulliver's writing at all below himself, that 'tis agreed that Part was not writ by the same Hand, tho' this hath its defenders too. It hath pass'd Lords and Commons, *nemine contradicente*; and the whole town, men, women, and children are quite full of it.

NOTE

1. A reference to Gulliver's sexual humiliations in Book II, chapter 5, about which Swift exchanged mutually ribald letters with Henrietta Howard, Countess of Suffolk – a 'maid of honour' in the household of the Princess of Wales (see below). [Ed.]

MRS HOWARD TO SWIFT   17 NOVEMBER 1726

. . . I cannot conclude without telling you that our Island is in great Joy; one of our Yahoo's having been diliver'd of a Creature, half Ram, and half Yahoo; and an other has brought forth four perfect Black Rabits. may we not hope? and with some probabillity expect that in time our female Yahoo's will produce a race of Houyhnhnms. I am Sir Your most | humble Ser^t | Sieve Yahoo[1]

NOTE

1. In Swift's Laputian glossary (Book III, chapter 6) 'Sieve' = court lady. [Ed.]

SWIFT TO MRS HOWARD   27 NOVEMBER 1726

Madam.

When I received your Letter I thought it the most unaccountable one I ever saw in my Life, and was not able to comprehend three words of it together. The Perverseness of your Lines astonished me, which tended downwards to the right on one Page, and upward in the two others. This I thought impossible to be done by any Person who did not squint with both Eyes; an Infirmity I never observed in you. However, one thing I was pleased with, that after you had writ me *down*, you repented, and writ me *up*. But I continued four days at a loss for your meaning, till a Bookseller sent me the Travells of one Cap^tn Gulliver, who proved a very good Explainer, although at the same time, I thought it hard to be forced to read a Book of seven hundred Pages in order to understand a Letter of fifty lines; especially since those of our Faculty are already but too much pestered with Commentators. The Stuffs you require are making, because the Weaver piques himself upon having them in perfection, but he has read Gulliver's Book, and has no Conception of what you mean by returning Money, for he is become a Proselyte of the Houyhnhnms, whose great Principle (if I rightly remember) is Benevolence. And as to my self, I am rightly affronted with such a base Proposall, that I am determined to complain of you to her Royal Highness, that you are a mercenary Yahoo fond of shining Pebbles. What have I to do with you or your Court further than to show the Esteem I have for your Person, because you happen to deserve it, and my Gratitude to Her Royal Highness, who was pleased, a little to distinguish me; which, by the way is the greatest Compliment I ever made, and may probably be the last. For I am not such a prostitute Flatterer as Gulliver; whose chief Study is to extenuate the Vices, and magnify the Virtues, of Mankind, and perpetually dins our Ears with the Praises of his Country, in the midst of Corruptions, and for that Reason alone, hath found so many readers; and probably will have a Pension, which, I suppose, was his chief design in writing : As for his Compliments to the Ladyes, I can easily forgive him as a naturall Effect of that Devotion which our Sex always ought to pay to Yours.

SWIFT TO ALEXANDER POPE   27 NOVEMBER 1726

I am just come from answering a Letter of Mrs. Howard's writ in such mystical terms, that I should never have found out the meaning, if a Book had not been sent me called *Gulliver's Travellers*, of which you say so much in yours. I read the Book over, and in the second volume observe several passages which appear to be patched and altered, and the style of a different sort (unless I am much mistaken) Dr. Arbuthnot likes the Projectors least, others you tell me, the Flying island; some think it wrong to be so hard upon whole Bodies or Corporations, yet the general opinion is, that reflections on particular persons are most to be blamed: so that in these cases, I think the best method is to let censure and opinion take their course. A Bishop here said, that Book was full of improbable lies, and for his part, he hardly believed a word of it; and so much for Gulliver. . . . Let me add, that if I were Gulliver's friend, I would desire all my acquaintance to give out that his copy was basely mangled, and abused, and added to, and blotted out by the printer; for so to me it seems, in the second volume particularly. | Adieu.

'LEMUEL GULLIVER' TO MRS HOWARD
28 NOVEMBER 1726

Madam

My correspondents have informed me that your Lady^p has done me the honor to answer severall objections that ignorance, malice, and party have made to my Travells, and bin so charitable as to justifie the fidelity and veracity of the Author. This Zeal you have shown for Truth calls for my particular thanks, and at the same time encourages me to beg you would continue your goodness to me by reconcileing me to the Maids of Honour whom they say I have most grievously offended. I am so stupid as not to find out how I have disobliged them; Is there any harm in a young Ladys reading of romances? Or did I make use of an improper Engine to extinguish a fire that was kindled by a Maid of Honour? And I will venture to affirm, that if ever the Young Ladies of your Court should meet with a man of as little consequence in this country, as I was in Brobdingnag, they would use him with as much contempt: But I submit my self and my cause to your better judgment, and beg leave to lay the crown of Lilliput at your feet, as a small acknowledgment of your favours to my book & person. . . .

B

In 1727 Desfontaines published a French translation, with an introduction which slighted the puerilities of the original. In June he
wrote a rather shifty explanation to Swift. This is a translation of
part of Swift's reply (*Corr.*, III, 226, in French). [Ed.]

Translators, for the most part, give excessive praise to the works
they translate, and imagine perhaps that their reputations depend
in some way on that of the authors they have chosen. But you
have felt your powers, which place you above such precautions,
capable of correcting a bad book, a more difficult task than that of
composing a good one. You have not feared to give the public a
translation of a work which, you assure them, is full of foolish-
ness, puerilities, etc. We agree here that the tastes of Nations are
not always the same, but we are led to believe that good taste is
the same wherever there are people of wit, of judgement, and of
learning. If, then, the writings of Mr. Gulliver are intended only
for the British Isles, that traveller must pass for a very pitiable
writer. The same vices and the same follies reign everywhere, at
least in all the civilised countries of Europe, and the author who
writes only for a town, a province, a kingdom, or even a century,
deserves so little to be translated that he does not deserve to be
read.

The Partisans of this Gulliver, who are yet very numerous
among us, maintain that his book will last as long as our language,
because its merit lies not in certain modes or manners of thinking
and speaking, but in a succession of observations on the imper-
fections, the follies, and the vices of mankind.

You judge rightly that the people I tell you of do not much
approve your criticism, and you will no doubt be surprised to
know that they regard this ship's surgeon as a grave author, who
never departs from seriousness, who assumes no disguise, who
takes no pride in the possession of wit, and who is content to com-
municate to the public, in a simple and artless narration, the
adventures which befell him, and the things he saw or heard tell
of during his travels.

EARLY COMMENTS

Dean Swift gives the most exact account of kings, ministers, bishops and the courts of justice that is possible to be writ. He has certainly a vast deal of wit; and since he could contribute so much to the pulling down the most honest and best-intentioned ministry that ever I knew, with the help only of Abigail and one or two more, and has certainly stopped the finishing stroke to ruin the Irish in the project of the halfpence, in spite of all the ministry could do, I could not help wishing that we had had his assistance in the opposition; for I could easily forgive him all the slaps he has given me and the Duke of Marlborough, and have thanked him heartily whenever he would please to do good. I never saw him in my life; and though his writings have entertained me very much, yet I see he writes sometimes for interest; for in his books he gives my Lord Oxford as great a character as if he was speaking of Socrates or Marcus Antoninus. But when I am dead the reverse of that character will come out with vouchers to it under his own hand.

SOURCE: *Memoirs of Sarah, Duchess of Marlborough, together with her Characters of her Contemporaries and her Opinions*, ed. William King (1930) p. 313.

JOHN BOYLE, LORD ORRERY   1752

. . . It is with great reluctance, I shall make some remarks on GULLIVER's voyage to the *Houyhnhnms*. In this last part of his imaginary travels, SWIFT has indulged a misanthropy that is intolerable. The representation which he has given us of human nature, must terrify, and even debase the mind of the reader who views it. His sallies of wit and humour lose all their force, nothing remaining but a melancholy, and disagreeable impression: and, as I have said to you, on other parts of his works, we are disgusted, not entertained; we are shocked, not instructed by the fable. I should therefore chuse to take no notice of his YAHOOS, did I not think it necessary to assert the vindication of human nature, and thereby, in some measure, to pay my duty to the great author of our species, who has created us in a very fearful, and a very wonderful manner.

. . . In painting YAHOOS he becomes one himself. Nor is the picture, which he draws of the *Houyhnhnms*, inviting or amusing. It wants both light and shade to adorn it. It is cold and insipid. We there view the pure instincts of brutes, unassisted by any knowledge of letters, acting within their own narrow sphere, merely for their immediate preservation. They are incapable of doing wrong, therefore they act right. It is surely a very low character given to creatures, in whom the author would insinuate some degree of reason, that they act inoffensively, when they have neither the motive nor the power to act otherwise. Their virtuous qualities are only negative. SWIFT himself, amidst all his irony, must have confessed, that to moderate our passions, to extend our munificence to others, to enlarge our understanding, and to raise our idea of the Almighty by contemplating his works, is not only the business, but often the practice, and the study of the human mind. It is too certain, that no one individual has ever possessed every qualification and excellence: however such an assemblage of different virtues, may still be collected from different persons, as are sufficient to place the dignity of human nature in an amiable, and exalted station. We must lament indeed the many instances of those who degenerate, or go astray from the end and intention of their being. The true source of this depravity is often owing to the want of education, to the false indulgence of parents, or to some other bad causes, which are constantly prevalent in every nation. Many of these errors are finely ridiculed in the foregoing

parts of this romance : but the voyage to the *Houyhnhnms* is a
real insult upon mankind.

S O U R C E : *Remarks on the Life and Writings of Dr. Jona-
than Swift, Dean of St. Patrick's, Dublin. In a Series of
Letters from John Earl of Orrery to his Son, the Honourable
Hamilton Boyle* (1752) pp. 132–6, 184–90, extracts.

DEANE SWIFT   1755

Deane Swift, Jonathan's cousin, is concerned to refute the opinions
of Lord Orrery and Patrick Delaney (who also refuted Orrery, but
lamely).

. . . I have been told that some others, beside the grand remarker
upon the works of DR. SWIFT, have thought proper to censure
GULLIVER'S voyage to the HOUYHNHNMS. But whether indeed their animadversions proceeded from the infirmity of their
judgment, or from some YAHOO depravity in their own nature,
I shall not vouchsafe to enquire; as the daily occurrences of this
wretched world prove, illustrate, and confirm all the sarcasms of
the Doctor. Shall we praise that excellent moralist, the humorous
HOGARTH, for exposing midnight revels, debaucheries, and a
thousand other vices and follies of humankind, in a series of hiero-
glyphicks, suited to the improvement and the correction of the
wild, the gay, the frolick, and the extravagant? And shall we
condemn a preacher of righteousness, for exposing under the
character of a nasty unteachable YAHOO the deformity, the
blackness, the filthiness and corruption of those hellish, abominable vices, which inflame the wrath of GOD against the children of
disobedience; and subject them without repentance, that is, without a thorough change of life and practice, to everlasting per-
dition? Ought a preacher of righteousness; ought a watchman
of the Christian faith, (who is accountable for his talents, and
obliged to warn the innocent, as well as terrify the wicked and
the prophane) to hold his peace, like a dumb dog that cannot

bark, when avarice, fraud, cheating, violence, rapine, extortion, cruelty, oppression, tyranny, rancour, envy, malice, detraction, hatred, revenge, murder, whoredom, adultery, lasciviousness, bribery, corruption, pimping, lying, perjury, subordination, treachery, ingratitude, gaming, flattery, drunkenness, gluttony, luxury, vanity, effeminacy, cowardice, pride, impudence, hypocrisy, infidelity, blasphemy, idolatry, sodomy, and innumerable other vices are as epidemical as the pox, and many of them the notorious characteristicks of the bulk of humankind? . . .

S o u r c e : *Essay upon the Life, Writings and Character of Dr. Jonathan Swift* (1755) p. 220.

JOHN HAWKESWORTH   1755

(Books I and II)
From the whole of these two voyages to Lilliput and Brobdingnag, arises one general remark, which, however obvious, has been overlooked by those who consider them as little more than the sport of a wanton imagination. When human actions are ascribed to pigmies and giants, there are few that do not excite either contempt, disgust, or horror. To ascribe them therefore to such beings, was perhaps the most probable method of engaging the mind to examine them with attention, and judge of them with impartiality, by suspending the fascination of habit, and exhibiting familiar objects in a new light. The use of the fable then is not less apparent, than important and extensive; and that this use was intended by the author, can be doubted only by those who are disposed to affirm, that order and regularity are the effects of chance.

(Book IV, Chapter I)
Whoever is disgusted with this picture of a *Yahoo*, would do well to reflect, that it becomes his own in exact proportion as he deviates from virtue, for virtue is the perfection of reason. The

appetites of those abandoned to vice, are not less brutal and sordid, than that of a *Yahoo* for asses flesh; nor is their life a state of less abject servility.

(Book IV, Chapter V)
It would perhaps be impossible, by the most laboured argument or forcible eloquence to shew the absurd injustice and horrid cruelty of war as effectually, as by this simple exhibition of them in a new light: with war, including every species of iniquity and every art of destruction, we become familiar by degrees under specious terms, which are seldom examined, because they are learned at an age, in which the mind implicitly receives and retains whatever is imprest: thus it happens, that when one man murders another to gratify his lust, we shudder; but when one man murders a million to gratify his vanity, we approve and we admire, we envy and we applaud. If, when this and the preceding pages are read, we discover with astonishment, that when the same events have occurred in history we felt no emotion, and acquiesced in wars which we could not but know to have been commenced for such causes, and carried on by such means; let not him be censured for too much debasing his species, who has contributed to their felicity and preservation by stripping off the veil of custom and prejudice, and holding up in their native deformity the vices by which they become wretched, and the arts by which they are destroyed.

(Books I–IV)
To mortify pride, which indeed was not made for man, and produces not only the most ridiculous follies, but the most extensive calamity, appears to have been one general view of the author in every part of these *Travels*. Personal strength and beauty, the wisdom and the virtue of mankind, become objects, not of pride, but of humility, in the diminutive stature, and contemptible weakness of the Lilliputians; in the horrid deformity of the Brobding-

nagians; in the learned folly of the Laputians; and in the parallel
drawn between our manners and those of the Houyhnhnms.

SOURCE: from the critical notes in Hawkesworth's *The
Works of Jonathan Swift* (1755) vol 1, part 2, pp. 139, 217,
234–5, 286.

JAMES BEATTIE   1783

Beattie (1735–1803) was the author of *The Minstrel*, among other
poems, and professor of Moral Philosophy at Marischal College,
Aberdeen.

Gulliver's Travels are a sort of allegory; but rather Satirical and
Political, than Moral. The work is in every body's hands; and has
been criticised by many eminent writers. As far as the satire is
levelled at human pride and folly; at the abuses of human learning; at the absurdity of speculative projectors; at those criminal
or blundering expedients in policy, which we are apt to overlook,
or even to applaud, because custom has made them familiar; so
far the author deserves our warmest approbation, and his satire
will be allowed to be perfectly just, as well as exquisitely severe.
His fable is well conducted, and, for the most part consistent
with itself, and connected with probable circumstances. He per-
sonates a sea-faring man; and with wonderful propriety supports
the plainness and simplicity of the character. And this gives to
the whole narrative an air of truth; which forms an entertaining
contraste, when we compare it with the wildness of the fiction.
The style too deserves particular notice. It is not free from in-
accuracy: but as a model of easy and graceful simplicity, it has
not been exceeded by any thing in our language; and well deserves to be studied by every person, who wishes to write pure
English. – These, I think, are the chief merits of this celebrated
work; which has been more read, than any other publication of
the present century. Gulliver has something in him to hit every
taste. The statesman, the philosopher, and the critick, will admire
his keenness of satire, energy of description, and vivacity of lan-

guage: the vulgar, and even children, who cannot enter into these refinements, will find their account in the story, and be highly amused with it.

But I must not be understood to praise the whole indiscriminately. The last of the four voyages, though the author has exerted himself in it to the utmost, is an absurd, and an abominable fiction. It is absurd: because, in presenting us with rational beasts, and irrational men, it proceeds upon a direct contradiction to the most obvious laws of Nature, without deriving any support from either the dreams of the credulous, or the prejudices of the ignorant. And it is abominable: because it abounds in filthy and indecent images; because the general tenor of the satire is exaggerated into absolute falsehood; and because there must be something of an irreligious tendency in a work, which, like this, ascribes the perfection of reason, and of happiness, to a race of beings, who are said to be destitute of every religious idea. – But, what is yet worse, if any thing can be worse, this tale represents human nature itself as the object of contempt and abhorrence. Let the ridicule of wit be pointed at the follies, and let the scourge of satire be brandished at the crimes of mankind: all this is both pardonable, and praiseworthy; because it may be done with a good intention, and produce good effects. But when a writer endeavours to make us dislike and despise, every one his neighbour, and be dissatisfied with that Providence, who has made us what we are, and whose dispensations toward the human race are so peculiarly, and so divinely beneficent; such a writer, in so doing, provides himself the enemy, not of man only, but of goodness itself; and his work can never be allowed to be innocent, till impiety, malevolence, and misery, cease to be evils.

SOURCE: 'On Fable and Romance', *Dissertations Moral and Critical* (1783) pp. 514–16.

Son of Swift's friend, the Rev. Thomas Sheridan, and father of
R. B. Sheridan.

. . . The last charge, as before mentioned against Swift, and which
has gained most general credit, is that of perfect misanthropy;
and this is chiefly founded upon his supposed satire on human
nature, in the picture he has drawn of the yahoos. . . . But it may
be asked, to what end has such an odious animal been produced
to view? The answer is obvious: The design of the author, in the
whole of this apologue, is, to place before the eyes of man a picture of the two different parts of his frame, detached from each
other, in order that he may the better estimate the true value of
each, and see the necessity there is that the one should have an
absolute command over the other. In your merely animal capacity, says he to man, without reason to guide you, and actuated
only by a blind instinct, I will show you that you would be degraded below the beasts of the field. That very form, that very
body, you are now so proud of, as giving you such a superiority
over all other animals, I will show you owe all their beauty, and
all their greatest powers, to their being actuated by a rational
soul. Let that be withdrawn, let the body be inhabited by the
mind of a brute, let it be prone as theirs are, and suffered like
theirs to take its natural course, without any assistance from art,
you would in that case be the most deformed, as to your external
appearance, the most detestable of all creatures. And with regard
to your internal frame, filled with all the evil dispositions, and
malignant passions of mankind, you would be the most miserable
of beings, living in a continued state of internal vexation, and of
hatred and warfare with each other.

On the other hand, I will show another picture of an animal
endowed with a rational soul, and acting uniformly up to the
dictates of right reason. Here you may see collected all the virtues,
all the great qualities, which dignify man's nature, and constitute
the happiness of his life. What is the natural inference to be
drawn from these two different representations? Is it not evi-

dently a lesson to mankind, warning them not to suffer the animal part to be predominant in them, lest they resemble the vile Yahoo, and fall into vice and misery; but to emulate the noble and generous Houyhnhnm, by cultivating the rational faculty to the utmost; which will lead them to a life of virtue and happiness.

Is it not very extraordinary that mankind in general should so readily acknowledge their resemblance to the Yahoo, whose similitude to man consists only in the make of its body, and the evil dispositions of its mind; and that they should see no resemblance to themselves, in a creature possessed of their chief characteristical marks, reason and speech, and endowed with every virtue, with every noble quality, which constitute the dignity of man's nature, which distinguish and elevate the human above the brute species? Shall they arraign the author of writing a malignant satire against human nature, when reduced to its most abject brutal state, and wholly under the dominion of the passions; and shall they give him no credit for the exalted view in which he has placed the nobler part of our nature, when wholly under the direction of right reason? Or are mankind so stupid, as in an avowed fable, to stop at the outside, the vehicle, without diving into the concealed moral, which is the object of all fable? Do they really take the Yahoo for a man, because it has the form of a man; and the Houyhnhnm for a horse, because it has the form of a horse?

S o u r c e : *The Life of the Reverend Jonathan Swift* (1801) vol. i, p. 478 ff.

PART TWO

Romantics and Victorians

Nathan Drake, 1766–1836, Physician and Critic.

. . . This singular work displays a most fertile imagination, a deep insight into the follies, vices, and infirmities of mankind, and a fund of acute observation on ethics, politics, and literature. Its principal aim appears to have been to mortify the pride of human nature, whether arising from personal or mental accomplishments: the satire, however, has been carried too far, and degenerates into a libel on the species. The fourth part, especially, notwithstanding all that has been said in its defence by Sheridan and Berkeley, apparently exhibits such a malignant wish to degrade and brutalize the human race, that with every reader of feeling and benevolence it can occasion nothing but a mingled sensation of abhorrence and disgust. Let us hope, though the tendency be such as we have described, that it was not in the contemplation of Swift; but that he was betrayed into this degrading and exaggerated picture, by that habitual and gloomy discontent which long preyed upon his spirits, which at length terminated in insanity, and which for ever veiled from his eyes the fairest portion of humanity.

SOURCE: *Essays, Biographical, Critical, and Historical, Illustrative of the Tatler, Spectator and Guardian* (1805).

. . . The voyage to the land of the Houyhnhnms is what an editor of Swift must ever consider with pain. The source of such a diatribe against human nature could only be, that fierce indignation which he has described in his epitaph as so long gnawing his heart. Dwelling in a land where he considered the human race as divided between petty tyrants and oppressed slaves, and being himself a worshipper of that freedom and independence which he beheld daily trampled upon, the unrestrained violence of his feelings drove him to loath the very species by whom such iniquity was done and suffered. To this must be added, his personal health, broken and worn down by the recurring attacks of a frightful disorder; his social comfort destroyed by the death of one beloved object, and the daily decay and peril of another; his life decayed into autumn, and its remainder, after so many flattering and ambitious prospects, condemned to a country which he disliked, and banished from that in which he had formed his hopes, and left his affections : – when all these considerations are combined, they form some excuse for that general misanthropy which never prevented a single deed of individual benevolence. Such apologies are personal to the author, but there are also excuses for the work itself. The picture of the Yahoos, utterly odious and hateful as it is, presents to the reader a moral use. It was never designed as a representation of mankind in the state to which religion, and even the lights of nature, encourage men to aspire, but of that to which our species is degraded by the wilful subservience of mental qualities to animal instincts, of man, such as he may be found in the degraded ranks of every society, when brutalized by ignorance and gross vice. In this view, the more coarse and disgusting the picture, the more impressive is the moral to be derived from it, since, in proportion as an individual indulges in sensuality, cruelty, or avarice, he approaches in resemblance to the detested Yahoo. It cannot, however, be denied, that even a moral purpose will not justify the nakedness with which Swift has sketched this horrible outline of mankind degraded to a bestial state; since a moralist ought to hold with the Romans, that crimes of atrocity should be exposed when punished, but those of flagitious impurity concealed. In point of probability, too, for there are degrees of probability proper even to the wildest fiction, the fourth part of *Gulliver* is inferior to the three others. Giants and pigmies the reader can conceive; for, not to mention their being the ordinary machinery of romance, we are accustomed to see, in the inferior orders of creation, a disproportion of size between those of the same generic description, which may parallel (among some reptile tribes at least) even the fiction of *Gulliver*. But the mind rejects, as utterly impossible, the supposition of a nation of horses placed in houses which they could not build, fed with corn which they could neither sow, reap, nor save, possessing cows which they could not milk, depositing that milk in vessels which they could not make, and, in short, performing an hundred purposes of rational and social life, for which their external structure altogether unfits them.

But under every objection, whether founded in reason or prejudice, the *Travels of Gulliver* were received with the most universal interest, merited indeed by their novelty, as well as their internal merit. Lucian, Rabelais, More, Bergerac, Alletz, and many other authors, had indeed composed works, in which may be traced such general resemblance as arises from the imaginary voyage of a supposed traveller to ideal realms. But every Utopia which had hitherto been devised, was upon a plan either extravagant from its puerile fictions, or dull from the speculative legislation of which the story was made the vehicle. It was reserved for Swift to enliven the morality of his work with humour; to relieve its absurdity with satire; and to give the most improbable events an appearance of reality, derived from the character and stile of the narrator. Even Robinson Crusoe (though detailing events so much more probable,) hardly excels Gulliver in gravity and

verisimilitude of narrative. The character of the imaginary traveller is exactly that of Dampier, or any other sturdy nautical wan-
derer of the period, endowed with courage and common sense,
who sailed through distant seas, without losing a single English
prejudice which he had brought from Portsmouth or Plymouth,
and on his return gave a grave and simple narrative of what he
had seen or heard in foreign countries. . . .

SOURCE: *The Works of Jonathan Swift, D.D., Dean of
St. Patrick's Dublin* (12 vols), 2nd ed. (1824) vol. 1, *Life
of Swift.*

Francis Jeffrey   *1816*

Lord Jeffrey, 1773–1850, editor of the *Edinburgh Review.*

. . . He was, without exception, the greatest and most efficient
libeller that ever exercised the trade; and possessed, in an eminent degree, all the qualifications which it requires : – a clear head
– a cold heart – a vindictive temper – no admiration of noble
qualities – no sympathy with suffering – not much conscience –
not much consistency – a ready wit – a sarcastic humour – a
thorough knowledge of the baser parts of human nature – and
a complete familiarity with everything that is low, homely, and
familiar in language. These were his gifts; – and he soon felt for
what ends they were given. Almost all his works are libels; gener-

ally upon individuals, sometimes upon sects and parties, sometimes upon human nature. Whatever be his end, however, personal abuse, direct, vehement, unsparing invective, is his
means. . . .

The voyages of Captain Lemuel Gulliver is indisputably his
greatest work. The idea of making fictitious travels the vehicle
of satire as well as of amusement, is at least as old as Lucian; but
has never been carried into execution with such success, spirit, and
originality, as in this celebrated performance. The brevity, the
minuteness, the homeliness, the unbroken seriousness of the narrative, all give a character of truth and simplicity to the work
which at once palliates the extravagance of the fiction, and en-
hances the effect of those weighty reflections and cutting severities
in which it abounds. Yet though it is probable enough, that without those touches of satire and observation the work would have
appeared childish and preposterous, we are persuaded that it
pleases chiefly by the novelty and vivacity of the extraordinary
pictures it presents, and the entertainment we receive from following the fortunes of the traveller in his several extraordinary
adventures. The greater part of the wisdom and satire at least
appears to us to be extremely vulgar and common-place; and
we have no idea that they could possibly appear either impressive
or entertaining, if presented without these accompaniments. . . .

That the interest does not arise from the satire but from the
plausible description of physical wonders, seems to be farther
proved by the fact, that the parts which please the least are those
in which there is most satire and least of those wonders. In the
voyage to Laputa, after the first description of the flying island,
the attention is almost exclusively directed to intellectual absurdities; and every one is aware of the dulness that is the result.
Even as a satire, indeed, this part is extremely poor and defective;
nor can any thing show more clearly the author's incapacity for
large and comprehensive views than his signal failure in all those
parts which invited him to such contemplations. In the multitude of his vulgar and farcical representations of particular errors
in philosophy, he nowhere appears to have any sense of its true
value or principles; but satisfies himself with collecting or imagin-

ing a number of fantastical quackeries, which tend to illustrate nothing but his contempt for human understanding. Even where his subject seems to invite him to something of a higher flight, he uniformly shrinks back from it, and takes shelter in commonplace derision. What, for instance, can be poorer than the use he makes of the evocation of the illustrious dead – in which Hannibal is brought in just to say, that he had not a drop of vinegar in his camp; and Aristotle, to ask two of his commentators, 'whether the rest of the tribe were as great dunces as themselves?' The voyage to the Houyhnhnms is commonly supposed to displease by its vile and degrading representations of human nature; but, if we do not strangely mistake our own feelings on the subject, the impression it produces is not so much that of disgust as of dulness. The picture is not only extravagant, but bald and tame in the highest degree; while the story is not enlivened by any of those numerous and uncommon incidents which are detailed in the two first parts, with such an inimitable air of probability as almost to persuade us of their reality. For the rest, we have observed already, that the scope of the whole work, and indeed of all his writings, is to degrade and vilify human nature; and though some of the images which occur in this part may be rather coarser than the others, we do not think the difference so considerable as to account for its admitted inferiority in the power of pleasing.

SOURCE: Jeffrey's review of Scott's edition, *Edinburgh Review,* xxvii (1816).

Samuel Taylor Coleridge (undated)

The great defect of the Houyhnhnms is not its misanthropy, and those who apply this word to it must really believe that the essence of human nature, that the *anthropos misoumenos*, consists in the shape of the body. Now, to show the falsity of this was Swift's great object : he would prove to our feelings and imaginations, and thereby teach *practically*, that it is Reason and Conscience which give all the loveliness and dignity not only to Man, but to the shape of Man; that deprived of these, and yet retaining the Understanding, he would be the most loathsome and hateful of all animals; that his understanding would manifest itself only as malignant cunning, his free will as obstinacy and unteachableness. And how true a picture this is every madhouse may convince any man; a brothel where highwaymen meet will convince every philosopher. But the defect of the work is its inconsistency; the Houyhnhnms are not rational creatures, *i.e.*, creatures of perfect reason; they are not progressive; they have servants without any reason for their natural inferiority or any explanation how the difference acted (?); and, above all, they – *i.e.*, Swift himself – has a perpetual affectation of being wiser than his Maker [see postscript], and of eradicating what God gave to be subordinated and used; *ex. gr.*, the maternal and paternal affection (σοργὴ). There is likewise a true Yahooism in the constant denial of the existence of Love, as not identical with Friendship, and yet distinct always and very often divided from Lust. The best defence is that it is a Satyr; still, it would have been felt a thousand times more deeply if Reason had been truly pourtrayed, and a finer imagination would have been evinced if the author had shown the effect of the possession of Reason and the moral sense in the outward form and gestures of the Horses. In short, critics in general complain of the Yahoos; I complain of the Houyhn-hnms.

As to the *wisdom* of adopting this mode of proving the great truths here exemplified, that is another question, which no feeling mind will find a difficulty in answering who has read and understood the Paradise scenes in *Paradise Lost*, and compared the moral effect on his heart and his virtuous aspirations of Milton's Adam with Swift's horses; but different men have different turns of genius; Swift's may be good, tho' very inferior to Milton's; they do not stand in each other's way.

S. T. C.

A case in point, and besides utterly inconsistent with the boasted Reason of the Houyhnhnms, may be seen, p. 194, 195 [chap. iv.], where the Horse discourses on the human frame with the grossest prejudices that could possibly be inspired by vanity and self-opinion. That Reason which commands man to admire the fitness of the horse and stag for superior speed, of the bird for flight, &c., &c. – must it not have necessitated the rational horse to have seen and acknowledged the admirable aptitude of the human hand, compared with his own fetlocks, of the human limbs for climbing, for the management of tools, &c.? In short, compare the *effect* of the Satire, when it is founded in truth and good sense (chap. v., for instance), with the wittiest of those passages which have their only support in spleen and want of reverence for the original frame of man, and the feelings of the Reader will be his faithful guide in the reperusal of the work, which I still think the highest effort of Swift's genius, unless we should except the *Tale of the Tub*. Then I would put Lilliput; next Brobdingnag; and Laputa I would expunge altogether. It is a wretched abortion, the product of spleen and ignorance and self-conceit.

SOURCE: These undated comments were found in a volume of Swift which belonged to Wordsworth. They are given here as transcribed by G. A. Aitken in 'Coleridge on *Gulliver's Travels*', *The Athenaeum*, no. 3590 (15 August 1896) p. 224. [Ed.]

. . . Oh, when shall we have such another Rector of Laracor! – *A Tale of a Tub* is one of the most masterly compositions in the language, whether for thought, wit, or style. It is so capital and undeniable a proof of the author's talents, that Dr. Johnson, who did not like Swift, would not allow that he wrote it. It is hard that the same performance should stand in the way of a man's promotion to a bishopric, as wanting gravity, and at the same time be denied to be his, as having too much wit. It is a pity the Doctor did not find out some graver author, for whom he felt a critical kindness, on whom to father this splendid but unacknowledged production. Dr. Johnson could not deny that *Gulliver's Travels* were his; he therefore disputed their merits, and said that after the first idea of them was conceived, thay were easy to execute; all the rest followed mechanically. I do not know how that may be; but the mechanism employed is something very different from any that the author of *Rasselas* was in the habit of bringing to bear on such occasions. There is nothing more futile, as well as invidious, than this mode of criticising a work of original genius. Its greatest merit is supposed to be in the invention; and you say, very wisely, that it is not *in the execution*. You might as well take away the merit in the invention of the telescope, by saying that, after its uses were explained and understood, any ordinary eyesight could look through it. Whether the excellence of *Gulliver's Travels* is in the conception or the execution, is of little consequence; the power is somewhere, and it is a power that has moved the world. The power is not that of big words and vaunting common places. Swift left these to those who wanted them; and has done what his acuteness and intensity of mind alone could enable any one to conceive or to perform. His object was to strip empty

. . . the imposing air which external circum-
. . . d them; and for this purpose he has cheated
. . . of the illusions which the prejudices of sense and
. . . a put upon it, by reducing every thing to the abstract
. . . nent of size. He enlarges or diminishes the scale, as he
. . . es to show the insignificance or the grossness of our over-
weening self-love. That he has done this with mathematical precision, with complete presence of mind and perfect keeping, in a
manner that comes equally home to the understanding of the
man and of the child, does not take away from the merit of the
work or the genius of the author. He has taken a new view of
human nature, such as a being of a higher sphere might take of
it; he has torn the scales from off his moral vision; he has tried an
experiment upon human life, and sifted its pretensions from the
alloy of circumstances; he has measured it with a rule, has weighed
it in a balance, and found it, for the most part, wanting and
worthless – in substance and in show. Nothing solid, nothing valuable is left in his system but virtue and wisdom. What a libel is
this upon mankind! What a convincing proof of misanthropy!
What presumption and what *malice prepense*, to show men what
they are, and to teach them what they ought to be! What a
mortifying stroke aimed at national glory, is that unlucky incident
of Gulliver's wading across the channel and carrying off the
whole fleet of Blefuscu! After that, we have only to consider
which of the contending parties was in the right. What a shock
to personal vanity is given in the account of Gulliver's nurse
Glumdalclitch! Still, notwithstanding the disparagement to her
personal charms, her good-nature remains the same amiable quality as before. I cannot see the harm, the misanthropy, the immoral and degrading tendency of this. The moral lesson is as fine
as the intellectual exhibition is amusing. It is an attempt to tear
off the mask of imposture from the world; and nothing but imposture has a right to complain of it. It is, indeed, the way with
our quacks in morality to preach up the dignity of human nature,
to pamper pride and hypocrisy with the idle mockeries of the
virtues they pretend to, and which they have not : but it was not
Swift's way to cant morality, or any thing else; nor did his genius

prompt him to write unmeaning panegyrics on mankind!

I do not, therefore, agree with the estimate of Swift's moral or intellectual character, given by an eminent critic, who does not seem to have forgotten the party politics of Swift. I do not carry my political resentments so far back: I can at this time of day forgive Swift for having been a Tory. I feel little disturbance (whatever I might think of them) at his political sentiments, which died with him, considering how much else he has left behind him of a more solid and imperishable nature! If he had, indeed, (like some others) merely left behind him the lasting infamy of a destroyer of his country, or the shining example of an apostate from liberty, I might have thought the case altered. . . .

SOURCE: *Lectures on the English Poets* (1818)
pp. 218–22.

. . . The grave and logical conduct of an absurd proposition, as exemplified in the cannibal proposal just mentioned,[1] is our author's constant method through all his works of humour. Given a country of people six inches or sixty feet high, and by the mere process of the logic, a thousand wonderful absurdities are evolved, at so many stages of the calculation. Turning to the First Minister who waited behind him with a white staff near as tall as the mainmast of the 'Royal Sovereign,' the King of Brobdingnag observes how contemptible a thing human grandeur is, as represented by such a contemptible little creature as Gulliver.

The Emperor of Lilliput's features are strong and masculine [what a surprising humour there is in this description!] – The Emperor's features, [Gulliver says] are strong and masculine, with an Austrian lip, an arched nose, his complexion olive, his countenance erect, his body and limbs well proportioned, and his deportment majestic. He is taller *by the breadth of my nail* than any of his Court, which alone is enough to strike an awe into beholders.

What a surprising humour there is in these descriptions! How noble the satire is here! how just and honest! How perfect the image! Mr. Macaulay has quoted the charming lines of the poet where the king of the pigmies is measured by the same standard. We have all read in Milton of the spear that was like 'the mast of some great ammiral;' but these images are surely likely to come to the comic poet originally. The subject is before him. He is turning it in a thousand ways. He is full of it. The figure suggests itself naturally to him, and comes out of his subject, as in that wonderful passage, when Gulliver's box having been dropped by the eagle into the sea, and Gulliver having been received into the ship's cabin, he calls upon the crew to bring the box into the cabin, and put it on the table, the cabin being only a quarter the size of the box. It is the *veracity* of the blunder which is so admirable. Had a man come from such a country as Brobding-nag, he would have blundered so.

But the best stroke of humour, if there be a best in that abounding book, is that where Gulliver, in the unpronounceable country, describes his parting from his master the horse:

I took [he says] a second leave of my master, but as I was going to prostrate myself to kiss his hoof, he did me the honour to raise it gently to my mouth. I am not ignorant how much I have been cen-sured for mentioning this last particular. Detractors are pleased to think it improbable that so illustrious a person should descend to give so great a mark of distinction to a creature so inferior as I. Neither have I forgotten how apt some travellers are to boast of extraordinary favours they have received. But if these censurers were better acquainted with the noble and courteous disposition of the Houyhnhnms they would soon change their opinion.

The surprise here, the audacity of circumstantial evidence, the astounding gravity of the speaker, who is not ignorant how much he has been censured, the nature of the favour conferred, and the respectful exultation at the receipt of it, are surely complete; it is truth topsy-turvy, entirely logical and absurd.

As for the humour and conduct of this famous fable, I suppose there is no person who reads but must admire; as for the moral, I think it horrible, shameful, unmanly, blasphemous; and giant and great as this Dean is, I say we should hoot him. Some of this audience mayn't have read the last part of *Gulliver*, and to such I would recall the advice of the venerable *Mr. Punch* to persons about to marry, and say 'Don't.' When Gulliver first lands among the Yahoos, the naked howling wretches clamber up trees and assault him, and he describes himself as 'almost stifled with the filth which fell about him.' The reader of the fourth part of *Gulliver's Travels* is like the hero himself in this instance. It is Yahoo language: a monster gibbering shrieks, and gnashing im-precations against mankind – tearing down all shreds of modesty, past all sense of manliness and shame; filthy in word, filthy in thought, furious, raging, obscene.

And dreadful it is to think that Swift knew the tendency of his creed – the fatal rocks towards which his logic desperately drifted. That last part of *Gulliver* is only a consequence of what has gone before; and the worthlessness of all mankind, the pettiness, cruelty, pride, imbecility, the general vanity, the foolish pretension, the mock greatness, the pompous dulness, the mean aims, the base successes – all these were present to him; it was with the din of these curses of the world, blasphemies against Heaven, shrieking in his ears, that he began to write his dreadful allegory – of which the meaning is that man is utterly wicked, desperate, and imbecile, and his passions are so monstrous, and his boasted powers so mean, that he is and deserves to be the slave of brutes, and ignorance is better than his vaunted reason. What had this man done? what secret remorse was rankling at his heart? what fever was boiling in him, that he should see all the world bloodshot? We view the world with our own eyes, each of us; and we make from within us the world we see. A weary heart gets no gladness out of sunshine; a selfish man is sceptical about friendship, as a man with no ear doesn't care for music. A frightful self-consciousness it must have been, which looked on mankind so darkly through those keen eyes of Swift.

SOURCE: *The English Humourists of the Eighteenth Century* (1851).

NOTE

1. Thackeray has, in the preceding paragraph of the original essay, misinterpreted *A Modest Proposal.*

. . . *Gulliver's Travels* belongs to a literary genus full of grotesque and anomalous forms. Its form is derived from some of the imaginary travels of which Lucian's *True History* – itself a burlesque of some early travellers' tales – is the first example. But it has an affinity also to such books as Bacon's *Atlantis*, and More's *Utopia*; and, again, to later philosophical romances like *Candide* and *Rasselas*; and not least, perhaps, to the ancient fables, such as *Reynard the Fox*, to which Swift refers in the *Tale of a Tub*. It may be compared, again, to the *Pilgrim's Progress,* and the whole family of allegories. The full-blown allegory resembles the game of chess said to have been played by some ancient monarch, in which the pieces were replaced by real human beings. . . . and such a book as *Gulliver* must be regarded as lying somewhere between the allegory and the direct revelation of truth, which is more or less implied in the work of every genuine artist. Its true purpose has thus rather puzzled critics. Hazlitt urges, for example, with his usual brilliancy, that Swift's purpose was to 'strip empty pride and grandeur of the imposing air which external circumstances throw around them.' Swift accordingly varies the scale, so as to show the insignificance or the grossness of our self-love. He does this with 'mathematical precision;' he tries an experiment upon human nature; and with the result that 'nothing solid, nothing valuable is left in his system but wisdom and virtue.' So Gulliver's carrying off the fleet of Blefuscu is 'a mortifying stroke, aimed at national glory.' 'After that, we have only to consider which of the contending parties was in the right.'

Hazlitt naturally can see nothing misanthropical or innocent in such a conclusion. The mask of imposture is torn off the world, and only imposture can complain. This view, which has no doubt its truth, suggests some obvious doubts. We are not invited, as a matter of fact, to attend to the question of right and wrong, as between Lilliput and Blefuscu. The real sentiment in Swift is that a war between these miserable pygmies is, in itself, contemptible; and therefore, as he infers, war between men six feet high is equally contemptible. The truth is that, although Swift's solution of the problem may be called mathematically precise, the precision does not extend to the supposed argument. If we insist upon treating the question as one of strict logic, the only conclusion which could be drawn from Gulliver is the very safe one that the interest of the human drama does not depend upon the size of the actors. A pygmy or a giant endowed with all our functions and thoughts would be exactly as interesting as a being of the normal stature. It does not require a journey to imaginary regions to teach us so much. And if we say that Swift has shown us in his pictures the real essence of human life, we only say for him what might be said with equal force of Shakspeare or Balzac, or any great artist. The bare proof that the essence is not dependent upon the external condition of size is superfluous and irrelevant; and we must admit that Swift's method is childish, or that it does not adhere to this strict logical canon.

Hazlitt, however, comes nearer the truth, as I think, when he says that Swift takes a view of human nature such as might be taken by a being of a higher sphere. That, at least, is his purpose; only, as I think, he pursues it by a neglect of 'scientific reasoning.' The use of the machinery is simply to bring us into a congenial frame of mind. He strikes the key-note of contempt by his imagery of dwarfs and giants. We despise the petty quarrels of beings six inches high; and therefore we are prepared to despise the wars carried on by a Marlborough and a Eugene. We transfer the contempt based upon mere size, to the motives, which are the same in big men and little. The argument, if argument there be, is a fallacy; but it is equally efficacious for the feelings. You see the pettiness and cruelty of the Lilliputians, who want to conquer an empire defended by toy-ships; and you are tacitly invited to consider whether the bigness of French men-of-war makes an attack upon them more respectable. The force of the satire de-

pends ultimately upon the vigour with which Swift has described
the real passions of human beings, big or little. He really means
to express a bitter contempt for statesmen and warriors, and
seduces us to his side, for the moment, by asking us to look at a
diminutive representation of the same beings. The quarrels which
depend upon the difference between the high-boots and the low-
heeled shoes; or upon breaking eggs at the big or little end; the
party intrigues which are settled by cutting capers on the tight-
rope, are meant, of course, in ridicule of political and religious
parties; and its force depends upon our previous conviction that
the party-quarrels between our fellows are, in fact, equally contemptible. Swift's satire is congenial to the mental attitude of all
who have persuaded themselves that men are, in fact, a set of
contemptible fools and knaves, in whose quarrels and mutual
slaughterings the wise and good could not persuade themselves
to take a serious interest. He 'proves' nothing, mathematically or
otherwise. If you do not share his sentiments, there is nothing
in the mere alteration of the scale to convince you that they are
right; you may say, with Hazlitt, that heroism is as admirable in
a Lilliputian as in a Brobdingnagian, and believe that war calls
forth patriotism, and often advances civilisation. What Swift has
really done is to provide for the man who despises his species a
number of exceedingly effective symbols for the utterance of his
contempt. A child is simply amused with Bigendians and Little-
endians; a philosopher thinks that the questions really at the bottom of church quarrels are in reality of more serious import : but
the cynic who has learnt to disbelieve in the nobility or wisdom of
the great mass of his species finds a most convenient metaphor
for expressing his disbelief. In this way *Gulliver's Travels* contains a whole gallery of caricatures thoroughly congenial to the
despisers of humanity.

[Stephen goes on to speak of Swift's 'morbid interest in the
physically disgusting', and how 'he nurses his misanthropy, as he
might tear his flesh to keep his mortality before his eyes'.]

SOURCE: *Swift* (English Men of Letters series, 1882).

. . . In Brobdingnag, the humour is not less, but the satire is far
more bitter and intense. Brobdingnag is not merely Lilliput seen,
as Scott puts it, through the other end of the telescope. To ridicule mankind by comparing them with pigmies was one thing:
to make them contemptible by using them as a means of ele-
vating a superior order of beings, was quite another. In Lilliput
the humour is on the surface: the satire is only occasional: in
Brobdingnag the satire never allows itself to be forgotten long.
Human nature seemed to Swift contemptible chiefly for its infinite pettiness and triviality, for its endless and futile restlessness:
for its pigmy strainings to create difficulties, for the blind folly
with which it entangled itself in labours beyond its strength. In
the natives of Brobdingnag the leading feature is that massive
simplicity after which Swift's soul longed. Political science they
deem a waste of time. They have ceased to multiply books. Of
philosophy they are fortunate in having no conception. To pursue
legal niceties is, with them, a capital crime. They are wise enough
to see their own counterpart in creatures so contemptible as
human beings, and are not blind to their own faults, reflected
in these, 'the most pernicious race of little odious vermin, that
nature ever suffered to crawl upon the surface of the earth.' But
human nature, in Gulliver, is content 'to wink at its own little-
ness,' and to forget the gulf between itself and the giants by which
it is surrounded.

Yet bitter as is the drift of the satire in Brobdingnag, it is not
without relief. We are carried on by the story, and in amusement
at the mishaps of Gulliver we forget that we are laughing at ourselves. But in Laputa, and the Houyhnhnms, we advance a step
further. The spirit of the allegory is changed. We miss the nicely-

adjusted proportions, and the careful construction of the preceding voyages. It is not without purpose that Gulliver is made
to return from Lilliput and Brobdingnag, by vaguely described
and almost miraculous means; while from Laputa he sails to the
allied empire of Japan, and from the Houyhnhnms prepares for
his homeward voyage as he would have done in starting from
Rotherhithe. In the latter region we are no longer in realms of
pure fancy, but only in places where the ordinary laws of nature
are confounded in a bewildering jumble. Fancy and reality are
constantly intermingled. As the Academy of Lagado comes
nearer to the type of human crotchet-mongers, and as the Yahoo
typifies more closely humanity, so the construction of the allegory
fails, but so also the directness of the satire is increased. In Lagado
we are in the midst of our familiar wits and Greshamites : in
Glubbdubdrib we see the falsities of our own history exposed : in
the Struldbrugs of Luggnagg we see the hideousness that human
nature would present, were it but permitted to ripen to full maturity. So in the Yahoos we see a counterpart of human nature, free
only from the dangerous ingredient of 'a little reason,' which
makes humanity more detestable. Swift speaks no longer with
the mouth of Scriblerus, but with a voice whose reality falsifies the
original scheme, and from a heart torn by that fierce anger that
he vented on his kind. . . .

If it is the voyages to Lilliput and to Brobdingnag, in which
no thought of the satire they contain mingles with the interest of
the story, that have proved most attractive to children, it is the
voyage to the Houyhnhnms which is likely to excite most interest
amongst men. On its coarseness we need not dwell. But beyond
that fault, we may admit that the fable is clumsy : that the comparison between the Houyhnhnms and their counterparts is often
mere verbal quibbling : that in the fancy of horses ruling men,
there is no great depth of satiric force. We may admit further
that Swift deserts matter of general concern, and here also attacks
particular classes from motives of personal irritation. But all this
fails to affect the real interest of the satire. Its central feature is
contrast between the Houyhnhnm, representing, in himself, and
as the negation of all human attributes, the type of Stoical and

c

impassive dignity; and the Yahoo, as the picture of degradation,
the points of distinction between whom and human beings gradually drop away, leaving humanity without one shred of defence
for its own self-respect. Step by step the force of the contrast gains
upon us: from a picture full of warning, it changes into a sentence of despair: with ruthless hand it throws down the fancied
dignity of humanity, strips off the trappings and disguises with
which we deceive ourselves, and leaves us face to face with the
stern realities of our nature and our lot. Scathing, indeed, must
have been the contempt for his kind, unrelenting the clearness of
vision, that had to seek relief from smooth conventionalities by
pitiless delineation such as this. But a further question still remains. We can scarcely doubt that Swift summed up the book
in this contrast betyeen Houyhnhnm and Yahoo. But did he
satisfy himself with the ideal Houyhnhnm? Was the formal Stoicism, typified in the ruling caste, Swift's conception of the highest
morality? Was that absence of passion and emotion, that negation of natural affection, that level and unlovable monotony,
what Swift most admired? If it was so, then his ideals were shaped
in a mould strangely different from anything in his own consciousness. If it was not so, was this picture but another ply of
the satire on humanity, whose best ideals could be attained only
by eliminating all that made life worth living, but whose passions
and emotions, when ripened to full maturity, ended only in the
loathsomeness of the Yahoo?

S o u r c e : *Life of Jonathan Swift* (1882) vol. 2.

PART THREE

Modern Studies

C. H. Firth

THE POLITICAL SIGNIFICANCE OF
GULLIVER'S TRAVELS (1919)

A critic who seeks to explain the political significance of *Gulliver's Travels* may be guilty of too much ingenuity, but he cannot fairly be charged with exaggerated curiosity. He is searching for a secret which Swift tells us is hidden there, and endeavouring to solve riddles which were intended to exercise his wits. Swift loved to mystify the public; he often preferred to speak in parables when there was no reason for doing so. In this case there was good reason for his preference. At that time, and for many years later, it was dangerous to write plainly about public affairs, or to criticize public men with any freedom.

When Swift wrote his *History of the Last Four Years of the Queen* he proposed to prefix to it characters of the party leaders of that period in order to make it more intelligible. In 1738 he contemplated the publication of this *History*. Though it was about five-and-twenty years after the events described, he was warned by his friend Erasmus Lewis, that if the characters he had drawn were published as they stood 'nothing could save the author's printer and publishers from some grievous punishment'.[1] Accordingly it was not published till 1758, thirteen years after Swift's death.

Authors who wrote about public affairs immediately after they had happened and about ministers of state while they were actually in office were obliged to use literary artifices of various kinds in order to express their opinions with impunity. But it was not without some compensating advantage, for to be allusive and indirect, while it protected the author, stimulated the curiosity of the reader.

In *Gulliver's Travels* many figures which seem to be imaginary
are meant to depict real personages, or at all events are drawn
from them. Swift says in one of his earlier writings : 'In describing
the virtues and vices of mankind, it is convenient, upon every
article, to have some eminent person in our eye, from whence we
copy our description.' Again he says : 'I have thought of another
expedient, frequently practised with great safety and success by
satirical writers; which is that of looking into history for some
character bearing a resemblance to the person we would describe;
and with the absolute power of altering, adding, or suppressing
what circumstances we please, I conceive we must have very bad
luck or very little skill to fail.' He admitted that this method of
writing had one serious drawback. 'Though the present age may
understand well enough the little hints we give, the parallels we
draw, and the characters we describe, yet this will all be lost
to the next. However, if these papers should happen to live till
our grandchildren are men, I hope they may have curiosity
enough to consult annals and compare dates, in order to find
out.'[2]

Gulliver's Travels was published on October 28, 1726, but
some portions of the book were written much earlier. They were
intended to be a contribution to the *Memoirs of Martinus Scriblerus*. 'It was from a part of these memoirs', Pope told Spence,
'that Dr. Swift took his first hints for *Gulliver*. There were pigmies in Schreibler's *Travels*; and the projects of Laputa.'[3]

As Pope's statement is confirmed by internal evidence, and is
inherently probable, it may be accepted in an inquiry into the
composition of the *Travels*, and parts of the First and Third
Voyages may be assigned to the year 1714.[4] At that date, as
Swift's correspondence shows, Swift and a circle of his friends
were engaged upon the *Memoirs*. Swift's return to Ireland and
the political revolution which followed Queen Anne's death
(August 1, 1714) broke up the circle, and it was not till 1741
that the *Memoirs of Scriblerus* were printed. In the meantime
Swift's intended contribution to the joint work had been trans-
formed into the Travels of Captain Lemuel Gulliver.

The development was a slow process. After the revolution of

1714 Swift had no heart to continue his story. 'I must be a little easy in my mind before I think of Scriblerus', he wrote on June 28, 1715. 'You know how well I loved both Lord Oxford and Bolingbroke, and how dear the Duke of Ormond is to me. Do you imagine I can be easy while their enemies are trying to take off their heads? . . . Truly I must be a little easy in my mind before I can think of Scriblerus.'

Five or six years later he had regained his ease of mind, and he began to write again. He took up his pen in defence of Ireland, writing about May 1720 his *Proposal for the Universal Use of Irish Manufacture*. He took out of his desk his half-finished contribution to the *Memoirs of Scriblerus*, and converted it into the *Voyages of Captain Gulliver*. In a letter written to Charles Ford and dated April 15, 1721, he says, 'I am now writing a History of my Travels, which will be a large volume, and gives account of countries hitherto unknown; but they go on slowly for want of health and humor.' Three years later the *Travels* were nearly completed. 'I have left the Country of Horses,' he told Ford on January 19, 1724, 'and am in the Flying Island, where I shall not stay long, and my two last journeys will be soon over.' He was able to tell his friend on August 14, 1725: 'I have finished my *Travels*, and I am now transcribing them; they are admirable things, and will wonderfully mend the world.' On September 29 in the same year he told Pope: 'I have employed my time in finishing, correcting, amending, and transcribing my *Travels* in four parts complete, newly augmented, and intended for the press when the world shall deserve them, or rather when a printer shall be found brave enough to venture his ears.' This reference to the printer's ears is an acknowledgement that the book contained political allusions which might bring the publisher to the pillory, and draw upon him the fate which befell Defoe.

Political allusions abound in the *Travels*. Some are to the events of the end of Queen Anne's reign, others to events in the reign of George I. Naturally those events which happened during the five years in which the *Travels* were completed left most traces on the work. In England at the beginning of the period there was

the South Sea Bubble (1720), which was followed by the return
of Walpole to office (1721) and by the return of Bolingbroke
from exile (1723), by the ejection of Carteret from the English
cabinet (1724), and by the supremacy of Walpole in it (1725).
In Ireland during the same period the struggle over Wood's
patent began and ended (1722–5).

These references to public events and public personages are
most frequent in the First and Third Voyages. Each of these
Voyages consist of a part which was written about 1714, as
Pope's statement proves, and internal evidence confirms. Each
of these Voyages also contains other parts written later, as Swift's
letters indicate, and the contents of the additions show. Moreover, there are signs in the text itself, such as repetitions, explanations, and alterations, which show where the matter was added.

Let us begin by examining the Voyage to Lilliput. The first
part of it, which contains the story of Gulliver's shipwreck, and
of his early adventures among the pigmies, has no political significance. It is simply what Shakespeare terms 'very gracious fool-
ing'. This no doubt represents the part written in 1714. On the
other hand, the account of the laws and customs of Lilliput contained in Chapter VI was probably written later. It seems to be
an afterthought, because in Chapter IV Gulliver had announced
that he proposed to reserve 'for a greater work' the very subjects treated of in Chapter VI.[5] There is also a distinct change of
tone; a serious didactic purpose becomes apparent. The institutions of Lilliput are described for the instruction of Swift's fellow
countrymen, just as Sir Thomas More described the institutions
of Utopia. 'There are some laws and customs in this empire very
peculiar,' says Gulliver; 'and if they were not so directly contrary to those of my own dear country, I should be tempted to
say a little in their justification.' Thus he directs the attention of
his readers to the impunity of certain crimes in England and the
shortcomings of English education.

By a curious contradiction, as soon as Swift turns to describe
the politics of Lilliput it ceases to be Utopia and becomes England
itself, instead of being an example to England. 'We labour', says
Gulliver's informant, 'under two mighty evils: a violent faction

at home and the danger of an invasion by a most potent enemy from abroad.'

In Lilliput there are two struggling parties called 'Tramecksan and Slamecksan, from the high and low heels on their shoes, by which they distinguish themselves.' These typify the High Church and Low Church parties, or the Tories and Whigs. The potent enemy abroad is the island of Blefuscu, which typifies France, engaged in an obstinate struggle with its neighbour for a whole generation. The conversion of Lilliput into England marks the change of plan made by Swift when he took up the half-finished story of the First Voyage again, about 1720, and turned his story into a political allegory. This change involved other changes. The majestic Emperor of Lilliput of the second chapter, with his 'Austrian lip and arched nose', was a purely conventional monarch, not representing George I or any other real king. It was now necessary to convert this personage into George I, which was effected by making him a Whig 'determined to make use of only Low Heels in the administration of the government', and wearing himself heels lower than any of his court. The parallel was emphasized by making the heir to the throne show an inclination to the High Heels, as the Prince of Wales did to the Tories. Finally Swift inserted an ironical passage on the lenity and mercy of the King, intended to call to the minds of his readers the executions which had taken place after the rebellion in 1715, and the encomiums on the King's mercy which the Government had published at the time.

The King was not the only personage who underwent a sort of transformation when Swift took his half-told story in hand again. Gulliver is changed too. At first Gulliver to a certain extent represented Swift himself – that is, certain incidents in Gulliver's adventures were an allegorical representation of certain incidents in Swift's life. Editors of *Gulliver's Travels* rightly agree in their interpretation of the story of Gulliver's extinction of the fire in the palace at Lilliput, and of the resentment of the Empress in consequence.[6] Sir Walter Scott says: 'It is perhaps a strained interpretation of this incident to suppose that our author recollected the prejudices of Queen Anne against the indecency and immorality of his own satirical vein, though it was so serviceable to the cause of her ministry.'[7] Mr. Dennis says: 'Queen Anne was so much disgusted with the *Tale of a Tub* that in spite of Swift's political services she could never be induced to give him preferment in the Church.'[8] J. F. Waller and W. C. Taylor, in their editions of *Gulliver*, interpret the incident in a similar fashion. It is not an unreasonable interpretation, for it is clear that Swift's satirical writings stood in the way of his promotion. He failed to obtain the Irish bishopric which he hoped to get in 1708,[9] and it was with great difficulty that he obtained a deanery in 1713.[10]

The tradition is that the first failure was due to the influence of Dr. Sharp, the Archbishop of York, who showed the Queen the *Tale of a Tub*.[11] The second, it is alleged, was due to the influence of the Duchess of Somerset, incensed by Swift's *Windsor Prophecy*, written in December 1711.[12] Swift believed that this was the case, and in the lines entitled 'The Author on Himself', written in 1714, he mentioned both causes, and spoke of Queen Anne as 'a royal prude', whose opposition to his preferment was due to the efforts of his enemies. In that poem he names firstly the Duchess of Somerset and the Archbishop of York, and secondly the Earl of Nottingham and Robert Walpole as the enemies in question.

In *Gulliver's Travels* the captain's chief enemy is a certain lord named Bolgolam, who was pleased, says Gulliver, 'without provocation to be my mortal enemy. . . . That minister was Galbet, or Admiral of the Realm, very much in his master's confidence, and a person well versed in affairs, but of a morose and sour complexion.' He is referred to later as Gulliver's 'mortal enemy', and his 'malice' is mentioned and insisted upon.

This person is clearly intended to represent the Earl of Nottingham. The 'morose and sour complexion' attributed to Bolgolam at once suggests the identification. In one of his pamphlets Swift says that Nottingham's 'adust complexion disposeth him to rigour and severity', and time after time he refers to him by his nickname of 'Dismal'. 'Dismal, so men call him from his looks', explains Swift to Stella.[13] The earl had long been Swift's personal enemy. In 1711, when Nottingham joined the Whigs in their attack on the foreign policy of the Government, Swift wrote two ballads against him, 'An Orator Dismal from Nottinghamshire' and 'Toland's Invitation to Dismal'.[14] Nottingham retaliated by using whatever private influence he possessed at court to stop Swift's preferment, and finally by an open and bitter attack upon him in Parliament. On June 1, 1714, when the Schism Act was debated in the House of Lords, Nottingham opposed the bill, saying that it was dangerous because it gave too much power to the bishops, 'though now they had the happiness of having so worthy bishops, yet it possibly might happen that a person who wrote lewdly, nay, even atheistically, might by having a false undeserved character given him be promoted to a bishopric by her Majesty.'[15] Another version makes Nottingham say : 'I own I tremble when I think that a certain divine who is hardly suspected of being a Christian, is in a fair way of being a Bishop.'[16] More than any other statesman of the period, he might be described with justice as Swift's 'mortal enemy'. On the other hand, it is more difficult to explain why Nottingham should be designated 'High Admiral'. There was no Lord High Admiral in England after 1709, and the different noblemen who held the post of First Lord of the Admiralty between 1709 and 1726 were none of them enemies of Swift. One reason for the designation can be suggested. Nottingham had been First Lord from February 1680 to May 1684, and ever afterwards 'piqued himself upon understanding sea affairs'. In William III's reign, when he was Secretary of State, he was continually interfering in the management of the fleet. 'All men', says Lord Dartmouth, 'that had been bred to that profession unanimously agreed that he was totally ignorant in their science, and were highly provoked when he pretended to contradict or give them directions.'[17] To term Nottingham 'High Admiral' may be an ironical reference to this notorious foible.

Nottingham was President of the Council in the first Ministry of George I, and held that post till February 29, 1716, when he was dismissed because he pressed for the pardon of the leaders of the late rebellion.[18] This attack upon him under the character of Bolgolam must have been written in the summer of 1714, when his offences against Swift were fresh and Swift's anger against him was hot. The prose character is the counterpart of the verses entitled 'The Author on Himself', which belong to the same summer. It is not likely that it was written after 1716, when Nottingham's clemency had led to his fall from office.

When Swift, in 1719 or 1720, took up his unfinished story again, and converted it into a political allegory, he changed his plan, developed, as we have seen, the character of the Emperor, and shadowed forth under the misfortunes of Gulliver the fate of Bolingbroke. That statesman must have been much in Swift's mind about that time. He had resumed his correspondence with his exiled friend in February 1719, at which time there was some prospect of Bolingbroke's pardon and his return to England, though the hope was not realized till 1723. During that period several long letters passed between them. It was towards the end of 1721 that Swift seems to have mentioned his *Travels* to Bolingbroke. 'I long to see your *Travels*', wrote the latter, answering on January 1, 1722, a letter from Swift dated September 29, 1721.

The parallel between the fate of Bolingbroke and that of Gulliver was very close. Like Gulliver, Bolingbroke had brought a great war to an end and concluded a peace 'upon conditions very advantageous' to his country, but was denounced by his political opponents for not prosecuting the war to the complete subjugation of the enemy. He was accused of treasonable intercourse with the ambassadors of France, as Gulliver was with those of Blefuscu. Gulliver fled from Lilliput because he felt that he could not obtain a fair trial, 'having in my life', says he, 'perused many state trials, which I ever observed to terminate as the judges thought fit to direct,' and because he knew that powerful enemies sought his life. Bolingbroke declared that he fled from England because 'I had certain and repeated information from some who are in the secret of affairs, that a resolution was taken by those who have power to execute it to pursue me to the scaffold. My blood was to have been the cement of a new alliance; nor could my innocence be any security, after it had once been demanded from abroad, and resolved on at home, that it was necessary to cut me off.'[19]

Bolingbroke was pardoned in May 1723, and returned from exile in July 1723. In April 1725 he was restored to his ancestral estates, but remained excluded from the House of Lords because Walpole refused to agree to his complete restoration. The enmity between the two, which was concealed between 1723 and 1725, when Bolingbroke was hoping to obtain full restitution, and endeavouring to earn it by services to the Government, broke out once more about 1725, when he found his hopes were vain.[20]

One result of the transformation of Gulliver into Bolingbroke was the development of the character of Flimnap, who was obviously designed to represent Walpole, as all commentators agree. The Flimnap of the first version of the Voyage to Lilliput was a somewhat colourless character, secretly hostile to Gulliver because the prodigious appetite of the monster made him a burden to the treasury, but not his mortal enemy as Bolgolam was. At the end of Queen Anne's reign Walpole was not a personage of the first rank in English politics; in 1721 he became one of the most powerful members of the Government, and by 1726 he was practically Prime Minister. Hence three or four additional touches were added to give Flimnap additional importance, and to bring out the resemblance to Walpole.

Candidates for great employments in Lilliput competed for them by dancing on a rope for the entertainment of the Emperor. 'Flimnap, the Treasurer,' says Gulliver, 'is allowed to cut a caper on the straight rope at least an inch higher than any other lord in the whole empire.' This symbolizes Walpole's dexterity in parliamentary tactics and political intrigues. 'The King's cushion', which broke Flimnap's fall when he leaped too high, and saved him from breaking his neck, is agreed to symbolize the Duchess of Kendal, one of the King's mistresses, by whose influence Walpole, after his fall from power in 1717, was again restored to favour.

Another passage in the text must have been added just before the publication of the *Travels*. It is the account of the silken threads, green, red, and blue, given to the courtiers who showed most agility in leaping over or creeping under a stick. The green thread typifies the order of the Thistle, revived by Queen Anne in 1703. The red typifies the order of the Bath, revived by George I in May 1725. Its revival, according to Horace Walpole, was due to Sir Robert 'and was an artful bank of thirty-six ribands to supply a fund of favours in lieu of places'. The blue thread typifies the order of the Garter, which was bestowed on Sir Robert himself in May 1726, after which he was known to satirists by the title of Sir Blue-String. Swift's verses on the revival of the order of the Bath explain the meaning of his prose.[21]

A third passage is more difficult to explain. It is the account of Flimnap's jealousy of his wife, who was reported to have conceived a violent affection for Gulliver, and the story is introduced to explain the Treasurer's enmity to Gulliver. This may be an ironical hit at Walpole, whose first wife, Catherine Shorter, was not above suspicion, while Walpole's indifference to her levities was notorious. Pope hints at it when he calls Walpole 'a tyrant to his wife'.[22]

Another explanation is that the episode is a reference to Bolingbroke's attempt to win the favour of the Duchess of Kendal, hitherto Walpole's firmest ally, in order to utilize her influence with George I to Walpole's detriment. Sir Robert, who was aware of the intrigue, 'bestowed some fitting language on her Grace, and said she would at any time have sold her influence with the King for a shilling advance to the best bidder.' Bolingbroke, according to Walpole, had paid her £11,000 for her support, and she was entirely in his interest.[23]

Besides Flimnap, another minister of the Lilliputian court is mentioned. Gulliver says: 'My friend Reldresal, Principal Secretary for Private Affairs, is in my opinion, if I am not partial, the second after the Treasurer.' Reldresal was the lord who explained to Gulliver the intricacies of Lilliputian politics and proved himself throughout his true friend. Commentators have not identified him, but it is clear that the person meant is Lord Carteret. He was Secretary of State from March 5, 1721, to April 14, 1724, and stood so high in the King's favour that he might fairly be described as the second man in the Government at that time. 'Principal Secretary of State' or one of our 'Principal Secretaries of State' was Carteret's official title. As the two Secretaries of State who then existed divided the conduct of foreign affairs between them, and the care of home affairs was the common function of both of them, there was strictly no 'Principal Secretary for Private Affairs' at the time. The choice lies between Carteret and his colleague Townshend; as Carteret was Swift's friend he must be the person meant. In April 1724 Walpole got rid of Carteret by making him Lord Lieutenant of Ireland. In that capacity Carteret was obliged to issue a proclamation (October 27, 1724) offering a reward of £300 for the discovery of the author of the *Drapier's Letter to the People of Ireland*, just as Reldresal was obliged to suggest a method of punishing his friend Gulliver.[24]

The Second Voyage, the Voyage to Brobdingnag, requires less commentary. It was written at one time and is all of a piece. There are no references to persons which require explaining, and the allusions to contemporary politics are only general. Some of the institutions and customs of Brobdingnag are briefly described and praised; for instance, the brevity of the laws, the cultivation of useful knowledge rather than speculative philosophy or abstract sciences, and the simplicity of the literary style in fashion. The method adopted throughout is not to hold up ideal institutions for imitation as in the case of Lilliput, but to describe existing institutions so as to show their defects. In five interviews Gulliver explains to the King the constitution and government of England, and then the King, by astute 'doubts, queries, and objections', forces him to reveal the difference between the practice and the theory of the institutions described. Gulliver has to admit that the working of the parliamentary government is vitiated by the method of selecting peers, bishops, and members of the House of Commons, so that, as the King points out, the original idea of the institution is 'blurred and blotted by corruptions'.

The comments of the King of Brobdingnag express on many questions the political views of Swift's party. He was amazed, says Gulliver, 'to hear me talk of a mercenary army in the midst of peace and among a free people.' Every year, over the Mutiny

Act or the Estimates, the House of Commons resounded with
denunciations of standing armies, and Chesterfield recommended
the question to his son as the best subject for a young member's
maiden speech. In the same way the King of Brobdingnag echoed
the criticisms of the Tories on the financial system, and their
alarm at the existence of the National Debt.[25]

On most questions, however, the King is the mouthpiece of
Swift, not merely that of the Tory party, and the opinions he
expresses are those Swift had already set forth in his pamphlets.
Swift's condemnation of gaming, Swift's complaint of the neglected education of the upper classes, Swift's theory of the best
way of treating Dissenters and his rooted animosity to lawyers,
lose nothing in vigour in issuing from the King's lips :

I shall never forget, [says Swift at the close of the *Drapier's Letters*] what I once ventured to say to a great man in England : 'that
few politicians, with all their schemes, are half so useful members
of a commonwealth, as an honest farmer, who by skilful draining,
fencing, manuring, and planting hath increased the intrinsic value
of a piece of land, and thereby done a perpetual service to his country'; which it is a great controversy whether any of the former ever
did, since the creation of the world.

The King of Brobdingnag puts this in a more epigrammatic form.
'He gave it for his opinion, that whoever could make two ears of
corn or two blades of grass to grow upon a spot of ground where
only one grew before, would deserve better of mankind, and do
more essential service to his country than the whole race of politicians put together.'

In this way the specific reference to Ireland in the *Drapier's
Letters* is made a general maxim in *Gulliver's Travels*, but at the
back of Swift's mind there is always the thought of Ireland. In a
letter written in 1732 he makes his meaning still clearer. 'There
is not an acre of land in Ireland turned to half its advantage, yet
it is better improved than the people; and all these evils are effects
of English tyranny, so your sons and grandchildren will find it to
their sorrow.'[26]

There is another passage in the Second Voyage suggested by Irish conditions, and that is an incident in Gulliver's visit to the capital of Brobdingnag. As the carriage in which he and his nurse were conveyed stopped at a shop 'the beggars watching their opportunity crowded to the sides of the coach and gave me the most horrible spectacle that ever an European eye beheld.' He describes with horrid minuteness the exhibition of their sores, and there can be no doubt that the description was inspired by the beggars of Dublin, on whom he has much to say in his pamphlets and sermons.

These passages show that while Swift was entirely wrapt up in English politics when he wrote the First Voyage, Irish social conditions were beginning to occupy his thoughts when the Second was written. . . .

S o u r c e : *Proceedings of the British Academy,* ix (1919–20) pp. 237–59, extract; since collected in *Essays Historical and Literary* (Oxford 1938).

NOTES

(16 notes in the original are here deleted)

1. *Correspondence,* ed. F. Elrington Ball, vi, 78.
2. *Works,* ed. Temple Scott, ix, 81, 101, 110; cf. 271 and v, 297.
3. Spence, *Conversations,* ed. Singer (1820) p. 10.
4. [Few critics now attach much credence to this suggestion, and Firth's interpretations of one or two passages have therefore been contested. See notes 6 and 24 below. Ed.]
5. *Gulliver's Travels,* pp. 48, 59. The edition referred to is that edited by G. R. Dennis in 1899, forming volume viii of the *Prose Works of Swift,* edited by Temple Scott.
6. [A. E. Case, *Four Essays* (Princeton, 1945), offers an alternative interpretation. Ed.]
7. *Works* (ed. 1824) xi, 74.
8. *Gulliver's Travels,* p. 57.
9. Craik, *Life of Swift* (1882) pp. 145, 183.
10. Craik, p. 259; *Correspondence,* ii, 22.

11. Craik, p. 114; *Correspondence*, I, 73, 152; II, 212; Johnson, *Lives of the Poets*, ed. Hill, III, 10, 68.

12. *Poems*, ed. W. E. Browning (1910) II, 150; Orrery's *Remarks*, p. 48; *Correspondence*, II, 212; *Works*, V, 463.

13. *Works*, II, 294; X, 29.

14. *Poems*, II, 148, 156.

15. *Wentworth Papers*, p. 385.

16. Mahon, *History of England*, I, 82.

17. Burnet, *History of My Own Time*, II, 95 (ed. 1833).

18. W. M. Torrens, *History of Cabinets* (1894) I, 116–18; Tindal, IV, 387.

19. W. Sichel, *Life of Bolingbroke* (1901) I, 523.

20. Ibid. II, 110, 155, 173, 191, 208–10, 258, *D.N.B.*, I, 138. Bolingbroke before exile, Torrens, I, 56, 62, 92, 97, 101, 141; return, 317, 326, 349.

21. *Poems*, II, 203; H. Walpole, *Letters* (ed. 1877) I cxiv.

22. Pope, *Works*, ed. Elwin and Courthope, III, 481.

23. Torrens, I, 348, 358; Sichel, II, 190, 208, 266.

24. *Works*, VI, 109, 235. [Again, A. E. Case argues differently. Ed.]

25. *Gulliver's Travels*, p. 134. The views expressed by the King refute Sir Walter Scott's opinion (*Swift*, XI, 8), that the monarch was perhaps drawn from William III.

26. *Correspondence*, IV, 312.

T. O. Wedel

ON THE PHILOSOPHICAL BACK-GROUND OF *GULLIVER'S TRAVELS* (1926)

Swift, the master of irony among the moderns, has achieved no greater ironic masterpiece than the posthumous reputation of *Gulliver's Travels*. Written to vex the world, not to divert it, hiding within its cloak of wit and romantic invention the savage indignation of a lifetime, the fiercest indictment of the pride of man yet penned in our language, it has become, forsooth, a children's book – an example, so Goethe thought, of the failure of allegory to make an idea prevail.[1]

Types and Fables, [so runs a passage in *A Tale of a Tub*[2] which could be applied prophetically to *Gulliver's Travels*,] the writer having been perhaps more careful and curious in adorning, than was altogether necessary, it has fared with these Vehicles after the usual Fate of Coaches, over-finely painted and gilt; that the transitory Gazers have so dazzled their Eyes, and fill'd their Imaginations with the outward lustre, as neither to regard or consider the Person or the Parts of the Owner within.

The failure of posterity to appreciate the philosophical thesis of Gulliver's travels, is not, however, due solely to the triumph of Swift's art. The year of our Lord 1726, when Gulliver appeared, was in no mood to put a proper value upon a work which spoke of *homo sapiens* as 'the most pernicious race of little odious vermin that nature ever suffered to crawl upon the surface of the earth.' We need only remind ourselves that the very year previous there

had appeared, in Swift's own Dublin, Hutcheson's first panegyric essay[3] on the soundness of man's benevolent instincts, a classic expression for the century of the new optimistic creed, and
itself the resultant of a respectable tradition. No, neither the
eighteenth century nor the nineteenth has expressed anything
but scorn for the view of man to be found in *Gulliver's Travels.*
Eighteenth-century criticism, in fact, is remarkably silent about
Swift. Yet when *Gulliver's Travels* is discussed by Orrery, Warton, Young, Jeffrey, or Scott, its philosophy is referred to as the
result of a diseased mind, blaspheming as it does a nature little
lower than that of the angels.[4] 'In what ordure,' exclaims Young
in his *Conjectures*,[5] 'hast thou dipped thy pencil! What a monster hast thou made of the "Human face divine!"' The German
Herder, to be sure, attempts to appreciate Swift's misanthropy,
at the same time preserving his constant enthusiasm for Shaftesbury. But it is John Wesley who, alone among eighteenth-century
readers, can cite the Voyage to the Houyhnhnms with real enthusiasm. In his longest written work, *The Doctrine of Original
Sin*,[6] it is Swift rather than St. Augustine upon whom he leans
for quotations.

Yet if Swift had written *Gulliver's Travels* a few generations
earlier, he would have given little cause for complaint. Pascal
would have understood him, as would La Rochefoucauld and
Boileau;[7] so would Montaigne; so would Bayle. For the transition
from the seventeenth century to the eighteenth was experiencing
a revolution in ethical thought. 'Rarely, if ever,' says Brunetière,[8] with perhaps too dogmatic assurance, 'has so profound a
transformation occurred more swiftly. Everything has changed.'
The pessimism of Pascal has given way to the optimism of Leibnitz; the theory of self-love of La Rochefoucauld to the theory of
benevolence of Hutcheson and Hume; the scepticism of Montaigne to the rationalism of Locke, Toland, and Clarke; the dualism of Nature and Grace to a monistic inclusion of Nature under
the rule of a beneficent God; the bold warfare between atheism
and faith to a mere gentlemen's quarrel between revealed and
natural religion. In fact, it is this revolutionary background which
alone can explain Swift's purpose in writing *Gulliver's Travels.*

Swift's darker meaning, to be sure, does not lie on the surface, for, as Johnson noted in his biographical sketch, he was the most reticent of men. Rarely does he reveal his opinions or his feelings without a cloak of irony; rarely does he quote an author. Indeed an article of his artistic creed discouraged quotation.[9] Pedantry is absent from his writings to a fault. While Bolingbroke, in the famous correspondence, overloads his page with learning, Swift turns out epigrams on Ireland or the weather. *Vive la bagatelle* was his motto. He might illustrate the saying of Joubert: 'The wise man is serious about few things.' Or he might have applied to himself his own maxim:[10] 'Some people take more care to hide their wisdom than their folly.'

Yet the student of Swift is not left entirely without guidance as to his philosophical opinions. The *Tale of a Tub*, for example, furnishes plentiful evidence of his distrust of metaphysics on the one hand, of his hatred of mystical enthusiasm on the other. A stray remark in his *Letter to a Young Clergyman* tells us that he did not approve of Locke's attack upon innate ideas. His *Sermon on the Trinity*, thought by Wesley to be one of the great sermons of the age, helps, when read in the light of contemporary thought, to define the same anti-rationalism which appears in *Gulliver's Travels* and which animated his attacks upon the Deists. The *Sermon on Conscience*, in turn, defending religion against the upholders of mere moral honesty and honour, reads like a rebuttal of both Shaftesbury and Mandeville. The *Correspondence* yields more than one hint that Swift felt himself to be on the side of the opposition with reference to the growing optimism of Pope and Bolingbroke. In two letters, in particular, Swift plays the truant to his creed of reticence, giving us in round terms his formula of misanthropy. I shall quote the respective passages in full. The first, indeed, constitutes the *locus classicus* for the critic of Gulliver.

I have ever hated all nations, professions, and communities, and all my love is toward individuals: for instance, I hate the tribe of lawyers, but I love Counsellor Such-a-one, and Judge Such-a-one . . . . But principally I hate and detest that animal called man, although I heartily love John, Peter, Thomas, and so forth. This is the system upon which I have governed myself many years, but do not tell, and so I shall go on till I have done with them. I have got materials toward a treatise, proving the falsity of that definition *animal rationale*, and to show it should be only *rationis capax*. Upon this great foundation of misanthropy, though not in Timon's manner, the whole building of my Travels is erected; and I will never have peace of mind till all honest men are of my opinion.

In the second and later letter Swift is dissuading Pope from undertaking a refutation of La Rochefoucauld, who, Swift says, 'is my favourite, because I found my whole character in him.'

I desire you and all my friends will take a special care that my disaffection to the world may not be imputed to my age, for I have credible witnesses ready to depose that it has never varied from the twenty-first to the fifty-eighth year of my life. . . . I tell you after all, that I do not hate mankind : it is *vous autres* who hate them, because you would have them reasonable animals, and are angry for being disappointed.

Finally, besides all such incidental aids for the critic, we have *Gulliver's Travels* itself – its views on education and politics; its attack on science; its satire on luxury, war, and commerce, bordering on a kind of primitivism; its dualism of Yahoos and Houyhnhnms; above all, its savage indignation at the animalism and pettiness of man, culminating in its magnificent peroration on pride.

And in trying to interpret in the light of the ethical revolution of his day, at least some of this provocative satire, I may begin with his misanthropic view in general, his hatred of the animal called man, his love for individuals – 'a sentiment,' so Thomas Warton thought,[11] voicing the general opinion of posterity, 'that dishonors him as a man, a Christian, and a philosopher.' A hard view of man it is, clearly, yet no more severe than that of the seventeenth century as a whole. Parallels to Swift's very words can be found several times over. Listen, for example, to Pascal :[12] 'The nature of man may be viewed in two ways : the one according to its end, and then he is great and incomparable; the other, according to the multitude, just as we judge of the nature of the horse and the dog, popularly, . . . and then man is abject and vile. . . . The nature of man is wholly natural, *omne animal.*' Or to a similar judgment of La Bruyère:[13] 'A reasonable man may hate mankind in general; he discovers in it so little of virtue. But he is ready to excuse the individual . . . and strives to deserve as little as possible a similar indulgence.' One is tempted to quote by way of contrast Hazlitt's confession,[14] equally typical of more recent centuries: 'I believe in the theoretical benevolence, but the practical malignity of man.'

In more general form, Swift's hard view of man could be duplicated scores of times even without resorting to the Ancients, the Fathers, or the Calvinists. Although, as we shall see, a more flattering doctrine had already appeared early in the seventeenth century, his is after all the prevailing judgment on human nature from Montaigne to Locke, among men of the world as well as ascetic Christians. Even Bayle at the turn of the new century, arch sceptic that he was, still clings to it. His article on Ovid, for example, in the *Dictionnaire*, quoting voluminously from Cicero and St. Augustine to Esprit and the Moderns, reads like a pedantic prospectus of *Gulliver's Travels*. In Bayle's view, man is still an ungovernable animal, ruled by self-love, given over to evil incomparably more than to good, the slight glimmering of reason which has been left him usually worsted in the fight against the passions, his only hope, apart from utilitarian virtue, being divine grace. Vauvenargues, a moralist writing in the middle of the eighteenth century, may well exclaim:[15] 'Man is at present in disgrace among all those who think; they heap upon him all manner of vices.' Only he adds: 'Perhaps he is soon to awake and to demand the restitution of his virtues.' By the year 1726, in England at least, the restitution of man's virtues was already well under way. The dignity of human nature is already on everyone's lips. Locke and the Deists had given man a new trust in Reason; the Cambridge Platonists and Shaftesbury were discovering in him a moral sense, even in the hitherto despised realm of the passions. Nothing seems more certain to the new age than the existence of a beneficent deity, and the consequent goodness of his creation. Optimistic theodicies are being written on all sides,[16] explaining away the evil from this best of all possible worlds.

Place the mind in its right posture, [declares a *Spectator* paper,][17] it will immediately discover its innate propension to beneficence. Persons conscious of their own integrity, satisfied with themselves and their condition, and full of confidence in a Supreme Being, and the hope of immortality, survey all about them with a flow of good-will. As trees which like their soil, they shoot out in expressions of kindness and bend beneath their own precious load, to the hand of the gatherer.

A popular article in the *Gentleman's Magazine* (1732) sets out to prove 'that men are as generally good, as they are represented bad.' Any other conclusion is declared to be a blasphemy against God; 'for neither God nor man can be good but by their works.'

Definitions of vice and virtue are at sixes and sevens. Evil and good, once set over against each other as equivalent to Nature and Grace, now oppose each other within the natural realm alone. Pride has become a virtue. When Pope proposed to refute La Rochefoucauld[18] by dissolving vices into virtues, as the cynic of the seventeenth century had dissolved virtues into vices, he set himself a supernumerary task. The thing was being done all around him. An unworldly definition of virtue had become almost unintelligible. Tindal, the Deist, asserts that the Sermon on the Mount is absurd for practical life.[19] 'Pascal and La Rochefou-cauld,' says Voltaire,[20] 'who were read by everyone, have accus-tomed the French public to interpret the word self-love always in a bad sense. Only in the eighteenth century did a change come about, so that the ideas of vice and pride were no longer neces-sarily attached to the word.' Precisely so. Mandeville gained a stormy hearing for his paradox of 'private vices, public benefits' simply because at least half of his terminology was being dropped from the new vocabulary.[21]

In theological terms, what was happening of course was the avowed, or tacit denial of the doctrine of original sin. Human nature was being absolved of corruption. The ancient Christian faith, in the words of Pascal, had rested on but two things, 'the

corruption of nature and redemption by Jesus Christ.' Half at
least of Pascal's formula is seldom spoken of after 1700. Even
before that date optimism and orthodoxy jostle each other in
unexpected places. Jeremy Taylor is already suspected of unor-
thodoxy on the subject of original sin. Tillotson, though he bows
to the traditional dogma,[22] became for the Deists a favorite prop
for their rationalistic doctrines. A popular version of both the old
and the new in theological thought is Bishop Burnet's naïve account (1680) of the death of the Earl of Rochester. Though
Rochester's views can lay no claim to consistency, he is at least
an optimist. Man's instincts must be restrained here and there
perhaps, but they are not evil. The story of Adam's fall is absurd
– one man cheating the whole world. The honest Bishop offers
no rational explanation; he merely asserts in the name of Platonism and Augustinian Christianity that 'common experience tells
us there is a great disorder in our Nature, which is not easily
rectified : all philosophers were sensible of it, and every man that
designs to govern himself by Reason, feels the struggle between
it and Nature. So that it is plain there is a lapse of the high powers
of the Soul.'[23]

With the turn of the century, however, words like these are
rarely heard. If anyone doubts that by the year 1700 a new philosophy was in the air, he need merely read a designedly orthodox
work such as Locke's *Reasonableness of Christianity*. Christianity
is no longer for Locke, what it was for Pascal, a healer of souls,
but a supernatural blunderbuss enforcing the police regulations
of natural morality. Adam's fall, so Locke argues, brought the
punishment of death upon the world, but implies no corruption
of nature. 'If by death, threatened to Adam, were meant the
corruption of human nature in his posterity, 'tis strange that the
New Testament should not anywhere take notice of it.'[24] Locke's
literalism is indeed daring in view of centuries of Pauline theology. And while occasionally a writer on divinity saw that here
lay the chief danger to the old orthodoxy in Locke's appealing
philosophy, the prevailing thought of the century passed on to
other issues, busying itself with asserting the necessity of revelation
for natural law, or, in Samuel Johnson's phrase, defending the

apostles against the charge of forgery once a week. Wesley, hark-
ing back to pagan antiquity for parallels to his own unflattering
view of man, and glancing at the new gospel, exclaims: 'But how
much more knowing than these old pagans are the present generation of Christians! How many laboured panegyrics do we now
read and hear on the dignity of human nature!' ... 'I cannot see
that we have much need of Christianity. Nay, not any at all; for
"they that are whole have no need of a physician!"' ... Nor can
Christian philosophy, whatever be thought of the pagan, be
more properly defined than in Plato's words: "the only true method of healing a distempered soul." But what need of this if we
are in perfect health?' And in refutation of contemporary optimism Wesley proceeds to unload upon the reader page upon page
of *Gulliver*.

In the world of political thought, the clash between old and
new is perhaps nowhere so concretely exhibited as in the contrasting theories regarding the state of nature. For not in *Gulliver*
only are Yahoos set over against Houyhnhnms. In fact it looks
like too simple a discovery to point out that in the last voyage
of the *Travels* we have, designedly or not, Hobbes contrasted
with Locke. And yet the parallel holds good surprisingly well.
Men in Hobbes' state of nature, like Swift's Yahoos, are 'in that
condition which is called war; and such a war, as is of every man
against every man ... with no arts, no letters, no society, and,
which is worst of all, continual fear of violent danger; and the
life of man, solitary, poor, nasty, brutish, and short.'[25] And while
Hobbes' brevity of description with regard to his state of war
prevents elaboration of the parallel, the corresponding similarity
between Locke and Swift is certainly tempting. Men in Locke's
state of nature, like the Houyhnhnms, are rational creatures, 'living together according to reason, without a common superior,' –
in a state of liberty without license, every one administering the
laws of nature for himself, laws of temperance and mutual benevolence.[26] The relation of Swift to Hobbes and to Locke is a subject for separate investigation. On the whole, I think (and Swift's
political writings would furnish evidence in abundance), he
stands nearer to Hobbes. In *Gulliver's Travels*, however, Swift

is clearly neither Hobbes nor Locke. Gulliver is neither Yahoo
nor Houyhnhnm. He cannot attain to the rational felicity of the
Houyhnhnms. Neither has he sunk to the level of the Yahoos,
though this is a doubtful advantage. He lacks the strength of a
healthy animal, and his glimmering of reason has unhappily bur-
dened him with responsibility of conscience.

Indeed, if Swift's own hints regarding the meaning of his book
are heeded, it is in the contrast between Yahoo and Houyhnhnm
that his main thesis lies hid. Gulliver, occupying a position between the two, part beast, part reason, is Swift's allegorical picture of the dual nature of man. He is not Houyhnhnm, *animal
rationale*, nor is he Yahoo. He is *rationis capax*. One could apply
to *Gulliver's Travels* a passage of Cicero, quoted with approval
by both St. Augustine and Bayle : 'Nature has been to man not a
mother, but a step-mother – sending him into the world naked,
frail, and infirm, toiling under a burden of care, fearful, slothful,
and given over to lust, but not without a spark of divine reason.'[27]

Animal rationale – animal rationis capax! Swift's somewhat
scholastic distinction turns out, in the light of seventeenth-century
thought, to be by no means scholastic. It symbolises, in fact, the
chief intellectual battle of the age. Swift seems to have seen clearly
enough that in assaulting man's pride in reason, he was attacking
the new optimism at its very root. His enmity to rationalistic dog-
matising was the one enduring intellectual passion of his life. It
animates his orthodoxy in his sermon on the Trinity; it prompts
the dangerous laughter of *A Tale of a Tub*; it explains his merci-
less satire of the Deists.

The phrase *animal rationale* can be traced at least as far back
as Seneca[28] and ancient Stoicism. This fact alone explains much.
For it is precisely the circle of ideas represented by Stoicism, however changed in form through centuries of filtration, which the
seventeenth century, like the fifth, was still finding it difficult to
assimilate. Stoicism has ever been associated with optimism. It
is the Stoic who worships pride. And despite the noble appeal of
its ethical heroism – or perhaps one had better say because of it –
Stoicism has constituted one of Christianity's gravest dangers.
Corruptio optimi pessima est. No Christian in the Augustinian

sense could have said with Epictetus: 'I was never hindered in my will or compelled against my wish. . . . Who can hinder me against my own judgments, or put compulsion on me? I am as safe as Zeus.'[29] The Stoic faith in a beneficent deity and a rational world robbed the universe of evil. To follow nature was to obey God and reason. The wise man, to be sure, had to conquer his passions; but the passions themselves were merely wrong opinion. The Stoic was still master of his fate.

It was Stoicism in the form of the Pelagian heresy against which St. Augustine threw the whole weight of his eloquence in the last great doctrinal war of his career. Man for Pelagius, too, was not by nature evil. 'For they think,' so St. Augustine defines the belief of his enemies, 'that, by the strength of their own will, they will fulfill the commands of the law; and wrapped up in their pride, they are not converted to assisting grace.'[30] Conceive of God as goodness and benevolence, of nature as His creation, include man in nature, let the myth of the Fall imply, as it did for Locke, merely a legal death penalty laid upon otherwise innocent descendants of Adam, who are rational beings, free to choose good and evil, and you have the Pelagian heresy.

Of the popularity of Stoicism in this period there can be no doubt. According to Strowski,[31] the author oftenest reprinted in the first half of the seventeenth century was Du Vair, whose *Philosophie Morale des Stoïques* was one of the chief Stoic texts, together with a similar compendium of Justus Lipsius. Coming to the fore by way of translation and paraphrase, Stoicism, as I shall try to show a little later, soon suffered a sea-change, and was destined in its new form, to conquer the world. For the moment, however, its victory was delayed, though the warfare against it was confused, and though many a skirmish was fought on secondary issues. The passions, for one thing, found defenders against the Stoic attitude of disdain. Positivistic observers of man simply denied that man was ruled by reason. Balzac[32] ridicules the Stoics as 'that inhuman sect which, in cutting off from man his passions and his feelings, desires to rob him of half of himself. In place of having created a wise man, the Stoics have merely created a statue.' Or as Swift himself puts it in one of his maxims:

'The Stoical scheme of supplying our wants by lopping off our
desires is like cutting off our feet, when we want shoes.'[33] La
Rochefoucauld, man of the world, sees human nature as merely
the dupe of the ruling passion of self-love. As the century advances, optimism itself takes to throwing stones at the Stoics, actually defending the passions as good in themselves. Sénault writes
a treatise[34] proving the Stoic wise man a fiction and the passions
useful in the moral life. A similar defense is found in the *Enchiri-
dion Ethicum* of the Cambridge Platonist, Henry More. The
Augustinian tradition, of course, is against the Stoics. Jansen's
Augustinus is an attack upon them; so is Arnauld's *Fréquente
Communion*.[35] And Pascal, dualist always, accepts neither the
man of the world's cynical acceptance of man as a creature of
the passions, nor the Stoic's pride in having conquered them. It
is he who expresses the conviction of the mystic : 'The heart has
its reasons, which the reason knows not of.'[36] Machiavellians,
Epicureans, and Christians are at one in laughing at the Stoic's
vain pretensions that the passions can be conquered, and that
the will is free.

Combatants of divergent loyalties again united in attacking
Stoic rationalism itself – Montaigne, Bayle, Pascal : Epicurean,
sceptic, and Christian. Montaigne indeed may be said to be all
three in one. And to understand Swift's own position, Montaigne
is of particular importance. The best commentary on *Gulliver's
Travels* is the great *Apologie de Raymond Sébonde*. According
to Busson's recent study of rationalism in the Renaissance, Montaigne sums up in popular form the scepticism of the preceding
centuries of enlightenment. Now the rationalism of the Renaissance differed from that of the eighteenth century precisely in
that it was a sceptical balancing of reason against faith, including
reason itself among the objects of doubt. *Que sais je?* asks Montaigne. What do I know? Montaigne's *Apologie*, like *Gulliver's
Travels* is a scathing attack upon Stoic pride. Man is placed on
a level almost lower than that of the dog and the horse. In fact
Montaigne's primitivism, imitated by Swift – his disgust with the
pompous boasts of civilization – is a good deal softened in *Gulliver's Travels*.[37] Montaigne mistrusts dogmatic theology on the

one hand, man's reason on the other. Hence, like Bayle a century later, he falls back on faith. It is absurd for man, so Montaigne closes his *Apologie*, to attempt to raise himself above humanity.

For to make the handful bigger than the hand, and the armful larger than the arm, and to hope to stride farther than our legs can reach, is impossible and monstrous; or that man should rise above himself and humanity; for he cannot see but with his own eyes, nor seize but with his power. He shall rise if God will extraordinarily lend him His hand; he shall rise by abandoning and renouncing his own proper means, and by suffering himself to be raised and elevated by means purely celestial. It belongs to our Christian faith, and not to his stoical virtue, to pretend to that divine and miraculous metamorphosis.

And however mystifying Montaigne's philosophy may be when viewed as a whole, it is, I think, a gross misunderstanding of the role which scepticism has played in religion to accuse either Montaigne or Bayle of entire bad faith. Upon the twin pillars of scepticism and the corruption of human nature Pascal built his own *apologie*, as did Newman in more recent times his defense of the Catholic church. Newman merely echoes Montaigne when he says: 'Quarry the granite rock with razors, or moor the vessel with a thread of silk; then you may hope with such keen and delicate instruments as human knowledge and human reason to contend against those giants, the passion and the pride of man.'[38]

But by the time that Swift wrote his own treatise to vex the world, scepticism and the belief in the corruption of human nature had given way to rationalism and an optimistic faith in man. The Stoic creed had suffered its sea-change. Sceptic, Epicurean, dualistic Christian had surrendered.

And the founder of the new faith was no other than the father of modern philosophy, Descartes himself. To the layman, burrowing his way into the history of ideas in the seventeenth century, it is almost disconcerting to discover how all roads lead to the author of the *Discourse on Method*. Let any one, after reading Montaigne's *Apologie*, turn to Descartes' treatise on the passions and a new planet swims into his ken. For the first assumption of

Descartes is precisely the Stoic faith in a beneficent God and an uncorrupted nature. A good God cannot deceive us, and our reason is from God; hence our reason is to be trusted. And while the Stoicism of Epictetus still left within man a dualism of reason and passion, this, too, is obliterated by Descartes. The passions become good. *Elles sont toutes bonnes.* Vicious and evil instincts are denied the name of passions – ingratitude, impudence, effrontery. Reversing the method of La Rochefoucauld, Descartes dissolves a bad passion into that good one which nearly resembles it. Envy, for example, becomes a praiseworthy love of distributive justice. Pride is good, except when wrongly applied. Humility is scored as evil when it persuades us that we are feeble or unable to exercise our free will. Descartes' treatise on the passions does not, of course, yet picture the man of sentiment of Vauvenargues, or Rousseau; man is still decidedly *animal rationale*, master over himself like the heroes of Corneille :

> Je suis, maître du moi, comme de l'univers ;
> Je le suis, je veux l'être.

But one may perhaps already see the eighteenth century in the offing – Deism, Shaftesbury, even the new anti-rationalism of Rousseau.

Though Cartesianism, as we have seen, found plentiful enemies in the seventeenth century, its ultimate victory was a foregone conclusion. It became for a time the ally of orthodoxy itself. Deceived by the first-fruits of the Cartesian method, resulting as it did in a dogmatic faith in God and immortality, the Church, fifty years later, discovered that she had fallen victim to seduction. The Deism of Toland, for example, is almost pure Descartes. Eighteenth-century orthodoxy, itself turned rationalist and optimist, found no weapons adequate to fight the Deists. Swift was one of few bold enough to oppose them squarely with an appeal to the weakness of human reason. Bossuet[39] still saw the danger, as did the light-hearted Bayle.[40] And Pascal rested his dualism precisely on the necessity of reconciling Montaigne and Descartes. Nowhere, perhaps, is the issue fought out in the seventeenth cen-

tury more clearly expressed than in Pascal's little dialogue between himself and M. de Saci, in which Montaigne is set over
against Epictetus – Montaigne, for whom man was on a level with
the beasts; Epictetus (Descartes), for whom man was a god.

Clearly Swift belongs with Montaigne, La Rochefoucauld,
and Bayle, among those who see man without illusion. But can he
also be said to be a disciple of Pascal, the Christian? I do not
think so. He did not, like Montaigne, achieve Epicurean tranquillity. He was decidedly not at ease in his inn. Neither could he
feel kinship with the saints as could Pascal. Swift was not a mystic.
One might apply to *Gulliver's Travels* Pascal's words : 'It is dangerous to make man see too clearly his equality with the brutes,
without showing him his greatness.'[41] Even Swift's Utopia is the
Utopia of Locke, not Plato's philosopher's kingdom, nor St.
Augustine's City of God. He was a rationalist with no faith in
reason. Against the language of the heart he harbored an almost
Freudian complex. Wesley, we may be sure, would have found
him strange company. Sceptic and misanthrope, Swift fell back
upon *saeva indignatio* and the established religion of his country.

Yet Swift's view of man, as Wesley perceived, and as Professor Bernbaum[42] has pointed out in our own time, is essentially
the view of the classical and Christian tradition. Almost any fair
definition of that tradition would absolve *Gulliver's Travels*
from the charge of being an isolated example of misanthropy. I
can, in truth, find no better closing comment on *Gulliver's Travels*
than a passage from Sainte-Beuve's *Port-Royal.*[43] It is a definition
of Christianity, written by one who was not himself a Christian,
who throughout his sympathetic study of seventeenth-century
mysticism preserved the calm detachment of the critic.

One of the most direct ways to conceive the essence of Christianity
is to accept the view of human nature as a fallen human nature,
exactly as do Hobbes, La Rochefoucauld, and Machiavelli [and
Sainte-Beuve might surely have added Swift], those great positive
observers of life. The more such a view arouses a feeling of sadness,
either in a soul not too hardened, or in a soul which, in spite of being
hardened, is capable of compassion and which yearns for happiness,

the more it disposes and provokes such a soul to accept the extreme remedy, the remedy of hope. Such a soul will ask itself if this is the true and final view of life, and will seek a way of escape beyond this earth and this state of misery, even in the vastnesses of heaven, in the awful infinite silences. This entering by the narrow gate, this unhoped-for way of escape to safety, this is Christianity. And I speak of that which is verifiable.

S o u r c e : *Studies in Philology,* xxiii (1926)
pp. 434–50.

NOTES

(9 notes in the original are here deleted, and 5 abbreviated.)

1. Goethe, *Werke* (Weimar, 1901) xl, 220 : 'Gulliver hat mehr als Mährchen gereizt, als seine Resultate unterrichtet und moralisch gebessert haben.'
2. *A Tale of a Tub,* ed. A. C. Guthkelch and D. Nichol Smith (Oxford, 1920) p. 66.
3. As republished in 1726, Hutcheson's two first essays bore the titles : *Inquiry concerning Beauty, Order, Harmony, and Design,* and *Inquiry concerning Moral Good and Evil.*
4. A typical modern comment is that of Courthope (*Liberal Movement in English Literature,* London, 1885, p. 112) : 'Chivalrous feeling could scarcely breathe in the same atmosphere as Gulliver.'
5. M. W. Steinke, *Edward Young's Conjectures on Original Composition* (New York, 1917) p. 59.
6. *The Doctrine of Original Sin* was written in 1757.
7. Boileau's eighth Satire constitutes, together with Montaigne's *Apologie de Raymond Sébonde,* perhaps the best parallel to Swift's picture of man as beast.
8. Brunetière's article on Bayle (*Études Critiques,* v, 116).
9. See his *Letter to a Young Clergyman* (*Prose Works,* ed. Temple Scott, London, 1909, iii, 211).
10. *Thoughts on Various Subjects* (*Prose Works,* i, 278).
11. See Pope's *Works,* ed. Elwin and Courthope, vii, 53.
12. Pascal, *Thoughts* (tr. Temple Classics), nos. 415, 94.
13. La Bruyère, *Caractères,* chap. 'De l'homme'.

D

14. Hazlitt, *Aphorisms on Man*, no. 46 (*Works*, ed. A. R. Waller and Arnold Glover, London, 1904–6, XII, 222).

15. Sainte-Beuve's article on Vauvenargues in the *Causeries du Lundi* (18 Nov. 1850).

16. Optimism is almost full-blown in Henry More's *Divine Dialogues* (1668). The *De Origine Mali* of William King, Swift's ecclesiastical superior, appeared in 1702; the *Théodicée* of Leibnitz in 1710.

17. *Spectator*, no. 610.

18. An interesting comment of Pope on La Rochefoucauld is preserved by Spence (*Anecdotes*, London, 1820, p. 9) : 'As L'Esprit, La Rochefoucauld, and that sort of people, prove that all virtues are disguised vices, I would engage to prove all vices to be disguised virtues. Neither, indeed, is true, but this would be a more agreeable subject, and would overturn their whole scheme.'

19. Tindal, *Christianity as Old as the Creation* (London, 1732) p. 312.

20. *Encyclopédie*, article 'Intérêt'.

21. The paradox of Mandeville runs through seventeenth-century thought, though not all of its proponents equal Mandeville in his Epicurean equanimity. In fact, the quarrel between morality and religion goes back at least as far as Bacon. One of the favourite texts of the Deists was a passage in Bacon's essay on Superstition : 'Atheism leaves a man to sense, to philosophy, to natural piety, to laws, to reputation; all of which may be guides to an outward moral virtue, though religion were not.'

22. See, for example, Tillotson's Sermon, *On the Goodness of God* (*Works*, 10 vols., London, 1820, Sermon no. 145).

23. G. Burnet, *Some Passages of the Life and Death of the Right Honourable John, Earl of Rochester* (London, 1680) p. 85.

24. Locke, *The Reasonableness of Christianity as delivered in the Scriptures* (London, 1695) p. 7.

25. Hobbes, *Leviathan*, Part I, chap. 13.

26. Locke, *Two Treatises on Government*, Book II, chaps. 2, 3.

27. Bayle, *Dictionnaire*, article 'Ovid', Remark E.

28. Seneca, *Epist.*, 41, 8.

29. Epictetus, *Discourses*, IV, 1, 12.

30. Augustine, *Anti-Pelagian Writings* (*Nicene and Post-Nicene Fathers*, ed. Schaff, New York, 1902) p. 412.

31. Strowski, *Pascal et son Temps* (Paris, 1907) I, 106.

32. Ibid, I, 104.

33. Swift, *Thoughts on Various Subjects* (*Prose Works*, I, 277).

34. Sénault, *De l'Usage des Passions* (Paris, 1641).

35. Strowski, op. cit., I, 124.

36. Pascal, *Thoughts* (Temple Classics) no. 277.

37. The problem of Swift's primitivism – his admiration for the simple government of Brobdingnag and the rational Utopia of the Houyhnhnms – is not easy of solution. In fact, the primitivistic tradition in the seventeenth century invites further investigation. Swift's position could be compared with a passage in Aristotle's *Politics* (Book I, chap. 2) : 'Man, when perfected, is the best of animals, but when separated from law and justice, he is the worst of all; since armed injustice is the more dangerous, and he is equipped at birth with the arms of intelligence and with moral qualities which he may use for the worst ends. Wherefore if he have not virtue, he is the most unruly and the most savage of animals, and the most full of lust and gluttony.'

38. Newman, *Idea of a University*, Discourse V (Longmans edition, New York, 1912) p. 121.

39. One of the most interesting comments by a contemporary on the course of ideas in the seventeenth century is a letter of Bossuet to a disciple of Malebranche criticising the Cartesian philosophy from many sides (21 May 1687, *Works*, Paris, 1888, IX, 59).

40. Bayle, *Dictionnaire*, article 'Hobbes', Remark E.

41. Pascal, *Thoughts*, no. 418.

42. *Gulliver's Travels*, ed. Bernbaum (New York, 1920) pp. x–xii.

43. Sainte-Beuve, *Port-Royal* (Paris, 1878) III, 238.

John F. Ross

THE FINAL COMEDY OF
LEMUEL GULLIVER (1941)

Nominally, everyone regards *Gulliver's Travels* as one of the world's very great satires; the difficult intellectual feat, apparently, is to realize how satiric it is. Critical appraisals of *Gulliver*, at any rate, fall into confusion over the fourth voyage. Confronted by Swift's most unrelenting and severe attack on the Yahoo nature of man, the critic, from some obscure fellow feeling, refuses to read *Gulliver* to the end as complex satire. He thereby misses the final comic absurdity inherent in what is the climax not only of the fourth voyage, but of the satire as a whole. Swift may not be a comic figure, but Gulliver decidedly is.

I

Consider, in this regard, the common evaluation of Gulliver as voiced by Thackeray, Leslie Stephen, and their twentieth-century followers. Whatever their differences, and they have many, they are in substantial agreement on several points. (1) *Gulliver* is one of the world's great satires, and perhaps the most severe. (2) Voyage IV is its climax. And this voyage is plainspoken, terrible, and overwhelming, upsetting in the extreme to our normally optimistic view of man's nature and achievement. (3) The Yahoos are not a true representation of mankind, nor can horses talk and reason. (4) It follows from (2) and (3) that the fourth voyage is indecent and shameful, an insult to humanity. (5) Since Swift lost his mind at an advanced age, he was insane when, years before, he wrote the fourth voyage. (6) Therefore (the conclusion is expressed or implicit) it is advisable not to read this particular work of art to its conclusion, but to stop halfway, – that is to say, with the end of the second voyage.

A more logical conclusion for those who hold this attitude is this : great and severe satire should never be written, and if written, should be publicly burned – and the satirist with it. But logic has little enough to do with the matter; the attitude is self-contradictory. It resolves itself really into an acknowledgment of Swift's greatness and an admission of the validity of his satiric attack even in the fourth voyage, coupled with a determined refusal to admit that his attack is valid. The rationalization of the situation is not convincing, even when Swift's insanity is thrown in for good measure.

More thoughtful modern critics have abandoned this attitude, yet they too are troubled by Voyage IV. Severe satire, insults to humanity, and madness appear to worry them little; they have other objections. Something has gone wrong with Swift's craftsmanship. The last voyage is psychologically unconvincing. Even if we accept the Yahoos, we cannot accept the Houhyhnhnms; and furthermore, the drab and limited life of the horses is wholly unsatisfactory as a Utopia, as Swift himself should have known. Perhaps it is simply that, carried away by the impetus of his severe attack, Swift has lost control. Of the fourth voyage, W. A. Eddy says in his critical study of *Gulliver*, 'someone has blundered, and I fear me it is Swift'. Ricardo Quintana, in his careful and penetrating study of Swift, has many doubts concerning the last voyage, and shakes his head over its 'sensationalism'. This modern type of analysis is on much firmer ground than the older attitude, and is not to be carelessly dismissed. Yet in it an old error persists : by identifying the later Gulliver too completely with Swift, it takes the fourth voyage much too literally as a statement of Swift's final position. For instance, W. A. Eddy writes :

Swift tells us that the Houyhnhnms are more reasonable than Gulliver, but the Houyhnhnms do not bear him out. To me the defect of the fourth voyage is not the brutality of satire, but the stupidity of the Houyhnhnms, whose judgments of Gulliver prove nothing beyond their own incompetence to judge. Gulliver is quick to recognize

the excellent qualities of the horses. How is it then that the Houyhnhnms, who we are assured are so much more sensible, are unable to
recognize that the human body is much more suitable than their own
for the common needs of life? ...

Swift was careless of his story; the fires of misanthropy obscured
his judgment, and vitiated his argument. Much may be said for
Swift's Yahoo conception of man, but much more against his misconception of the ideal Houyhnhnms. Powerfully as he reiterates
and supports his postulate that the horse is the better creature, the
Houyhnhnms refute it on every page.

Here Swift and Gulliver are completely identified, regarded as of
one mind. Actually, all the postulates are Gulliver's postulates.
It is Swift who permits Gulliver to reveal in his narrative the
horses' 'incompetence to judge'.

The most recent attempt to deal with the problem of the fourth
voyage is an essay in *Perilous Balance*, by W. B. C. Watkins. Here
the solution offered is that the fourth voyage leaves the realms of
satire for those of tragedy. The essay is admirable in stressing the
profound seriousness and significance of Swift's view of the problem of evil; but in holding that this view is essentially tragic the
author misses the demonstrable satiric structure and conclusion
of the voyage.

Since no one seems to have had difficulty in reading the first
two voyages of *Gulliver* as satire, whence arise the difficulties over
the last voyage? One chief source of trouble, I have no doubt, lies
outside of Swift and his book, in certain assumptions which are
so traditional and conventional that the critic may not only not
express them, but may even be unaware of them. It is commonplace to distinguish two modes of satire: the genial, laughing,
urbane satire of Horace, and the severe, lashing satire of Juvenal.
Whatever hostility the first mode may contain, it nevertheless
works largely in terms of laughter. For convenience, it may be
termed comic satire. The second mode emphasizes a severely
satiric attack in which laughter is at a minimum, or perhaps even
lacking. This may be termed caustic or corrosive satire. Swift, like
Juvenal, holds a commanding position as a satirist in large part
because of the corrosive satire of which he was capable. Yet – and

any considerable reading in the history and criticism of satire will support the view – most critics are repelled by corrosive satire and prefer rather to deal with comic satire. I share that preference, indeed, and regard comic satire as a richer, more complete treatment of humanity than purely corrosive satire; but if one unconsciously comes to identify good satire with comic satire only, he is almost certain to have trouble with the fourth voyage of *Gulliver*. Unconsciously expecting the smile or the laugh as a partial balm to severe satiric attack, and finding that this balm is scarcely present in the effective first nine chapters of the last voyage, he may decide that he is no longer reading satire, and hence miss Swift's rounding of the whole of *Gulliver* in a superb return of comic satire.

For we should not assume that, if someone has blundered in the last voyage, the blunderer was therefore Swift. That assumption is dangerously close to the idea that we are superior to Swift because we are superior to Lemuel Gulliver. But Swift paid his readers a higher compliment than most readers will pay him. He assumed, as any ironic satirist by the very nature of his work assumes, that he and his readers were on terms of equality in sharing an important secret, which is that there is far more in literal statement than meets the literal eye. It may be granted that for nine chapters the corrosive satire of the last voyage of *Gulliver* is of unparalleled intensity, and that its recurrent waves are overwhelming enough to swamp minds of considerable displacement, as well as cockleshell intellects. Yet Swift offers us the opportunity to ride out the storm with him, and even goes to some trouble to keep us afloat. If we choose to disregard Swift himself and the last part of Voyage iv, and to go down finally for the third time, with Gulliver, it is hardly Swift's blunder.

II

One of my main concerns here is to show that Gulliver in the last voyage is not Swift. That done, we shall be able to see how Swift, though his corrosive satire continues to the last page of the volume, superadds to it a comic satire of great significance. But our understanding of the last voyage will be made easier if we appreciate certain complex effects achieved by Swift in the earlier voyages. Just as a great composer has a variety of single orchestral instruments which he uses to produce complex music, so Swift has a variety of instruments wherewith he produces the complexity which is *Gulliver's Travels*. Ready to his hand he has the modes of straight narrative, of comedy, of comic satire, and of corrosive satire. And he has the double voice of irony.

Though the voyage to Lilliput is commonly held to be the merriest and most diverting of the four voyages, the greater part of it, quantitatively considered, holds our interest chiefly as ingenious narrative. In the first four chapters, besides a few comic and satiric touches, there is one outstanding passage of comic satire, that concerning the High-Heels and Low-Heels, and the Big-Endians and the Little-Endians. The narrative then resumes chief importance until we reach the end of chapter vi, with its comic passage in which Gulliver defends the reputation of the Lilliputian lady whose name had been scandalously linked with his.

In chapter vii occurs the severest satire of the first voyage. Gulliver, who has deserved the highest gratitude from the Lilliputians, is impeached for capital offenses – chiefly, for making water within the precincts of the burning royal palace 'under colour of extinguishing the fire', and for traitorously refusing to reduce the empire of Blefuscu to a province and put to death all the Big-Endian exiles. Though the episode is introduced with a trace of comic absurdity in the articles of impeachment, and in their pompous phrasing, the court's debate on how to dispose of Gulliver is corrosive satire, savage and ironic. It is suggested that Gulliver be put to a painful and ignominious death, his house set on fire, and thousands of poisoned arrows shot into his face and hands. His servants are to strew poisonous juices on his shirt, to make him tear his own flesh and die in the 'utmost torture'. At this point Reldresal proves himself Gulliver's 'true friend' by suggesting that blindness would be a sufficient punishment; but Gulliver's enemies argue against this proposal. His Imperial Majesty, gracious and lenient, holds out against the death sentence, but hints that punishments in addition to blindness may be inflicted on Gulliver. Finally, again through the friendship of Reldresal, it is decided to blind Gulliver and to starve him to death.

In this episode, which is the longest satiric passage in the first voyage and the climax of the voyage, the satiric attack is bitter. As Swift shows the refinements of hypocrisy, ingratitude, and cruelty achieved by the Lilliputian court, mirth leaves him, and he is as severe as in any part of Voyage IV.

Yet the general sense that the voyage is a merry one is sound. The one passage of essentially corrosive satire is largely outweighed by incidental comedy, by the famous passage of comic satire, and by the wealth of sheerly narrative detail. By the end of chapter vii the corrosive attack has ceased – Gulliver is in Blefuscu, lying on the ground in order to 'kiss his Majesty's and the Empress's hand'. In the final chapter he is returned to England, and is in familiar and kindly surroundings, enjoying the company of his 'dear pledges' and breeding Lilliputian sheep in the absurd hope of improving the English woolen manufacture. Furthermore, there is the basic comic absurdity which pervades the entire voyage, namely, Gulliver's attitude in reporting his experiences. Constantly before our eyes we have the incredible double scale of size, human and Lilliputian, reported without comment by Gulliver, who accepts the Lilliputian scale as easily as the human. It is the comic incongruity of inadequate reporting, felt as inadequate when we visualize the scenes and episodes described by Gulliver. And Swift permits Gulliver so great a use of specific visual detail, in which the two scales of size are constantly blended, that even the unimaginative reader has no difficulty in seeing the picture. Thus the scandal about Gulliver and the Lilliputian lady is immediately comic to the reader. But as Gulliver goes through his elaborate defense of her reputation (and his), the comedy is immensely heightened by the reader's realization of Gulliver's inadequate sense of the situation; in his long defense he never mentions the one particular that makes the scandal perfectly absurd, the difference in physical scale.

If one is thinking primarily of the writer, Swift, one may see in this aspect of Gulliver only a device for understatement. But

Swift is achieving his effects by means of a created character; and we see that it is not deliberate understatement for Gulliver, it is simply a result of his character. It is all he finds worth saying. He has definite limitations of mind, which in spite of his development he never outgrows, even in the last voyage.

The second voyage, like the first, has much interesting descriptive and narrative material that is essentially neither comic nor satiric. But there is an increased proportion of comic episode, and the corrosive satire carries far more weight than in the first voyage.

The increased comic effect is achieved principally at the expense of Gulliver, for in the second voyage he is reduced in status and becomes obviously an object of comic satire. He retains a pride and self-esteem which would be perfectly normal for him among his physical equals, but which is ridiculous under the circumstances, and which results in his being made the comic butt in several episodes. The increased corrosive effect is achieved principally by the long passage wherein Gulliver and the king discuss mankind. To this passage we need to give close attention, for the satiric structure of Voyage iv (although on a different plane) is in important ways parallel to it.

Swift permits Gulliver to give the king a favorable statement about the English system. The king perceives that all is not well with Gulliver's civilization; and being a reasonable, thoughtful monarch, he asks Gulliver a long series of questions. These questions are direct and to the point; the answers, which are obviously called for, show defects in Gulliver's world. In the passage thus far, there is little or no emotional, ironic, or comic effect as the king conducts his grave and judicial inquiry. Finally, when the king has thought over his audiences with Gulliver, he delivers quite calmly his famous criticism of the human race. As he concludes it, he courteously hopes that Gulliver may have escaped many vices of his kind – nevertheless the bulk of humanity is 'the most pernicious race of little odious vermin that nature ever suffered to crawl upon the surface of the earth.'

So much for the human race, apparently, as judged by a reasonable being who has heard the best case Gulliver can make out for his kind. And the quality is corrosive, not comic. Yet it is only a preliminary to the satire that follows. Gulliver's hope to impress the king has had the reverse effect, but Gulliver himself has not come off badly. Swift now proceeds to allow Gulliver to reveal himself as a typical member of the race, and at the same time drives the satiric attack deeper. Gulliver expresses his great embarrassment at hearing his 'noble and most beloved country' so injuriously treated. At this point, and for the first time in the long passage, Swift calls into play the double voice of irony. The squirming Gulliver reveals that he has given 'to every point a more favorable turn by many degrees than the strictness of truth would allow'; but nevertheless he condescendingly suggests that 'great allowances should be given to a King who lives so wholly secluded from the rest of the world' and hence must have an insufficiency of knowledge and 'a certain narrowness of thinking, from which we and the politer countries of Europe are wholly exempted'.

Gulliver's comments here have further worsened his case for mankind, besides revealing the absurdity of his sense of superiority to the king. Another satirist might pause at this point, but Swift has still to reach his satiric climax and to reduce Gulliver utterly. Gulliver blunders on: 'To confirm what I have now said, and further, to show the miserable effects of a confined education, I shall here insert a passage which will hardly obtain belief.' In a word, Gulliver offers the king the secret of gunpowder, giving a notion of its effectiveness by means of a few graphic and specific details. The king is horrified, regards Gulliver as inhuman in advancing such thoughts, and forbids him to mention the matter again. Gulliver is still blind, and shakes his head over the king's reaction, which seems to him 'a strange effect of narrow principles and short views'.

This long, satiric passage is relatively simple at first, but it becomes elaborate before it ends. We have, first, Gulliver's theme of the excellence of mankind. Next is added the calm and generalized, but corrosive, satire of the king's queries and final dismissal of mankind – a note which sounds through the rest of the passage. Swift then calls irony, and, when he is ready, adds the emotional impact of his most forceful and graphic prose (specific details concerning the effective use of gunpowder). Gulliver's bland assumption that he is doing the king a favor coexists in the reader's mind with the shocking demonstration of what man's inhumanity is capable of; Gulliver is demolishing himself with the reader as well as the king; and Swift is achieving a bitter yet comic irony in Gulliver's naïve unawareness and continued self-assurance. And underlying the whole satiric structure of the long passage is the substructure of physical absurdity : with all his fine words and superiority, Gulliver can be taken into the king's hand and stroked – he is 'little Grildrig'.

Even so brief an analysis as the foregoing reveals several points important to our discussion. Swift moves from the simpler to the more complex for his satiric climax; to corrosive satire he adds comic and ironic notes. And it is of particular significance to our view of Voyage IV that in achieving his effects Swift has caused Gulliver, unawares, to make a lamentable spectacle of himself.

As we accompany Gulliver to the end of the second voyage, we are in no danger of confusing him with Swift. Gulliver remains likeable – indeed he remains likeable to the end; but Swift always uses him deliberately, even ruthlessly, to further the Swiftian satiric purpose. And Gulliver's characteristics are admirable for this purpose. He is a man of some education, has traveled, and by the end of the second voyage has had very surprising experiences. But he is and remains a type of ordinary, normal man – even a rather simplified version of the type. He is capable with his hands, and quick to meet physical emergency. He is essentially a man of good will, friendly, honest, and ethical according to his lights. His mental make-up is simple and direct, and it permits almost no complexity. He is not torn by any inner conflict, for his psyche is unwilling to admit the diverse possibilities which make for such conflicts. He can be the Gulliver of the first voyage, a man whose normal humanity seems good in the light of petty and ungrateful Lilliputian policy. He can be the Gulliver of the second voyage, whose normal acceptance of the standards and values of his civilization seems bad in the light of largeness and humaneness of spirit. He is much the same man in these two voyages :

Swift has shown first the better side of ordinary values, secondly, the worser side. And Gulliver's mind is not at first closed; new experiences occur and give new directions to his thought, or – as in the fourth voyage – produce a shift in his attitude. But the simplicity and naïveté remain; his mind is a single-track one. It never compasses the complex and the contradictory; it cleaves to the best line it knows, but to that line alone.

That Gulliver's mind is not at first closed, but yet is limited, has important consequences. Thus, while he is open-minded, he can change from one attitude to another under the pressure of what he sees and hears about him. Although always a giant in Lilliput, he adopts easily the prevailing Lilliputian scale. Although he is miniature in Brobdingnag, being completely surrounded by a gigantic environment he comes to take the gigantic scale as normal. That new attitude having become habitual with him, the fact of his own minuteness (though constant to his experience) drops out of his mind and ceases to have any meaning. And his new, oversimplified attitude has a narrowness and rigidity which continues after he leaves the land of the giants, and results in comedy when he returns to a world built to his scale. Back in England, he says, 'I was afraid of trampling on every traveller I met, and often called aloud to have them stand out of the way, so that I had like to have gotten one or two broken heads for my impertinence.' He behaves so unaccountably toward his family that they conclude he has lost his wits. In effect, his new attitude prevents him from believing the evidence of his own eyes. But his mind is not closed, and gradually the physical realities recall him to a proper sense of scale. On Voyage IV, however, in the simple intellectual and moral environment of the Houyhnhnms, and horrified at the Yahoos, Gulliver has that final intellectual development and illumination which leads to the completely closed mind. It is a situation which permits Swift to develop his corrosive attack, but we ought not to be surprised to find that Swift remains superior to his puppet to the end, and reveals an attitude different from Gulliver's.

III

The first two voyages of *Gulliver* are two complementary parts
which make up one large unit of satire. The fourth part of the
book is not simply an additional voyage, more severely satirical
but on the whole to be read like the earlier voyages; it is a voyage
different in concept and in treatment, and hence it is not to be
judged by the same criteria.

We notice at once that the fourth voyage lacks the picturesque
and interesting descriptive and narrative detail so abundantly
present in the earlier voyages. There is, for instance, no double
physical scale, and there is little narrative action. Swift does, of
course, embody the chief elements of his satiric analysis in the
concrete symbols of the horse and the Yahoo, and he describes
the Yahoo in full and unpleasant detail. Even so, the spirit and
scheme of the fourth voyage employ far less narrative richness
than is expended on Lilliput and Brobdingnag, since Swift shifts
the emphasis of his attack. The satire of the earlier voyages is
concerned with the flaws and defects of man's actions. Voyage
IV cuts deeper. Actions and doings are symptomatic of man's
nature – the corrosive satire of the last voyage is concerned with
the springs and causes of action, in other words, with the inner
make-up of man. Hence, though there is a narrative thread in
Voyage IV, and considerable detail about the Yahoo, the voyage
is characterized less by fullness of narrative than by fullness of
analysis.

Another difference in the fourth voyage should be noted. Here
the reader himself is inescapably an object of satiric attack. In the
first voyage he may remain calm in the face of the satire. There is
not only a good deal else to divert his attention; there is also the
fact that the activities of monarchs and statesmen are the actions
of an exceedingly small group of people. The reader's withers are
unwrung. He may even remain relatively detached emotionally
in reading of Gulliver's offer of gunpowder to the Brobdingnagian king. After all, war has been so far only an intermittent activity of nations, and the reader probably disapproves of it in theory
as much as Swift does. But the reader cannot evade the attack in

the last voyage: Swift is attacking the Yahoo in each of us.

Furthermore, it has now become Swift's purpose to drive home the satire, insistently and relentlessly. Had he wished to achieve only the diverting and comic satire of Voyages I and II, with occasional touches of the severer sort, he need not have written the last voyage. But he chose to go on, and in the fourth voyage corrosive satire at last comes home deeply and profoundly to his readers. In truth, the constant protests against it are evidence of its effectiveness.

Mere narrative or comic detail concerning either the Yahoos or the Houyhnhnms would inevitably tend to weaken, divert, or block off the intensity of the attack; hence Swift makes little use of such detail. He sharply cuts human nature into two parts. He gives reason and benevolence to the Houyhnhnms. Unrestrained and selfish appetites, and a mere brutish awareness, are left for the Yahoo. Since he is writing satire rather than panegyric, the good qualities are given the nonhuman form of the horse, and the bad qualities the nearly human form of the Yahoo. Consider how much less effective the satire would have been had the Houyhnhnms been merely a superior human race – the reader would naturally evade the satiric attack by identifying himself as a Houyhnhnm. Again, for intensity of attack, Swift dwells with unpleasant particularity on Yahoo form and nature: the emphasis is necessarily on Yahoo form and nature. In this connection, it should be said that the unpleasant physical characteristics of the Yahoos are in themselves hardly as repellent as the disgusting physical details Gulliver has noted among the Brobdingnagians. The microscopic eye among the giants produces perhaps as repulsive a series of physical images as can be found in literature; but, for all that, we are aware of a fantastic enlargement, and this makes for relative unreality. The Yahoos are not giants, they resemble us all too closely in some ways, and their unpleasant physical traits are displayed to us without the variety of relief permitted in Voyage II.

Swift's aim in the last voyage is to spare us nothing. If we could chuckle and laugh at the Yahoos, or be diverted by their activities, by so much would Swift have weakened his corrosive satire. And the same exigency governs his treatment of the Houyhnhnms. To make much of them for comic or narrative effect would impair Swift's chief purpose.

One further point: In the first nine chapters of Voyage IV, Swift further simplifies and concentrates his attack by making almost no use of irony; the attack on Yahoo-man is not only severe, but literal and direct.

Is the misanthropy of the fourth voyage, then, too much to accept? Is Swift's hatred all-consuming? Has it abandoned itself to wanton and animus-ridden insult? Has the sanity of his rich and complex genius been dissipated? Before we agree with the many who have answered 'Yes' to such questions, let us contemplate the voyage as a whole. For Swift not only wrote the first nine chapters of Voyage IV; he also wrote the last three. To neglect these final chapters is like ignoring the final couplet in a Shakespearean sonnet, the last part of a tragi-comedy like *The Winter's Tale*, or the last three chapters of *Moby Dick*. It is true that Swift's final attitude may not be obvious to a superficial reader, or to one inhibited (perhaps unconsciously) from reading *Gulliver* as a complete satire. But great and complex artists usually make some demands on their readers, and Swift is no exception. *Gulliver's Travels* is easier to understand than *A Tale of a Tub*; but it by no means follows that Lemuel Gulliver's naïve and simple misanthropy can be equated with the sophisticated satirist who recounted Gulliver's adventures. One should be on guard against simplifying an elaborate ironist.

Swift himself has warned us, if we are at all wary. To say that the first nine chapters of the fourth voyage are almost continuous corrosive satire is not to say that there are not some narrative and comic touches. Swift obviously visualized the Houyhnhnms very definitely as horses. It must have been a temptation to his constructive and comic imagination to avail himself of the opportunities offered by the horse form. Generally he restrains himself: thus Gulliver remembers once seeing some Houyhnhnms 'employed in domestic business', but he does not specify what business. Yet Swift cannot resist an occasional bit of fun at the expense of the Houyhnhnms. They have an absolute self-assurance in the completeness of their knowledge and experience. The etymology of the word Houyhnhnm means 'horse', but also 'the perfection of nature'. Their intellectual limitations and arrogance are divertingly illustrated in the passage wherein the Houyhnhnm criticizes the human form. In every point wherein man and horse differ, the Houyhnhnm automatically and even absurdly assumes that the advantage lies obviously with the horse; for example, that four legs are better than two, or that the human anatomy is defective since Gulliver cannot eat without lifting one of his 'fore feet' to his mouth. While Swift, in pursuit of his purpose, is chary of making the horses absurd, there are enough comic touches to guard the attentive reader from assuming that Swift accepts Gulliver's worshipful attitude toward the horses.

Further evidence that Swift was well aware that the Houyhnhnms were, after all, horses, and that they offered more material for comedy than he had permitted himself to use in his text, may be found in a letter he wrote his publisher, Motte, concerning illustrations for a new edition of the *Travels*. Since he tells Motte that a return of his deafness has put him 'in an ill way to answer a letter which requires some thinking', and since the letter also indicates that he has not reread *Gulliver* but is trusting to memory, it may be presumed that his remarks indicate his normal attitude toward the book. The relevant part of his letter reads:

The Country of Horses, I think, would furnish many [occasions for illustration]. Gulliver brought to be compared with the Yahoos; the family at dinner and he waiting; the grand council of horses, assembled, sitting, one of them standing with a hoof extended, as if he were speaking; the she-Yahoo embracing Gulliver in the river, who turns away his head in disgust; the Yahoos got into a tree, to infest him under it; the Yahoos drawing carriages, and driven by a horse with a whip in his hoof. I can think of no more, but Mr. Gay will advise you.

Swift's suggestions for illustrations, added to the few ludicrous suggestions in the first nine chapters of the fourth voyage, indicate that he took as a matter of course that there was a certain amount of comic effect in the rather simple horses visualized in their relationship of superiority to Gulliver and the Yahoos. Since Gulliver's Houyhnhnm worship is a vital element in making the corrosive attack on Yahoo nature effective, it might seem that Swift had bungled his craft in permitting even slight evidences of the limitations of the Houyhnhnms. Actually, without weakening the main attack of the early part of the voyage, these slight hints foreshadow Swift's attitude in the last three chapters. As a composer of music, giving almost complete emphasis to a main theme, may suggest from time to time a new theme before he develops it fully, so Swift, while developing misanthropic and corrosive satire at length, hints from time to time at another theme.

The horses and Gulliver have it all their own way for the first nine chapters of the last voyage. Yahoo-man has been presented in all his horror; Swift has achieved the most blasting and unrelieved satiric attack possible, and at great length. What simple and indignant reason can say against the flaws and defects of human nature has been said, and said exhaustively. Gulliver's revolt against his kind is so complete that Swift is able to give the knife a final twist: mankind is, if anything, worse than the Yahoo, since man is afflicted by pride, and makes use of what mental power he has to achieve perversions and corruptions undreamed of by the Yahoo.

At this point of the satiric attack many readers have ceased really to read the book, and have concluded that this was Swift's final word because it is Gulliver's final word. Swept away by the force of the corrosive attack on Yahoo-man, they conclude that Gulliver is at last Swift. (Such a misconception is facilitated no doubt by Swift's temporary abandonment of irony for straightforward invective.) In the last three chapters, however, Swift shows that Gulliver's word cannot be final.

Swift, satirist and realist, is well aware that there is more of the Yahoo in humanity than there is of benevolence and reason. And he develops his attack as forcibly as he can, by means of corrosive satire, in terms of pessimism and misanthropy. But this is only a part of Swift. He is also perfectly aware that the problem is not so simply solved as it is for the Houyhnhnms and for Gulliver. He knows that there is much to be hated in the animal called man, but he knows also that there are individuals whom he loves. The horses have no room for anything between Houyhnhnm and Yahoo, and Gulliver takes over this too simple attitude. Just as his physical sense of proportion was upset by his voyage to the country of the giants, so here his intellectual sense of proportion is overbalanced. The limited, simplified Houyhnhnm point of view is obviously better to him than the Yahoo state; and he cleaves to it. Swift can keep clear the double physical scale of Gulliver and giant; not so, Gulliver. Swift can differentiate between Yahoo and Gulliver, and does – but Gulliver himself is convinced he is a Yahoo. The attentive reader will realize that Gulliver is the one actual human being present through the first nine blighting chapters of the last voyage. Hence he is not only a constant reminder that horse and Yahoo are symbols, but also a constant demonstration that a human being is not a Yahoo.

Swift has fun with Gulliver in chapter x. Gulliver has finally come to the conclusion that human beings are, if anything, worse than Yahoos. As much as possible he tries to transform himself into a horse:

By conversing with the Houyhnhnms, and looking upon them with delight, I fell to imitate their gait and gesture, which is now grown into a habit, and my friends often tell me in a blunt way, that I trot like a horse; which, however, I take for a great compliment. Neither shall I disown that in speaking I am apt to fall into the voice and manner of the Houyhnhnms . . .

And in the paragraph immediately following this excerpt, with Gulliver at the height of his enchantment, Swift has the horses, with more ruthlessness than benevolence, order Gulliver to leave the island and swim back to the place whence he came. Gulliver swoons. He is allowed two months to finish a boat, and is granted the assistance of a sorrel nag, who 'had a tenderness' for him. It is a diverting picture: Gulliver and the sorrel nag working away together to make a canoe, 'covering it with the skins of Yahoos well stitched together' and 'stopping all the chinks with Yahoos' tallow'. When the moment of parting comes:

His Honour, out of curiosity and perhaps (if I may speak it without vanity) partly out of kindness, was determined to see me in my canoe. . . . I took a second leave of my master; but as I was going to prostrate myself to kiss his hoof, he did me the honour to raise it gently to my mouth. I am not ignorant how much I have been censured for mentioning this last particular. For my detractors are pleased to think it improbable that so illustrious a person should descend to give so great a mark of distinction to a creature so inferior as I. . . .

My master and his friends continued on the shore till I was almost out of sight; and I often heard the sorrel nag (who always loved me) crying out, *Hnuy illa nyha majah Yahoo*, Take care of thyself, gentle Yahoo.

It is heartbreaking for Gulliver; but for Swift and the reader it is not wholly a matter for tears.

Gulliver's design is to make his way to an 'uninhabited island', but he is eventually found by the crew of a Portuguese ship. Gulliver's meeting with the crew returns him to the real world; he is no longer the sole representative of humanity, placed between horse and Yahoo. In the earlier voyages, Swift had spent only a few pages on Gulliver's return to the real world; in the last, he gives two chapters to it. Those chapters deserve very careful reading: they are, as the book now stands, the climax of Swift's whole satire as well as the end of the fourth voyage. Gulliver, hating himself and all men as Yahoos, is reintroduced to the world of actual men and women. What happens? If Swift's view is the same as Gulliver's, he ought to go on with his severe satire against mankind, now even deepening it with specific examples of Yahoo nature. He does nothing of the sort. Rather, he shows us very carefully and at some length the insufficiency of Gulliver's new attitude. Gulliver continues to 'tremble between fear and hatred' when confronted by human beings, while at the same time his own account of affairs shows that the persons with whom he comes into contact are essentially honest, kindly, and generous. It is the same limited mentality in Gulliver which has been noted in previous voyages. He has adopted a final rigid and oversimplified attitude, which so completely possesses him that he cannot believe the evidence of his own experience; since he now sees man only as Yahoo, he cannot even take in contradictory evidence when faced with it.

The Portuguese crew speak to Gulliver 'with great humanity' when they find him; but he is horrified. Concluding that his misfortunes have 'impaired his reason' (as indeed they have), they deliver him up to the captain.

[The captain's] name was Pedro de Mendez; he was a very courteous and generous person; he entreated me to give some account of myself, and desired to know what I would eat and drink; said I should be used as well as himself, and spoke so many obliging things, that I wondered to find such civilities in a Yahoo. However, I remained silent and sullen; I was ready to faint at the very smell of him and his men.

Gulliver finally promises the captain not to attempt anything against his own life, but at the same time protests that he will 'suffer the greatest hardships rather than return to live among Yahoos'. In the course of the voyage home, out of gratitude to Don Pedro, Gulliver sometimes sits with the captain and tries to conceal his antipathy to mankind. The captain offers Gulliver the best suit of clothes he has; Gulliver will accept only two clean shirts, which, he thinks, will not so much 'defile' him. In Lisbon, the captain still further aids Gulliver, takes him into his house, and persuades him to accept a newly made suit of clothes. Gulliver finds that his terror at humanity gradually lessens : the captain's 'whole deportment was so obliging, added to a very good *human* understanding, that I really began to tolerate his company'. But though the terror might lessen, Gulliver's 'hatred and contempt seemed to increase'.

Why does Swift give us Don Pedro, the kindly, generous individual? Obviously as a foil to Gulliver's misanthropy, as evidence that Gulliver has gone off the deep end and cannot recover himself from the nightmare view of Yahoo-man. Chapter xi is almost wholly a demonstration that Gulliver is absurd in his blind refusal to abandon his misanthropic convictions. His conduct upon his return home is the ultimate result of his aberration. His family receive him with joy, but the sight of them fills Gulliver

with hatred, contempt, and disgust. When his wife kisses him, he
falls 'into a swoon for almost an hour'. His adopted attitude of
mind, directed by the too simple Houyhnhnm view, permits him
to see only the Yahoo in man or woman. Even after five years
he will not permit any member of his family to take him by the
hand. But we may allow him to characterize his mode of life
himself : 'The first money I laid out was to buy two young stone-
horses, which I kept in a good stable, and next to them the groom
is my greatest favourite, for I feel my spirits revived by the smell
he contracts in the stable. My horses understand me tolerably
well; I converse with them at least four hours every day.'

Gulliver's attitude is not the solution, and Swift knew it. It is
too unbalanced and unrealistic for a final attitude, and Swift presents its absurdity – so clearly as to make one wonder how he
could have been so misunderstood. Gulliver's attitude is in effect
a complete quarrel with man, a final refusal to accept the nature
of mankind. To charge Swift with the same final refusal is to
ignore the evidence. In this connection a passage from the second
voyage, where surely Swift is speaking through Gulliver, is help-
ful. Gulliver has been reading a Brobdingnagian book, and says :

This writer went through all the usual topics of European moralists,
showing how diminutive, contemptible, and helpless was man in his
own nature [i.e., the sixty-foot nature of the Brobdingnagians]. . . .
The author drew several moral applications useful in the conduct of
life, but needless here to repeat. For my own part, I could not
avoid reflecting how universally this talent was spread, of drawing
lectures in morality, or indeed matter for discontent and repining,
from the quarrels we raise with nature.

I do not by any means wish to say that Swift was always superior
to drawing matter for discontent and repining from quarrels
raised with nature. He was clear-sighted and sensitive; he was an
ethical moralist and a satirist. Much in the nature of man was
hateful and detestable to him, and he often attacked it and quar-
reled with it in no uncertain terms. But, though Gulliver's soul
was completely discontented, completely repining, Swift could
rise to a far higher plane, and did so. Swift was much more than
a corrosive satirist only; he had a high sense of the comic, and in

the final satiric vision of the concluding chapters of *Gulliver* the Gulliverian discontent is supplemented by, and enclosed in, comic satire, with Gulliver himself as the butt.

In Voyage IV, Swift gives his severest satiric vision full scope, but knows that conclusions growing out of this nightmare vision are inadequate and invalid. He lets Gulliver go the whole horse, and up to the last page the negative, corrosive attack is present. But what else he does in those last chapters is unique in the history of satiric literature : the severe attack with its apparently rational basis and its horrifying conclusions continues to the end in the personal narrative of Swift's puppet. Thus severe satire remains the main theme, but the new theme of Gulliver's absurdity complicates the issue. By rising to a larger and more comprehensive view than he permits to Gulliver, Swift is satirically commenting on the insufficiency of the corrosive attitude. The evils in the world and in man are such that it is no wonder that a simple and ethical nature may be driven to despair and misanthropy. Nevertheless, such an attitude Swift demonstrates to be inadequate and absurd.

Gulliver's attitude, in its simplicity and finality, is a kind of misanthropic solution of the problem of evil. It is a tempting solution for a severe satirist; but Swift found it too limited and too unreal. So far as I can see, Swift offers no answer of his own, no solution. But he does transcend the misanthropic solution. He could see that his own severest satire was the result of a partial and one-sided view, which was therefore properly a subject for mirth.

This seems to me the final comedy of Lemuel Gulliver – that Swift could make an elaborate and subtle joke at the expense of a very important part of himself. We may leave Lemuel in amiable discourse in the stable, inhaling the grateful odor of horse. But Swift is not with him, Swift is above him in the realm of comic satire, still indignant at the Yahoo in man, but at the same time smiling at the absurdity of the view that can see *only* the Yahoo in man.

S o u r c e : *Studies in the Comic*, University of California Publications in English, vol. 8, no. 2 (1941) pp. 175–96.

Herbert Davis

MORAL SATIRE (1947)

> Sir, our *Accounts* are diff'rent quite,
> And your *Conjectures* are not right;
> 'Tis plain, his Writings were design'd
> To *please*, and to *reform* Mankind;
> And, if he often miss'd his Aim,
> The *World* must own it, to their *Shame*;
> The *Praise* is *His*, and *Theirs* the *Blame*.[1]

We have examined the method of Swift's satire, first, as he was concerned with the world of letters, the Author of *A Tale of a Tub*, writing as a wit with his reading fresh in his head, so that the result is very literary, full of parody and of echoes of seventeenth-century literature; and second, as he was concerned with the world of politics, both in London and in Dublin, when he appeared in the role of Tory Examiner and Drapier – not to show off his wit or his literature, but to support a party and bring about certain political action.

We must now try to observe him at work on a satire which he hoped would vex the world, and which was intended not merely to show off his wit or to reach a London or a Dublin audience, but which as he said later to the French translator of *Gulliver's Travels*, would be equally well understood abroad, and which was addressed both to his contemporaries and to posterity. If we were right in considering *A Tale of a Tub* as the final product of the seventeenth century, paradoxically growing out of it and at the same time satirizing it and repudiating so much of its spirit, so in like manner we may well regard *Gulliver's Travels* as, both in form and shape, wholly the product of the eighteenth century, while being at the same time the most violent satire of its hopes and dreams and a repudiation of much that it most valued. For it is typical of the century in a very general way, because it is, more than all Swift's so-called historical writings, his contribution to the favourite study of the age – history, not of course in the present sense of the term, but as it was practised by the eighteenth-century philosophers whether in France or in England, who were concerned, as Carl Becker has shown so conclusively in his *Heavenly City of the Eighteenth Century Philosophers*, all of them with a particular thesis on human behaviour, which they set out to prove, whether by a study of the Decline and Fall of the Roman Empire, or by the study of the history of England, or by a study of the spirit or ideas of Law.

They also like Swift used many of the weapons of the satirist – wit and ridicule and irony, even though their travels were limited to parts and places well-known. And Swift, like Gibbon, had learned his idea of liberty and justice from a study of the writers of Greece and Rome; he had given a good deal of attention to the study of government, and by his own direct experience had arrived at as complete a scepticism as any of theirs. But these eighteenth-century philosophers had 'demolished the Heavenly City of St. Augustine only to rebuild it with more up-to-date materials'; they remained optimists enough to believe in the possible enlightenment and rescue of the human race from its folly and from its superstition. Swift had an answer very different from theirs, which has continued to shock successive generations, even though the course of later history has hardly proved him wrong. He thought of himself as different even from his friends, and he remained apart from and unlike most of the philosophers of the century. He could not share their beliefs, and he termed them 'vous autres'. Perhaps it was the purpose of Gulliver to prove this to them, and to their followers.

When his first political career was coming to an end, Swift like many other discarded statesmen turned to the writing of memoirs. He had wished to be appointed officially historiographer to the Queen, in order that he might leave a record for posterity. So after his return to Ireland in 1714, and indeed earlier in England after he left London, despairing of being of further use to the Ministry, he had immediately set to work to put down his own record of the history of the last four years of the Queen. There are various manuscripts surviving from this period, one – *The Enquiry into the Behaviour of the Queen's last Ministry* – begun in the hand of Stella with corrections in the hand of Swift, but none of these memorials were printed in Swift's lifetime, and it was perhaps natural or inevitable that he should try to find some form in which he could make his comment on human behaviour for the benefit of his contemporaries as well as posterity. But this again could only be done safely and adequately in some disguise. For this purpose he could not appear as the London wit; a Bickerstaff would be too provincial and too literary, the Tory Examiner too political, the Dean too ecclesiastical, the linen draper of Dublin too Irish.

Once again he finds the solution by employing his favourite device of parody. He would write a book of Travels, in imitation of the most popular best sellers of the day, like Dampier's *Voyages*. It should not be forgotten also that in 1719, when Swift seems to have begun work seriously on *Gulliver's Travels*, that despised rival political pamphleteer, that secret henchman of Harley's, the fellow who was pilloried, whose name Swift could never remember, Daniel Defoe, delighted the world with his story of Robinson Crusoe. And so Swift settled down to read a lot of this trash, and turned over the pages of a seaman's manual in order to provide himself with the necessary flavour of nautical language, and emerged in an entirely new disguise, the one in which he is best known to the whole world – as the seaman, the plain honest traveller, not over learned or too literary (he had only been three years at Emmanuel College and after that had had some training as a surgeon and in navigation), a simple plain teachable man of unspoiled intelligence, who could serve as a sort of *Everyman*.

My Father had a small Estate in Nottinghamshire; I was the Third of five Sons. He sent me to Emanuel College in Cambridge, at Fourteen Years old, where I resided three Years, and applied my self

close to my Studies : But the Charge of maintaining me (although
I had a very scanty Allowance) being too great for a narrow Fortune; I was bound Apprentice to Mr. James Bates, an eminent
Surgeon in London, with whom I continued four Years; and my
Father now and then sending me small Sums of Money, I laid them
out in learning Navigation, and other Parts of the Mathematicks,
useful to those who intend to travel, as I always believed it would
be some time or other my Fortune to do. When I left Mr. Bates, I
went down to my Father; where, by the Assistance of him and my
Uncle John, and some other Relations, I got Forty Pounds, and a
Promise of Thirty Pounds a Year to maintain me at Leyden : There
I studied Physick two Years and seven Months, knowing it would
be useful in long Voyages.

. . . I was Surgeon successively in two Ships, and made several Voy-
ages, for six Years, to the East and West-Indies; by which I got some
Addition to my Fortune. My Hours of Leisure I spent in reading the
best Authors, ancient and modern; being always provided with a
good Number of Books; and when I was ashore, in observing the
Manners and Dispositions of the People, as well as learning their
Language; wherein I had a great Facility by the Strength of my
Memory.

This device would also provide him with a way to use all the
hints and plans that had remained from the evenings of the Brothers Club, or the satirical papers of Martin Scriblerus, or, even
before that, suggestions thrown out to Steele and Addison for a
Tatler : e.g., *Journal to Stella*, April 28, 1711 : 'Yesterday the
Spectator was made of a noble hint I gave him long ago for his
Tatlers, about an Indian supposed to write his Travels into England. I repent he ever had it. I intended to have written a book
on that subject.' It is not fanciful to find here the first source in
Swift's mind of some of the comments on English life of the King
of Brobdingnag or of the criticism of English morals made by
Gulliver's master in the land of the Houyhnhnms.

By employing the form of the travel book Swift was able to
use the satirical methods which he had perfected in his earliest
literary work, parody and raillery and irony, and to make use of
all his experience of the world gained during his active political
career, and make a masterpiece – the product of his mastery of

his art together with his mastery of the business of life. It is this, I think, which gives such finality to his ethical judgments. It is sometimes said that Swift was not a great intelligence, that he was no profound scholar, no outstanding political thinker, and no really original genius. But at least that well-prepared, sceptical intelligence which showed itself in *A Tale of a Tub* had been given a rather complete and varied experience of the ways of the world and of the characters of men and women in those thirty years between his earliest writings and the appearance of *Gulliver's Travels*. He had met and known intimately the greatest and best men of his time, and he had likewise come up against and suffered from some of the cleverest and most ruthless scoundrels; he had had a price set on his head, and he had known what it was to be the idol of the mob, or, as he called them later, his good friends the common people of Ireland. He had indeed been himself a great traveller, and had learned many things; his problem was to find a way in which he could set down the most significant of his observations upon human life, so that the world might be forced to read them. For even if he could not do any good, he might be able to vex the world and perhaps amuse some of his friends.

In the first and the third books of *Gulliver's Travels* he manages to include a great deal of satirical reference to the political events in which he had taken part, both in England and in Ireland. Both of these books are in fact confused and inconsistent, because they are constantly twisted to suit his immediate satirical purpose, whether he is concerned with the political situation or with very specific parody and burlesque of the experiments of contemporary scientists or the schemes of other projectors.

There is a good deal of fun in Lilliput, and with Gulliver we are able to assume a certain superior detachment and amusement at the ways of the pigmies. Like him we are protected from any serious danger at the hands of the Lilliputians. We are provided as it were with a buff jerkin, which is proof against all their arrows; we are on good terms with them, and could not be unduly disturbed by anything those little creatures might do, who could dance, five or six of them at a time on the palm of one of

our hands, or play at hide-and-seek in our hair. Even the diver-
sions of the court of Lilliput are therefore inevitably observed by
us with good humour, and we can laugh at the antics of the rope-
dancers, and the *leaping* and *creeping* of the ministers as the
Emperor advances or depresses his stick. It is just a joke to watch
them swearing an oath according to the strange method prescribed by their laws : 'hold the right foot in the left hand, place
the middle finger of the right hand on the crown of the head, and
the thumb on the tip of the right ear' – just another of the antics
of these minute ballet-dancers. And even the struggles between
the High Heels and the Low Heels, and between those who break
their Eggs at the Big End and at the Little End, seem to be a
matter for comedy; and that ugly ambition of the Emperor to
obtain all his enemy's ships, after their Navy had been brought
to him by Gulliver, in order to make himself monarch of the
whole world, does not frighten us unduly, especially as his ambition is not approved by the wisest part of his ministry.

We are indeed made very subtly to share the innocence of Gulliver, his unwillingness to believe evil of princes, his unprepared-
ness for their ingratitude and dishonesty. It was only after he had
been wrongly suspected of disaffection that he began to have
doubts : 'This was the first time [he says] I began to conceive
some imperfect Idea of Courts and Ministers.'

We cannot really believe any harm of them, as the Royal Family come to dine with him, sitting in their chairs of state, with
their guards about them, on a corner of his table, just over against
him; or as the members of the Court visited him, remaining in
their coaches drawn by two horses gently round his table. Even
when the articles of impeachment are drawn up against Gulliver,
and the fierceness of his enemies is disclosed, with their demand
that he should be horribly murdered, whereas the Emperor in
his lenity and tenderness was willing to condemn him only to the
loss of his eyes, he is still able to make use of the most delicate form
of irony :

Yet, as to myself, I must confess, having never been designed for a
Courtier, either by my Birth or Education, I was so ill a Judge of

Things, that I could not discover the *Lenity* and Favour of this Sentence; but conceived it (perhaps erroneously) rather to be rigorous than gentle. I sometimes thought of standing my Tryal; for although I could not deny the Facts alledged in the several Articles, yet I hoped they would admit of some Extenuations. But having in my life perused many State-Tryals, which I ever observed to terminate as the Judges thought fit to direct; I durst not rely on so dangerous a Decision, in so critical a Juncture, and against such powerful Enemies. Once I was strongly bent upon Resistance : For while I had Liberty, the whole Strength of that Empire could hardly subdue me, and I might easily with Stones pelt the Metropolis to Pieces; But I soon rejected that Project with Horror, by remembering the Oath I had made to the Emperor, the Favours I received from him, and the high Title of *Nardac* he conferred upon me. Neither had I so soon learned the Gratitude of Courtiers, to persuade myself that his Majesty's *present Severities acquitted me of all past Obligations.*

It is almost as though the very scale of the Lilliputians obliges him to handle them and their affairs with a sort of tenderness lest they break in pieces. The whole country remains inevitably in the imagination as a sort of toy-shop, invaded by a clumsy colossus who finds it difficult to move about without overturning houses and trampling on their inhabitants, unable even to see what is going on; amazed to observe 'a cook pulling a Lark, which was not so large as a common fly; and a young girl threading an invisible needle with invisible silk'. Only occasionally when Gulliver allows himself to make comments on the laws and customs of the land, and on their system of education, we sometimes forget the figure of Gulliver the colossus and the minute figures he is discussing, and hear rather the familiar comments of Dean Swift on education and life. It is surprising how easily the imagination is kept in leash if we are constantly given some one concrete detail, a goose the size of a sparrow, or a forest tree the top of which Gulliver can just reach with his closed fist; but likewise, a sentence or two can completely dispel the scene and banish us from this tiny commonwealth. 'In relating these and the following Laws, I would only be understood to mean the original Institutions, and not the most scandalous Corruptions into which these People are fallen by the degenerate Nature of Man.' Phrases like 'the degenerate nature of man', 'the great laws of nature', 'the miseries of human life' are somewhat too large for that tiny world and break down the willing suspension of our unbelief; and then it takes more than the word *Lilliputian* to restore it again.

Swift was to find a better way of handling this problem of keeping in due balance the imagined scene and the real world in books II and IV, so that he could use quite freely every phase of his experience, and bring it to be weighed in the scales provided by his hosts.

But in the Third book, which as I have said is also somewhat confused and lacking in unity, his difficulty was not so much in forcing his satire to adapt itself to the imaginary circumstances of the voyage; it is rather that the material in part has never been thoroughly assimilated through his own experience, and he seems sometimes to fall back almost on the method of the *Tale* in making fun of the extravagancies of the virtuosos, and the strange experiments of the scientists of the Royal Society. A great deal has been written about the details of this book, to prove how closely he was parodying, when describing the experiments in the Academy of Lagado, the actual accounts he had read in the *Philosophical Transactions of the Royal Society*. In thus using his favourite method of parody which for full enjoyment requires an immediate recognition of the original, Swift was appealing more directly to his contemporaries and especially to his London audience, but he doubtless trusted that the absurdities he slightly exaggerated would serve as symbols which everyone could recognize of the spirit of research he was eager to expose. Professor Everett Case in his *Essays on Gulliver's Travels* published by the Princeton Press just preceding his death, is I believe correct in emphasizing that the satire upon Projectors in this book was not limited to virtuosos and scientists; for Swift was equally if not more concerned to warn his readers against the political projectors and speculators, who had been responsible for such schemes as the South Sea Bubble, and other trade swindles of this sort.

The real reason why so many readers have felt that the Third book is confused and less effective than the others is not simply

that Swift was making use of old stuff remaining from the days of
the Scriblerus Club; it is rather that he was adding even after
the rest of the book was finished passages of political satire in
which he was tempted to celebrate his recent success in Ireland,
a section indeed which seemed to the printer to be of so immediate and dangerous significance that it was not even included by
Faulkner in his Dublin edition published ten years after the events
referred to. And further Marjorie Hope Nicolson's and Nora
Mohler's studies of the sources of the experiments in the Lagado
Academy would indicate the likelihood that Swift, caught by the
spirit of parody which he could never resist, went on even as late
as the spring of 1726, when he spent some weeks in the company
of Dr. Arbuthnot, collecting information about actual experiments then being carried out in order to burlesque them for his
main purpose. Sir Harold Williams in his introductory essay to
my edition of *Gulliver's Travels* has drawn attention to Dr. Arbuthnot's letter of October 1725, in which he offers the latest
information: '. . . before you put the finishing touch to it, it is
really necessary to be acquainted with some new improvements
of mankind that have appeared of late, and are daily appearing.
Mankind has an inexhaustible source of invention in the way of
folly and madness.' But he assumes that Swift did not avail himself of this offer, because a few days after the book was printed
Arbuthnot commented: 'I tell you freely, the part of the projectors is the least brilliant.'

I myself am tempted to interpret that in the opposite way, for
it must be remembered that they were two rivals in irony, and I
cannot imagine that Arbuthnot would have been so indelicate as
to have written just then almost in reproach, if Swift had indeed
rebuffed his offers to help. But what more natural if he had provided Swift with material and advice for this section, than that he
should say 'Of course the part of the book which I interfered with
is the least brilliant'?

In any case, the construction of parts of this book is less satis-
factory. The materials used have not been properly matured, the
wood is too green; and one would have to admit also that the
position of the satirist himself is not a very secure one in some

of his attacks upon the physical scientists, and the whirligig of time has given them their revenge.

But the real greatness of *Gulliver's Travels* is to be found when we recognize it as the final and completest satire on human life of this Christian moralist. That is the reason why so many people have been disturbed by the book. Some have said: Do not listen to this fellow, because he is mad; or, He is a monster, uttering blasphemies against mankind; or, He is abnormal, incapable of ordinary affection and loyalties; do not trust anything he says.

It is written by one who did not like the way of the world and was not unwilling to set down his testimony against it. There are two passages which seemed to the original publisher so unveiled, such unrestrained invective that he employed a clergyman, the Rev. Andrew Tooke, to rewrite them in more cautious language; but Swift was careful to have them restored in the edition he prepared for his collected works. The first is a comment on English political life: 'The Bulk of the People consisted wholly of Discoverers, Witnesses, Informers, Accusers, Prosecutors, Evidences, Swearers; together with their several subservient and subaltern Instruments; all under the Colours, the Conduct, and pay of Ministers and their Deputies.'

The second is a comment on the legal profession, with which it must be admitted Swift had had some unfortunate experiences: and perhaps it should also be remembered that Gulliver had been living some time in the land of the Houyhnhnms, and had doubtless been influenced by their simple views, before making this explanation to his master:

I said there was a Society of Men among us, bred up from their Youth in the Art of proving by Words multiplied for the Purpose, that *White* is *Black*, and *Black* is *White*, according as they are paid. To this Society all the rest of the People are Slaves.
. . . Now, your Honour is to know, that these Judges are Persons appointed to decide all Controversies of Property, as well as for the Tryal of Criminals; and picked out from the most dextrous Lawyers who are grown old or lazy: And having been byassed all their lives against Truth and Equity, are under such a fatal Necessity of favouring Fraud, Perjury and Oppression; that I have known

E

some of them to have refused a large Bribe from the Side where
Justice lay, rather than injure the *Faculty*, by doing any thing un-
becoming their Nature of their Office.

. . . In the Tryal of Persons accused for Crimes against the State, the
Method is much more short and commendable : The Judge first
sends to sound the Disposition of those in Power; after which he
can easily hang or save the Criminal, strictly preserving all the Forms
of Law.

But there were other comments which occur in the second
journey when Gulliver was trying to explain the glories of western
civilization to the simple-hearted king of the Brobdingnagians,
that the publisher did not bother to change, though the author's
intention and the possible effect might be considered dangerous,
for they were carefully covered in irony. Gulliver is still able to
boast of the past history of his own people and to try to describe
to the King some of the more important developments of society,
becoming quite eloquent as anyone may easily do when abroad
'to celebrate the Praise of our own dear country in a style equal
to its merits and felicity'. It took five audiences each of several
hours, and then in a sixth his majesty, consulting his notes, proposed many doubts, queries and objections upon every article;
and later he sums up his impressions in a fitting but unpleasant
figure : 'I cannot but conclude the Bulk of your Natives, to be the
most pernicious Race of little odious Vermin that Nature ever
suffered to crawl upon the Surface of the Earth.'

Great allowances of course have to be made for one living
wholly secluded from the world, unacquainted with the manners
and customs of other nations; and Gulliver adds another story to
illustrate the effect of narrow principles and short views, resulting
from a confined education :

I shall here insert a Passage which will hardly obtain Belief. In hopes
to ingratiate my self farther into his Majesty's Favour, I told him of
an Invention discovered between three and four hundred Years ago,
to make a certain Powder; into an heap of which the smallest Spark
of Fire falling, would kindle the whole in a Moment, although it
were as big as a Mountain; and make it all fly up in the Air together,
with a Noise and Agitation greater than Thunder. That, a proper

Quantity of this Powder rammed into an hollow Tube of Brass or Iron, according to its Bigness, would drive a Ball of Iron or Lead with such Violence and Speed, as nothing was able to sustain its Force. That, the largest Balls thus discharged, would not only Destroy whole Ranks of an Army at once; but batter the strongest Walls to the Ground; sink down Ships with a thousand Men in each, to the Bottom of the Sea; and when linked together by a Chain, would cut through Masts and Rigging; divide Hundreds of Bodies in the Middle, and lay all Waste before them. That we often put this Powder into large hollow Balls of Iron, and discharged them by an Engine into some City we were besieging; which would rip up the Pavement, tear the Houses to Pieces, burst and throw Splinters on every Side, dashing out the Brains of all who came near. That I knew the Ingredients very well, which were Cheap, and common; I understood the Manner of compounding them, and could direct his Workmen how to make those Tubes of a Size proportionable to all other Things in his Majesty's Kingdom; and the largest need not be above two hundred foot long; twenty or thirty of which Tubes, charged with the proper Quantity of Powder and Balls, would batter down the Walls of the strongest Town in his Dominions in a few Hours; or destroy the whole Metropolis, if ever it should pretend to dispute his absolute Commands. This I humbly offered to his Majesty, as a small Tribute of Acknowledgment in return of so many Marks that I had received of his Royal Favour and Protection.

The King was struck with Horror at the Description I had given of those terrible Engines, and the Proposal I had made. He was amazed how so impotent and groveling an Insect as I (these were his Expressions) could entertain such inhuman Ideas, and in so familiar a Manner as to appear wholly unmoved at all the Scenes of Blood and Desolation, which I had painted as the common Effects of those destructive Machines; whereof he said, some evil Genius, Enemy to Mankind, must have been the first Contriver. As for himself, he protested, that although few Things delighted him so much as new Discoveries in Art or in Nature; yet he would rather lose half his Kingdom than be privy to such a Secret; which he commanded me, as I valued my Life, never to mention any more.

But it is after all the fable of the Fourth book which has most shocked Swift's readers, though it is a simple and traditional moral

tale, rather vividly dramatized with the help of animal symbolism. It is perhaps a little mediaeval in its extravagant and sometimes unpleasant burlesque of some of the qualities of man's brute
nature, and in the complete separation of his rational qualities as
they might conceivably exist in some utopian world. But the real
source of our fear of Swift's satire is that we are progressively led
on with Gulliver from a comparatively happy condition in which
we were in that blessed state of being well deceived – the serene
peaceful state of being a fool among knaves – until we have made
the painful discovery of the knavery of human life and of the
stupidity and malice of mankind. But many moralists and pro-
phets and satirists have made this same discovery and travelled
by this same road, and have found the world a wilderness and life
a sorry condition, and they have turned to the past or the future
or to another world for consolation, and in some way or other
have justified the fact of life. But Swift leaves us no escape, no
place for dreams or imaginings; he can see no reason for it at
all. He has not been able to keep out at any point in his travels
this plain dislike of human existence, the protest of the individual
against the sum of things,

> a stranger and afraid
> In a world I never made.[2]

But his protest is put in a quite simple non-romantic way, some
development of the theme stated in one of his own Pensées,
printed under the title, *Thoughts on Religion.*

Although reason were intended by providence to govern our passions, yet it seems that, in two points of the greatest moment to
the being and continuance of the world, God hath intended our
passions to prevail over reason. The first is, the propagation of our
species, since no wise man ever married from the dictates of reason.
The other is, the love of life, which, from the dictates of reason every
man would despise, and wish it at an end, or that it never had a
beginning.

This colours that passage in the sixth chapter of the Voyage to
Lilliput concerning the relations between parents and children :

they will never allow, that a Child is under any Obligation to his Father for begetting him, or to his Mother for bringing him into the World; which, considering the Miseries of human Life, was neither a Benefit in itself, nor intended so by his Parents, whose Thoughts in their Love-encounters were otherwise employed. Upon these, and the like Reasonings, their Opinion is, that Parents are the last of all others to be trusted with the Education of their own Children :

More dramatically and more memorably he plays with the same theme at the end of the Fourth book, when, returning from his experience of a rational Utopia under the influence of beings who were the perfection of nature, Gulliver freely confesses that the sight of his wife and family filled him 'only with Hatred, Disgust and Contempt; and the more, by reflecting on the near Alliance [he] had to them'.

But even this is not such a violent satire upon 'love of life' as Swift reserved for the last episode of the third voyage, which may well have been in point of composition the last chapter he wrote. For we know that he wrote the Fourth book mainly in 1723, and did not complete the Third – apart from final revisions – until 1725. It is a chapter entirely complete in itself – a perfect little irony. I cannot understand why it has not been more praised, and used in anthologies, or in books of piety. Swift himself draws particular attention to it, and evidently considered it to be quite original. He says: 'I thought this account of the Struldbrugs might be some Entertainment to the Reader, because it seems to be a little out of the common Way; at least, I do not remember to have met the like in any Book of Travels that hath come to my Hands.' Gulliver is asked one day whether he had seen any of their immortals, and after hearing an account of them, indulges in his most endearingly innocent way in extravagant expressions of rapture at the thought of a people so blessed. He is then asked by his amused hosts what he would do if he were an immortal. After enlarging upon many topics 'which the natural desire of endless life and sublunary happiness could easily furnish', he is told what the Struldbrugs are really like and finally has an opportunity to see five or six of them, the youngest not above two hundred years old. 'They were the most mortifying Sight

I ever beheld . . . and my keen Appetite for Perpetuity of Life was much abated.' He would have been glad to send a couple home to arm people against the fear of death, but that was forbidden by the laws of the kingdom. Nevertheless, he tells us again with disarming innocence, he was led to believe that if he were to write down a simple and wholly truthful account of his travels, it might possibly do his countrymen some good. He can claim to be above any possible censure, having avoided every fault commonly charged against writers of travels : 'I write for the noblest End, to inform and instruct Mankind, over whom I may, without Breach of Modesty, pretend to some Superiority, from the Advantages I received by conversing so long among the most accomplished *Houyhnhnms*. I write without any View towards Profit or Praise.'

Is Gulliver then after all only another moral tale, another rationalist's utopian dream to turn men from the folly of their ways and bring about some improvement in human society? Swift indeed allows Lemuel Gulliver to enter unsuspectingly the company of the eighteenth-century philosophers, and to believe for a while, as even the most sceptical of them did, even a Hume or a Voltaire, that humanity could enter into a heavenly city of its own if only it could be released from the bonds of superstition and ignorance. But Swift allowed Gulliver to go thus far only to undeceive him utterly, and take from him his last illusion.

When the book appeared for the first time pretty much as Swift had written it, published under his direction in Dublin in 1735, it had been provided with an epilogue, in the form of a letter from Captain Gulliver to his cousin Richard Sympson, who had been responsible for getting the book printed. In this final statement Swift is careful to separate himself from the other historians and philosophers, and even from the rest of the satirists, turning his satire full upon them and their vain hopes to do something to improve the human species :

I do in the next place complain of my own great Want of Judgment, in being prevailed upon . . . very much against my own Opinion, to suffer my Travels to be published. Pray bring to your Mind how often I desired you to consider, when you insisted on the Motive of

publick Good; that the Yahoos were a species of animal utterly incapable of Amendment by Precepts or Examples : And so it hath
proved; for instead of seeing a full Stop put to all Abuses and Corruptions, at least in this little Island, as I had reason to expect : Behold, after above six Months Warning, I cannot learn that my Book
hath produced one single Effect according to my Intentions : . . .
And, it must be owned, that seven Months were a sufficient Time to
correct every Vice and Folly to which Yahoos are subject; if their
Natures had been capable of the least Disposition to Virtue or Wisdom.

Swift could not escape from this final irony. He did not wish
to prescribe for the sickness of humanity, having no hope of its
recovery; but he could not refrain from probing, anatomizing
and diagnosing its malady, though convinced that the further he
went the more he would find to stir his indignation and his pity.
And from his youth he had known it and written it down with a
kind of foolish pride, that he was one

> . . . whose lash just Heaven has long decreed
> Shall on a day make sin and folly bleed.[3]

To the end it was his peculiar satisfaction as a moralist and a
satirist, in all his various disguises, and employing all the tricks of
his trades, to make us see what a world we live in, to make us feel
its brutality and its degradation, to disturb all our complacencies
and to leave us unreconciled to the 'unestimable sum of human
pain'. . . .

SOURCE: from 'Moral Satire', *The Satire of Jonathan
Swift* (1947), as revised in *Jonathan Swift: Essays on his
Satire and other Studies* (1964) pp. 143–58.

NOTES

(16 references in the original are here omitted.)

1. *Poems*, p. 550.
2. A. E. Housman, *Last Poems*, p. 28.
3. *Poems*, p. 47.

Kathleen Williams

GULLIVER'S VOYAGE TO THE HOUYHNHNMS (1951)

It has long been recognised that the fourth Voyage of *Gulliver's Travels*, far from being the outburst of a misanthrope who delighted in 'degrading human Nature', is the culmination of Swift's lifelong attack on the pride of man, especially the pride which convinces him that he can live by the light of his unaided reason, the pride that Swift himself sums up, in the title of one of his imaginary discourses in *A Tale of a Tub*, as 'An Universal Rule of Reason, or Every Man his own Carver'. In particular, he is taking up a position opposed to the doctrines of natural goodness which pervade eighteenth-century thought and which find systematic expression in the writings of 'Toland, Collins, Tindal, and others of the fraternity', who, as Swift remarks, all talk much the same language and whose ideas are dismissed in the *Argument against Abolishing Christianity* as 'Trumpery'. It is clear, both from the satires and the religious writings, that Swift was hostile to all doctrines of the natural self-sufficiency of man, whether they were expressed in Deistic terms or in the related pride of neo-Stoicism; and the Fourth Voyage of *Gulliver's Travels* embodies that hostility. But while the object of attack is established, it is not immediately clear, from the Voyage itself, whether any positive position is implied in the Houyhnhnms or in the other characters. The Yahoos, clearly, embody the negative intention, and are to be condemned. This is what happens to man when he tries to live by reason and nature; he falls, as has been pointed out,[1] into a 'state of nature' nearer to that envisaged by Hobbes than that of Locke's *Two Treatises of Govern-*

Adam
Eve

ment. It is significant that, according to one Houyhnhnm theory, the Yahoos were descended from a pair of human beings, driven to the country by sea: 'coming to Land and being forsaken by their Companions, they retired to the Mountains, and degenerating by Degrees, became in Process of Time, much more savage than those of their own Species in the Country from whence these two Originals came.' Presumably these originals, forced into self-reliance, had degenerated because their feeble human reason had been overwhelmed by an irrational 'nature', and more adequate guides had been forgotten.

The ambiguity of the Fourth Voyage lies not in the Yahoos, but in the positions of Gulliver and, especially, of the Houyhnhnms. The function of the Houyhnhnms may be to present an ideal of the true life of reason, to be admired even if unattainable, and to be contrasted with the Yahoos to chasten the pride of that lump of deformity, man, by showing him the vanity of his pretensions. But if Swift did intend the Houyhnhnms to stand as an ideal contrast, he has badly mismanaged the matter. The Houyhnhnms do not strike the reader as altogether admirable beings; indeed they are sometimes absurd, and even repellent, and we are disgusted by Gulliver's exaggerated devotion to them. The dispassionate arguments of the assembly, for instance, about the nature and future fate of Gulliver and the Yahoos, show the characteristic and unpleasant coldness of the Houyhnhnm race; while Gulliver's master displays their equally characteristic self-satisfaction, carried here to the point of absurdity, when he criticises Gulliver's physical qualities. Gulliver tells us how his master interrupted his account of the relations of the European Yahoos with their horses, to point out the inferiority for all practical purposes of the Yahoo shape – 'the Flatness of my Face, the Prominence of my Nose, mine Eyes placed directly in Front, so that I could not look on either Side without turning my Head; that I was not able to feed myself without lifting one of my fore Feet to my Mouth; and therefore Nature had placed those Joints to answer that Necessity.' Throughout the book there are obvious blunders which cannot be explained away by the inevitable lack of positive attraction in rational Utopias. One of Swift's most at-

tractive characters, Don Pedro de Mendez, is placed in a position
at the end of the book where comparison with the Houyhnhnms
is inevitable, and our sympathies are alienated by the humour-
less arrogance both of the Houyhnhnms themselves, and of
Gulliver when, absorbed in admiration of his former master, he
avoids his own family to concentrate on 'the neighing of those two
degenerate Houyhnhnms I keep in my stable'. Clumsiness of
this kind is not usual with Swift, who is well aware, as a rule, of
the way to enlist our sympathy for a character, and shews his
awareness in the drawing of M. B. Drapier, and of Gulliver in
the Voyage to Lilliput. The whole course of his work makes it
unlikely that he could be unaware of the unpleasantness of such
passages as these. Possibly, then, the effect is a deliberate one, and
the Houyhnhnms, far from being a model of perfection, are intended to show the inadequacy of the life of reason. This would
be in keeping with the usual method of Swift's satire, and with
the negative quality which has been observed in it. The characteristic of Swift's satire is precisely his inability, or his refusal, to
present us straightforwardly with a positive to aim at. It may be,
at bottom, a psychological or a spiritual weakness; he turns it to
satiric strength, and produces satire which is comfortless but is
also disturbing and courageous. He will leave us with nothing
more than a few scattered hints of what is desirable and attainable, or sometimes, when what is desirable is clearly not to be
had, with a half-ironic acceptance of the best that is to hand. A
full, clear, and wholly unambiguous account of a state of life to
aim at would be unusual and unexpected in Swift. It is his habit
to look sceptically, not only at the evils of the world, but at those,
including himself, who criticise such evils, and at those who present schemes for the betterment of mankind. Gulliver is quaintly
indignant and surprised at the evils which still exist six months
after the publication of his travels, and in *A Tale of a Tub* the
Digression on Madness ends with a confession which undermines
the whole: 'Even I myself, the Author of these Momentous
Truths, am a person whose Imaginations are hardmouth'd, and
exceedingly Disposed to run away with his Reason.' In fact, there
is not usually a 'norm' in Swift's satire, positively and unequivoc-

ally stated. As far as any positive position can be discovered, it must be by piecing together the hints and implications and indirections typical of Swift's whole method; it is foreign to that method to embody in one person or one race a state of things of which he fully approves. It is, indeed, more than a matter of satiric method for a man 'betwixt two Ages cast', who had little of which he could approve wholeheartedly. The spirit of compromise and commonsense, the love of the middle way, affected him sufficiently to undermine any more rigorous standards, while failing to satisfy him as it satisfied his younger contemporaries; and his position was further complicated by a strong feeling for existing forms and a dislike of innovation, which, like Dryden, he regards as dangerous. Any suggestion of radical remedies is distrusted by him even as he presents it, and he will withdraw from it into irony, or fall back into compromise, as he does in the ambiguous *Argument against Abolishing Christianity*.

In *Gulliver's Travels*, this characteristic method re-appears. In the first two books, no one person or group of persons is put forward for our approval, and neither the Lilliputians, the Brobdingnagians, nor Gulliver himself, can be regarded as a consistent satiric norm against which the moral and political vagaries of eighteenth-century England are to be precisely measured. Swift slips from one side to another according as his isolated satiric points require it, and we are at one moment to admire, at another to dislike, the creatures of his imagination. Even in Laputa, a set of serious political schemes, such as the visionary project of 'persuading Monarchs to chuse Favourites upon the Score of their Wisdom, Capacity, and Virtue', appears among the absurdities of the projectors. Gulliver himself is now honest and kindly, now credulous or pompous, according to the momentary demands of the satire. During his adventures in Brobdingnag he is frequently ridiculous and on one occasion definitely unpleasant; his complacent attitude to warfare, in chapter VI, horrifies the giant King. In none of the first three books are we left with a consistent standard embodied in any creature, and it would seem that if the Houyhnhnms are presented fairly and squarely for our approval a change is involved not only in Swift's normal method but in his whole attitude of mind. He would hardly present the radical primitivism and rationalism of Houyhnhnm-land as desirable, at least without the ironic and sceptical withdrawal which his uncertain temperament demanded.

One would expect to find that Swift uses the Houyhnhnms in the same indirect way as he does the peoples of the earlier books, not as a complete statement of the right kind of man or society, attainable or not, but as a satiric contrast in which good and less good are mixed in a proportion which we must decide for ourselves, with the aid of such hints of the author's as we can piece together. And in fact Swift is just as ready to sacrifice the consistency of the Houyhnhnms to their satiric function of innocent comment on unknown humanity as he is any of his other creatures. The opinion of Gulliver's master on the 'prodigious Abilities of Mind' of English lawyers, which should qualify them to instruct others in wisdom and knowledge, leads to a valid satiric point, but does not show the Houyhnhnm in a very good light when one considers the damning account he has just heard of their moral depravity and lack of intellectual integrity. No doubt one reason why the Houyhnhnms are a race of animals is for satiric distance; but of course Swift's insistence on the animal in Book IV has a significance beyond that of satiric effectiveness. Several of the Houyhnhnms' characteristics seem to be intended to show their remoteness, and their irrelevance to the ordinary life and standards of mankind. Primitivism is used for this effect; they have great difficulty in understanding such humanly simple matters as Gulliver's clothes, his ship, his writing, and the Houyhnhnm in his dealings with Gulliver in chapter III is not only unattractive, but unattractive in a particular way. 'He brought me into all Company,' Gulliver says of him, 'and made them treat me with Civility because as he told them privately, this would put me into good Humour and make me more diverting.' This may be intended to lessen Gulliver's status and lower his pride, but Swift could hardly have missed its effect of displaying the lack of humanity and sympathy, the cold curiosity of the Houyhnhnms. There is, too, the solemn criticism of Gulliver's physical characteristics in chapter IV, part of which has already been quoted. This passage stresses the fact that man is not well endowed, either physically or mentally, to live a 'natural' life; but it also shows the Houyhnhnm's inability to grasp the human point of view, his self-righteousness, and his determination to belittle these creatures who in their own land claim to rule over the Houyhnhnm race. The Houyhnhnms are alien and unsympathetic creatures, not man at his best, as Godwin suggested, or man as he might be, but a kind of life with which humanity has nothing to do. The word Houyhnhnm, we are told, means 'Perfection of Nature'. These are not human beings, but virtuous animals, perfect but limited natural creatures, of a 'nature' not simply unattainable by man, but irrelevant to him, and incapable not only of the depths, but also of the heights, to which humanity can reach. The Houyhnhnms have no shame, no temptations, no conception of sin : they are totally unable to comprehend the purpose of lying or other common temptations of man. They can live by reason because they have been created passionless. In man, we know, the passions are apt to get astride of the reason, which is not strong enough to restrain them, and the result in its extremest form is seen in the Yahoos, but the Houyhnhnms have no passions to control : 'As these noble Houyhnhnms are endowed by Nature with a general Disposition to all Virtues, and have no Conceptions or Ideas of what is evil in a rational Creature, so their grand Maxim is, to cultivate Reason, and to be wholly governed by it.' The point of the description lies in 'as' and 'so'. The Houyhnhnms can live harmlessly by reason because their nature is different from ours.

Swift makes much of the differing natures of the Houyhnhnms, the Yahoos, and Gulliver himself. In the Houyhnhnms, nature and reason are one and the same. They have no 'natural affections' in our sense; Nature, they say, has taught them to be equally benevolent to everyone, and to make a distinction of persons only on the rational grounds of 'a superior Degree of Virtue'. Marriage is undertaken simply as 'one of the necessary Actions in a reasonable Being'. Nor have they any fear of death, which they greet with the same complete absence of emotion that they show towards every other event, great or small. These attitudes

are not those which Nature teaches human beings, as Swift recognises both in *Gulliver's Travels* and elsewhere; man has
affections and passions, and Swift seems not to regard them as
wholly bad. The painful and universal fear of death in mankind
was a subject which particularly interested and affected him,
and the curious episode of the immortal Struldbrugs in the Third
Voyage is an attempt to deal with it. Gulliver wished to take some
of the Struldbrugs back with him to England, 'to arm our People
against the Fear of Death', that dread which Nature has im-
planted in us, but not in the Houyhnhnms. In the *Thoughts on
Religion* reason is brought to bear on the problem : 'It is impossible that anything so natural, so necessary, and so universal as
death, should ever have been designed by providence as an evil to
mankind.' But reason is powerless against man's fear of death,
and his clinging to life on any terms; and Swift puts forward the
idea that although in general reason was intended by Providence
to govern our passions, in this God intended our passions to prevail over reason. Man cannot in all respects govern his passions
by reason, he suggests, because he has not been equipped by Providence to do so; perhaps both love of life and the propagation
of the species are passions exempted by Providence, for particular
purposes, from the control of reason. The precise amount of irony
in such statements is always difficult to gauge, though the
Thoughts on Religion are not satirically intended; but at least
the passage shows Swift's feeling that such deep-rooted passions
as these are part of the nature of man, created by God, and cannot and perhaps should not be ruled by reason. The Houyhnhnms are rational even in those things in which the wisest man's
passions inevitably and even perhaps rightly rule him, and the
handling of them seems to suggest not only the remoteness but
the inadequacy by human standards, of the life of Reason. They
have only the negative virtue of blamelessness.

The Houyhnhnms refer repeatedly to Gulliver's fellow-humans
in terms which press home the contrast between themselves and
mankind. Men are creatures 'pretending to Reason', the character of a rational creature was one which mankind 'had no Pretence to challenge'. Again the Houyhnhnms thought that 'Nature

and Reason were sufficient Guides for a reasonable Animal, as we pretended to be.' Man has no right to lay claim to the life of Reason, for in him nature and reason are not, as in the Houyhnhnms, identical, and there is that in his nature which is outside reason's legitimate control. But this is not necessarily to say that man's nature is thoroughly evil, and his situation hopeless, as in the case of the degenerate Yahoos, nor is man treated in these terms. Gulliver and the other humans of Book IV are clearly distinguished from the Yahoos as well as from the Houyhnhnms, and the difference in their mental and physical habits is strongly insisted upon. They stand apart from the two races of this animal world, separated from both by characteristics of which neither the naturally virtuous and rational animals, nor the vicious and irrational ones, have any knowledge – in fact by the characteristics proper to humanity. Man does indeed share the Yahoos' propensity to evil, but he has compensating qualities which the bestial Yahoos have not possessed since their first degeneration; and with these qualities he may surpass the cold rational virtue of the Houyhnhnms. The member of that race who is treated with most sympathy by Swift is the humble sorrel nag, one of the servant breeds who were 'not born with equal Talents of Mind'. Into the incompletely rational mind of the nag, some near-human warmth and devotion can creep, and he is the only creature in Houyhnhnm-land to show any affection; Gulliver's last link with the country as he sails away is the voice of the 'Sorrel Nag (who always loved me) crying out . . . Take Care of thyself, gentle Yahoo'.

With this partial exception, there is no sign among the Houyhnhnms of kindness, compassion, or self-sacrifice, yet elsewhere in *Gulliver's Travels* there is sympathetic treatment of love, pity, and a deliberate intervention of one man in the life of another, very different from the Houyhnhnm's equal benevolence, detachment, and rational respect for virtue. Even in Book I, where moral satire is not at its most serious, there is an insistence on the importance of gratitude among the Lilliputians, by whom, we are told in chapter VI, ingratitude is regarded as a capital crime. Gratitude is shown in action in Gulliver's behaviour to the Lilliputian King, when despite the King's unjust sentence upon him he cannot bring himself to retaliate, for, he tells us, 'Neither had I so soon learned the Gratitude of Courtiers, to persuade myself that his Majesty's present Severities quitted me of all past Obligations.' In Book II there is the forbearance of the Giant King and the affection between Gulliver and the protective Glumdalclitch, and in Book IV great prominence is given to the Captain and crew of the ship which rescues Gulliver. Swift makes it plain that the Portuguese sailors are admirable human beings, and emphasizes in them the very qualities which the Houyhnhnms neither possess nor would understand. It is Don Pedro who persuades Gulliver to abandon his design of living as a recluse, following as far as he can the life of a rational detached virtue which the Houyhnhnms have taught him to admire, and instead to commit himself once more to the human relationships proper to mankind. Gulliver's duty as Don Pedro sees it is to return to a life of humanity, tolerance, and affection among his own people, and Gulliver, finding he can do no better, reluctantly agrees. But his behaviour towards his own family, set in a place where it contrasts forcibly with the tolerant practical goodwill of Don Pedro, is exaggerated to the point of madness. Only with difficulty can he endure the sight of the wife and children for whom he had shown so charming a fondness in the past. Gulliver, once a normal affectionate human being, concerned with the well-being of his friends, is now a solitary misanthrope, absurd and yet terrible in his self-concentration and his loathing of those he had once loved. He had been, he tells us, a great lover of mankind, and his conduct in the previous voyages shows that he was particularly affectionate to his own family. Now they 'dare not presume to touch my Bread, or drink out of the same Cup'. To this point Gulliver has been led by his pride in the unaided reason. He has become inhuman, losing the specifically human virtues in his attempt to achieve something for which humanity is not fitted. He is ruined as a human being, and the failure of his fellows to attain his own alien standards has made him hate them. We are reminded of Swift's letter (of the 26th November, 1725) to Pope: 'I tell you after all, that I do not hate mankind : it is "vous autres" who hate them, because you would have them reasonable animals, and are angry for being disappointed.' Gulliver is one of 'vous autres', for to set for humanity the irrelevant standards of absolute reason is to end as Gulliver ended, in hatred and defeat. Swift was well aware of the process of disillusionment which has been attributed to him, and he exemplifies it in Gulliver, the true misanthrope, who believes man should try to rule himself by 'Reason alone'.

On this interpretation, neither the master Houyhnhnm nor the misanthropic Gulliver who once thought so highly of mankind is presented as an ideal of behaviour. Like all the peoples of the *Travels* the Houyhnhnms have some characteristics, such as honesty and truthfulness, which we might well try to follow, and they are used for particular satiric points, but as a whole they represent an inadequate and inhuman rationalism, and the negativeness of their blameless life is part of Swift's deliberate intention. For us, with our less perfect but also less limited nature, to try to live like them would be to do as the Stoics did, according to Swift's remark in his *Thoughts on Various Subjects* : 'The Stoical Scheme of Supplying our Wants by lopping off our Desires, is like cutting off our Feet when we want Shoes.' It would mean abandoning the purely human possibilities as well as the disadvantages of our own nature. The Houyhnhnms may indeed be compared with the passionless Stoics of the Sermon *Upon the Excellency of Christianity*, who are contrasted with the Christian ideal of positive charity. Gulliver, in his turn, shows the loss of hope, proportion, and even common humanity in a man who tries to limit the complex nature of man to 'Reason alone'. Something more than Houyhnhnm harmlessness is needed in a world of human beings, and in so far as there is any positive presentation of right living to be found in *Gulliver's Travels*, it is in the representatives of that humanity which Gulliver rejects. For it is not, after all, a purely destructive view of humanity that Swift shows us. 'Reason and Nature', indeed are set up only to be shown as inadequate. Swift never doubted that man should make use of reason to control his bad instincts where he can, but to live by reason alone is neither possible nor desirable if we are to remain human beings. Yet we have the generous King of Brobdingnag, whose people are the 'least corrupted' of Yahoos or humans, and of whom Swift says, with his habitual indirection, 'it would be hard indeed, if so remote a Prince's Notions of Virtue and Vice were to be offered as a Standard for all Mankind.' And there is Don Pedro de Mendez, who shows to what unselfish goodness man can attain. Don Pedro is guided by 'Honour and Conscience', and for Swift, as we know from the sermons, conscience was not a natural sense of right and wrong, or Shaftesbury's 'aesthetic perception of the harmony of the universe', but a faculty which must itself be guided, by the divine laws which we can know only from a source outside ourselves, from revelation. 'There is no solid, firm Foundation for Virtue,' he tells us in the sermon *On the Testimony of Conscience*, 'but on a Conscience which is guided by Religion.' 'There is no other Tie thro' which the Pride, or Lust, or Avarice, or Ambition of Mankind will not certainly break one time or other.' For him, as for so many Churchmen concerned with the controversies of the period, Reason is an insufficient guide without Revelation. The sermons, with their systematic attack on the supposed sufficiency of the moral sense, the scheme of virtue without religion, are clearly relevant to the theme of the fourth Voyage of *Gulliver's Travels*, and here we find the positive aspect of Swift's intention more explicitly set out. The sermon *Upon the Excellency of Christianity* shows, in its account of the ideal Christian, a creature who is meek and lowly, 'affable and courteous, gentle and kind, without any morose leaven of pride or vanity, which entered into the composition of most Heathen schemes'. The description applies far more nearly to Don Pedro and the early Gulliver than to the Houyhnhnms, or to Gulliver the misanthrope, into whose composition pride certainly enters. While allowing a place to the passions and affections, and their possibility, under guidance, for good, Swift does not fall into the Tillotsonian position that human nature's 'mild and merciful' inclinations and the maternal and other natural affections are more important than revealed religion. An implied disapproval of such a position is expressed in Swift's version of Anthony Collins' *Discourse of Freethinking*, in which Tillotson, naturally, is praised. Both affections and reason have their place in the well-regulated man, but they are to be subjected to the laws of God. Reason and gratitude may both suggest to a man that he should obey his parents, but the surest and most lasting cause of obedience must be the consideration 'that his Reason is the Gift of God; that God commanded him to be obedient to the Laws, and did moreover in a particular manner enjoin him to be Dutiful to his Parents' (*On the Testimony of Conscience*). Swift would no doubt have agreed with that passage from Butler's sermon *Upon Compassion* (published in the same year as *Gulliver's Travels*) in which passions and affections, carefully guided, are treated as necessary in creatures who are imperfect and interdependent, 'who naturally and, from the condition we are placed in, necessarily depend upon each other. With respect to such creatures, it would be found of as bad consequence to eradicate all natural affections, as to be entirely governed by them. This would almost sink us to the condition of brutes; and that would leave us without a sufficient principle of action.' The passage forms a comment on the contrasting creatures of Houyhnhnm-land, for Swift is as well aware as Butler of the complex nature of man, the possessor not only of evil impulses but of passions and affections which under the guidance of conscience and religion (to which reason must be subject) can issue in virtuous action, especially that compassionate assistance to our fellow men, whether or not our reason judges them worthy of it, which 'the Gentile philosophy' fails to produce. In *Gulliver's Travels* there is not only a traditional Christian pessimism; there may well be a positive Christian ideal suggested in the conduct of the good humans, though it is presented with Swift's habitual obliquity and restraint.

S o u r c e : *ELH, A Journal of English Literary History,*
xviii (1951) pp. 275–86.

NOTE

1. By T. O. Wedel, 'On the Philosophical Background of *Gulliver's Travels*', *Studies in Philology,* xxiii (1926).

R. S. Crane

THE RATIONALE OF THE FOURTH
VOYAGE (1955)

I have busied myself off and on for many years with the problem
of what Swift was trying to do in the 'Voyage to the Country
of the Houyhnhnms'; and in spite of numerous failures to solve
the problem to more than my temporary satisfaction, I have
recently come back to it with renewed hope, fortified by the current upsurge of scholarly writing on the rationale of the fourth
Voyage and by the suggestions and criticisms of friends. The problem turns, I think, on three principal questions, and it is with
the comparative merits of the different and conflicting answers
which these appear to admit of that I shall attempt to deal.[1] The
first question has to do with the terms in which the satirical
thought of the Voyage is framed; the second with the general
method of the Voyage; the third with the form and purpose of
its unifying argument.

The most obvious answer to the question of what the satire of
the fourth Voyage is in general about is that suggested by the
text itself. It would seem from this that the basic terms of reference in the Voyage are psychological and moral in a broadly
human and non-sectarian sense. It is in such terms, clearly, that
Gulliver narrates his encounter with the Yahoos and the Houyhnhnms and depicts the radical change in his thoughts and emotions
about mankind that results from this encounter. But may it not
be that there are other concepts lying behind these, of a more
particularized sort, which constitute, in Swift's intention, the real
substance and point of the work? That this is the case has been
urged upon us in several recent studies, the common thesis of

which is that Swift conceived his characters and his story as he
did for the sake of enforcing a specifically religious and Christian
view of things – either negatively by attacking current doctrines
incompatible with the dogma of original sin (this would account
for the assimilation of men to the Yahoos) or positively also by
insisting on the reality of divine grace and the scheme of redemption (this would explain the commonly felt limitations of the
Houyhnhnms and the presence in the narrative of the good Don
Pedro).

I find it hard, I must admit, to accept this theory. There is no
doubt that Swift could have conceived the fourth Voyage, had he
wished, as a theological allegory: the materials for a satirical
defence of religion were certainly in his possession. I cannot, however, find any decisive evidence, internal or external, that he
actually did so conceive it.

We might expect that if Swift had meant his story to be a contribution to Christian apologetics, there would be some unequi-
vocal hints of this in his correspondence, or that his closest friends,
like Pope and Arbuthnot, would have been aware of the fact.
But no such testimonies have come to light. We might also expect that in an age like the early eighteenth century, when it was
no disgrace to speak out on behalf of religion, a satire that turned
primarily on theological issues would make its intention evident
in the text itself. But where in the fourth Part of Gulliver are
there any clear indices that we ought to think, as we read it,
about original sin, divine grace, the necessity of religion, or the
heresies of Shaftesbury and the deists? Imagine the 'Voyage to
the Houyhnhnms, to be a completely anonymous work, and judge
then how nearly impossible it would be for a good scholar to
prove, by internal evidence, that its writer was a clergyman with
strong orthodox convictions, or even a Christian at all.

It is not difficult, of course, knowing who the writer was, to
find symbolic equivalents in the details of the story for the terms
and doctrines of whatever theological argument our hypothesis
presupposes. But of all the passages so used in the various theological readings of the fourth Voyage that I have seen, there
are none that do not seem to me capable of other, and usually

much simpler, constructions in the moral and psychological terms of Gulliver's own narrative. And it is significant, furthermore, that these readings (along with most of the current non-theological readings) have been based on an assumption about the general method of the Voyage, as a work of literary art, which is at the very least debatable.

The crucial question about Swift's method in the fourth Voyage can be put very simply. Is it primarily an allegorical or symbolic method, or is it not? Must we construe the main figures of the story – the Houyhnhnms and the Yahoos especially – as embodiments, in imaginative forms, of general concepts, or is it sufficient to regard them merely as actors in what the eighteenth century would call a marvelous fable?

The question has nearly always been answered in favor of the first alternative. The fourth Voyage has most commonly been considered to be a work that has to be interpreted, like *Everyman* or *The Pilgrim's Progress*, by finding abstract meanings for its characters in some scheme of moral, psychological, or theological principles.

This may indeed be the right view; but if so, we might expect that critics reading the Voyage as popular allegory would agree more completely than they have done on what the meanings are. The Houyhnhnms, for example, have been equated sometimes with man as he ought to be and sometimes, especially of late, with almost the reverse of that. And the contrast between the Houyhnhnms and the Yahoos has also been given a wide range of differing allegorical interpretations. For one critic, it represents the antithesis between man in the state of nature according to Locke and man in the state of nature according to Hobbes; for another, the discrepancy between beings who have escaped the Fall and beings in whom the evil effects of the Fall are carried to an extreme; for still another, the 'war' in Gulliver's self between the rational and animal parts of his nature (as if the Voyage were a body-and-soul debate); and for various other critics, various other things.

It is natural to suspect, therefore, that this diversity of interpretation – to which there seems to be no limit – may be not so much a sign of the richness, or obscurity, of Swift's thought as of the fact that these interpreters have been working on a false assumption about his technique. Why do we have to look for allegory in the fourth Voyage at all? The Voyage can be perfectly well understood as merely what it purports to be; namely, a marvelous or fantastic fable, literally narrated, in which the Houyhnhnms and the Yahoos are not metaphors or symbols standing for general ideas, but two species of concrete beings, the one beyond any known human experience, the other all-too-possible anywhere, whom Gulliver has been thrown with in his travels and has come to venerate and abhor respectively. The moral or thesis of the fable, on this assumption, is brought home to the reader directly through the story itself, which is essentially the story of how Gulliver, seeing the virtues of the Houyhnhnms 'in opposite view to human corruptions' and realizing the 'entire congruity' between men and the Yahoos, undergoes an extreme revolution in his opinions and feelings about 'human kind'. And we apprehend and respond to the moral simply by following this story and drawing such inferences from it concerning ourselves as it is calculated to produce in us.

This conception of the general method of the Voyage has just as much antecedent probability, I think, as the more usual conception, and it involves us, besides, in many fewer difficulties of interpretation. It is entirely in harmony, moreover, with either of the two ways of understanding the form and point of Swift's main argument in the Voyage which I shall now go on to discuss.

The question of the satirical point of the fourth Voyage has been made to center, in most recent studies, on the problem of Gulliver's misanthropy and of how far this final state of mind of Swift's hero can be thought to reflect the state of mind of Swift himself. When the issue is put in this way, I am bound to agree with the almost unanimous verdict of contemporary writers on the Voyage and its author that a simple identification of Gulliver's creator with Gulliver is absurdly naïve. I do not think, however, that I am obliged to draw all the consequences from this sensible position that have been drawn from it of late, as to the formula of the satire itself.

For it has been assumed by a growing number of critics that if Swift is not Gulliver (as he certainly is not), then Gulliver must be in error when he reacts to some or all of his experiences as he does, and hence must be designed to strike us, at the end of the Voyage and perhaps before that also, as a comic or ironical figure, who is surely right in recognizing and hating the Yahoo elements in man but just as surely ridiculous, or worse, in seeing only those elements and in admiring so unqualifiedly the rational horses.

This theory, or some variant of it, has been advanced by critics who consider the Voyage to be a satirical defence of Christianity and by critics who do not. And the contention in both cases is that Swift, in constructing the narrative of Gulliver's transformation from a 'lover of mankind' into a perfectionist misanthrope, went out of his way to introduce various signs into the story the natural effect of which would be to discredit, for attentive readers, the extreme conclusions drawn by Gulliver himself from his stay in Houyhnhnm-land. Such devices have been found in Swift's depiction of the Houyhnhnms, in his characterization of Gulliver, and in his invention and treatment of the episode of Don Pedro.

The Houyhnhnms, it is argued, impress us as both coldly repellent and as funny: how could they then have been intended as proper objects of Gulliver's 'love and veneration'? As for Gulliver himself, he is, on the one hand, in his basic excellence of character, a striking rebuttal – we are told – of his own final view of human nature and, on the other hand, in his excesses at the end, when he shuns his family, walks and neighs like a horse, and spends much of his time in his stable, obviously a victim of comic mania. The function of the incident of Don Pedro – with his conspicuously kind treatment of Gulliver and Gulliver's merely sullen toleration of him – is thought to be no less clear. Had Swift meant us to take seriously Gulliver's 'antipathy to human kind', wouldn't he have made his rescuer an unmistakable Yahoo? And isn't his emphasis on Don Pedro's virtues a plain indication, therefore, that he wanted us to think of Gulliver, at this final stage, as a person so infatuated with a false or one-sided theory of human nature that he is blind to any facts which contradict it?

Thus has Swift been saved from the old charge of morbid misanthropy at the expense of his hero, who now becomes the vehicle of an argument which does indeed discourage us from thinking over-well of our fellow men but which, in its ultimate point, is more than a little reassuring as to the capacity of at least some human beings for rising far above the Yahoo level.

I owe it to several of my friends that I now see more clearly than I once did the weaknesses of this hypothesis and the possibility of a perhaps more convincing alternative. It is very hard to reconcile it for one thing, with the plain statement of Swift that 'the chief end' he proposed, in his writings in general and in *Gulliver* in particular, was 'to vex the world rather than divert it'. For who is going to be greatly vexed by a satire the grand climax of which – if it was really meant to be taken as many have recently read it – will always provide an alibi for even the most Yahoo-like individual, since all he has to do is to identify himself, complacently, with such exceptions to the general attack as Gulliver and Don Pedro?

But also, and more important, the reasonings employed in support of this current view are by no means as persuasive as they appear to be at first glance. I need to make, I think, only one assumption, which is surely warranted by what we know of Swift's literary habits – namely, that he was capable, in a satire with a straight serious intention, of making light of his subject and characters, perhaps at times too much, in the interest of fantasy and humor, and also of pushing his main point, hyperbolically, as far as it would go, perhaps even farther. But if this is granted, then we are no longer forced to posit an ironical thesis, at the expense of Gulliver, in order to explain why, in the fourth Voyage, the Houyhnhnms and Gulliver are often comic, or why Gulliver's misanthropy is rendered in such extreme terms.

And the other supposed signs of Gulliver's error admit similarly of alternative constructions. The Houyhnhnms are charged with being humanly unsympathetic, and so they are. But what if Swift really wanted his readers to take the same view of their superiority to human corruptions that Gulliver takes? It would surely then have been an artistic error to endow them with the

amiable weaknesses of human beings. It is not true, moreover,
that they strike us as merely repellent all or even most of the time.
Consider only whether we, too, are not very often put sharply on
the defensive, along with Gulliver, when his Houyhnhnm 'master' marvels how creatures 'pretending to reason' can do, without
shame, all the evil things Gulliver assures him that men are accus-
tomed to do. The Houyhnhnms are undoubtedly the least satis-
factory part of the Voyage, but that is owing in large measure,
I think, to the intrinsic difficulty of Swift's task: try to think of
any writer who has ever given us wholly convincing and attractive
images of perfect excellence in either non-human or human
shape. The argument from the deficiencies of the Houyhnhnms
is thus not very strong. Nor need we take Gulliver's own admirable disposition as necessarily a sign that he is absurd in looking
up to the Houyhnhnms: he had to be a man good enough to be
able to recognize and admire 'virtues and ideas' superior to his,
or his story, as he tells it, would not make sense. And the episode
of Don Pedro is likewise susceptible of a non-ironical interpretation. For suppose that what has happened to Gulliver, in Swift's
conception of the fable, is not essentially distinct from what Gulliver himself thinks has happened; suppose Swift's point is that
Gulliver really has seen for the first time virtue and reason in their
fullest living manifestations: we should certainly expect him, on
his return, to be so blinded for a while by his vision as to be able
at best only to tolerate even the worthiest members of his own
species. A worse kind of rescuer than Don Pedro would consequently have been a blunder, since the whole logic of the satirical
argument would be spoiled.

These last remarks may suggest what I think that argument in
general is. It is an argument broadly moral and psychological
rather than specifically Christian in its reference, worked out not
allegorically but by means of a marvelous fable, and dependent,
for its satirical point, on our taking Gulliver's misanthropy not as
an error but as, in substance though not in degree, the natural
and proper consequence of the experience he has had. The best
analogue to it I can think of is the old argument familiar to all of
us – and perhaps also to Swift, though I do not know – in the

myth which Socrates relates to Glaucon in the seventh Book of the *Republic* : how the prisoners in the cave sit facing the wall with their backs to the distant light and thus see only the shadows of things, not their reality; how one of them is then taken forcibly up out of the cave and brought face to face with the sun; how, when he has become used to the brightness of this, he congratulates himself on his good fortune and feels sorry for the prisoners still in the cave, thinking that he would rather be anything else in the world than live and think as they do; and how, on being finally taken back to the cave, his eyes are 'blinded by the darkness', because he has come in suddenly out of the light, and so, for a time, he tends to 'blunder and make a fool of himself', and his companions say that his visit to the upper world has ruined his sight. It is not surprising, says Socrates, if those who have caught a glimpse of the absolute form of the Good are unwilling to return to mundane affairs, if they seem to act foolishly when they do return, and if their minds long to remain among higher things.

The argument of the 'Voyage to the Houyhnhnms' is, I suggest, of the same general order as this in its essential form – only transposed into an eighteenth-century key of humor and satiric hyperbole and given a moral instead of an intellectual emphasis. As embodied in the fable of Gulliver, who has seen not the sun but merely the noblest of animals and who reacts to the sight and to his enforced return to mankind even more extravagantly than the prisoner, the argument is well calculated to serve Swift's avowed end of vexing the world by shocking it violently but wittily out of its complacency with itself; and it does this, let me add, in a way that no more compels us to identify Swift with his hero than we are obliged to identify Socrates – or Plato – with the man who blundered and made a fool of himself, for a while, on being brought back to the cave.

S O U R C E : *Gulliver's Travels: An Annotated Text with Critical Essays*, ed. R. A. Greenberg (1961) pp. 300–7.

NOTE

1. A paper read at the annual meeting of the Modern Language Association in December 1955. I have since uncovered a body of historical evidence which tends, I think, to support the thesis about Swift's argument in the fourth Voyage I have developed here. [Professor Crane published this evidence in 1962 : see Bibliography; Ed.] On the general question of Swift's 'Platonism' see Jeffrey Hart, 'The Idealogue as Artist : Some Notes on *Gulliver's Travels*', *Criticism*, II (1960) especially pp. 129–31.

A. E. Dyson

SWIFT: THE METAMORPHOSIS OF IRONY (1958)

In an age of few or shifting values irony becomes, very often, a tone of urbane amusement; assuming the right to be amused, but offering no very precise positives behind the right. It can degenerate into a mere gesture of superiority, superficially polished and civilized, but too morally irresponsible to be really so. *Eminent Victorians* is an example of such irony which springs to mind. Lytton Strachey uses the tone of Gibbon in order to deflate the Victorians, but divorces the tone from any firm moral viewpoint, and so makes of it a negative and somewhat vicious instrument.

Irony can, also, become a mode of escape, as we have good cause to know in the twentieth century. To laugh at the terrors of life is in some sense to evade them. To laugh at oneself is to become less vulnerable to the scorn or indifference of others. An ironic attitude is, as we should all now agree, complex and unpredictable : fluctuating with mood and situation, and too subtle in its possibilities for any simple definition in terms of moral purpose or a 'test of truth' to be generally applicable.

This is not, however, a state of affairs as new, or unusual, as we might be tempted to think. Even in that great age of moral irony, the eighteenth century, the technique is far from being simple. Irony is, in its very nature, the most ambivalent of modes, constantly changing colour and texture, and occasionally suffering a sea-change into something decidedly rich and strange. In the work of Swift, who will concern us here, we find, at characteristic moments, that the irony takes a leap. It escapes from its supposed

or apparent purpose, and does something not only entirely different from what it set out to do, but even diametrically opposite.
Nor is this just a matter of lost artistic control or structural weakness. At the moments I have in mind the irony is at its most complex and memorable. It seems, in undergoing its metamorphosis,
to bring us nearer to Swift's inner vision of man and the universe.
It ceases to be a functional technique serving a moral purpose, and
becomes the embodiment of an attitude to life. And just as Alice
was forced, on consideration, to accept the metamorphosis of
the Duchess's baby into a pig as an improvement ('it would have
made a dreadfully ugly child : but it makes rather a handsome
pig, I think'), so the readers of Swift will have to agree that the
final impact of his irony, however disturbing, is more real, and
therefore more worth while, than its continuation as simple moral
satire would have been.

But this is to anticipate. We must begin by reminding ourselves that Swift *is* a satirist : and that satire, fiercer than comedy
in its moral intentions, measures human conduct not against a
norm but against an ideal. The intention is reformative. The
satirist holds up for his readers to see a distorted image, and the
reader is to be shocked into a realization that the image is his own.
Exaggeration of the most extreme kind is central to the shock
tactics. The reader must see himself as a monster, in order to
learn how far he is from being a saint.

The Augustan age, as Professor Willey has most interestingly
shown, was especially adapted to satiric writing. An age which
does not really believe in sin, and which imagines that its most
rational and enlightened ideals have been actualized as a norm,
is bound to be aware also, at times, of a radical gulf between theory and practice. '. . . if you worship "Nature and Reason", you will be the more afflicted by human unreason; and
perhaps only the effort to see man as the world's glory will reveal
how far he is really its jest and riddle.'[1]

Economic and acquisitive motives were coming more and more
into the open as mainsprings of individual and social action;
Hobbes's sombre account of human nature in terms of competition and conflict was altogether too plausible on the practical

level for the comfort of gentlemen philosophers who rejected it, as a theory, out of hand. The turning of Science, Britannia and The Moderns into idols was bound, in any case, to produce sooner or later some iconoclasm of the Swiftian kind. Satire thrives on moral extremes: and at this period, with Hobbes at hand to provide a view of man which was at once alarmingly possible and entirely opposite to the prevailing one, satire was bound to be very much at home.

It should follow from this, and to some extent really does, that Swift was a moralist, concerned, as he himself puts it, to 'wonderfully mend the world', in accordance with the world's most ideal picture of itself. *Gulliver's Travels* is far more complex and elusive, however, than this intention would suggest. It is, indeed, a baffling work: I have been re-reading a number of excellent and stimulating commentaries on Book IV, and find that there are disagreements upon even the most fundamental points of interpretation.[2] Clearly, we cannot arrive at Swift's 'true' meaning merely by reversing what he actually says. The illusion that he is establishing important positives with fine, intellectual precision breaks down when we try to state what these positives *are*.

On the surface, at least, the irony does work in ways that can be precisely defined. Swift has a number of techniques which he is skilled in using either singly, or in powerful combination. At one moment he will make outrageously inhuman proposals, with a show of great reasonableness, and an affected certainty that we shall find them acceptable; at another, he will make soundly moral or Christian proposals, which are confidently held up for scorn. Again, we find him offering, with apparent sympathy and pride, an account of our actual doings, but in the presence of a virtuous outsider whose horrified reactions are sufficient index of their true worth. Swift can, notoriously, shift from one technique to another with huge dexterity; setting his readers a problem in mental and moral gymnastics if they are to evade all of his traps. In Book III, for example, the Professors at Balnibarbi are presented as progressive scientists, of a kind whom the Augustan reader would instinctively be prepared to admire. We quickly find that they are devoid of all common sense; and that unless we are to approve of such extravagant projects as 'softening marble for pincushions' we have to dissociate ourselves from them entirely. But when we do this, Swift is still ready for us. 'In the school of political projectors', says Gulliver, 'I was but ill entertained; the Professors appearing in my judgement wholly out of their senses' (a pleasant reassurance, this, that we have done well to come to a similar conclusion some time before). The crowning absurdity is that these 'unhappy people were proposing schemes for persuading monarchs to choose favourites upon the score of their wisdom, capacity and virtue . . . of rewarding merit, great abilities and eminent services . . .' and so on. Dissociated from the Professors, we find ourselves, once more, in Swift's snare.

The technique is, of course, one of betrayal. A state of tension, not to say war, exists between Swift and his readers. The very tone in which he writes is turned into a weapon. It is the tone of polite conversation, friendly, and apparently dealing in commonplaces. Naturally our assent is captured, since the polite style, the guarantee of gentlemanly equality, is the last one in which we expect to be attacked or betrayed. But the propositions to which we find ourselves agreeing are in varying degrees monstrous, warped or absurd. The result is the distinctively satiric challenge: why, we have to ask, are we so easily trapped into thinking so? And is this, perhaps, the way we really do think, despite our normal professions to the contrary?

The technique of betrayal is made all the more insidious by Swift's masterly use of misdirection. No conjuror is more adept at making us look the wrong way. His use of the polite style for betrayal is matched by his use of the traveller's tale. The apparently factual and straightforward narrative with which *Gulliver's Travels* opens (the style of *Robinson Crusoe*), precludes suspicion. We readily accept Gulliver as a representative Englishman fallen into the hands of an absurd crew of midgets, and only gradually realize that the midgets, in fact, are ourselves, and Gulliver, in this instance, the outside observer. The same technique is used, I shall argue, in Book iv: though there, the misdirection is even more subtle, and the way to extricate ourselves from a disastrous committal to Gulliver's point of view far more difficult to discover.

So much, then, for the purpose of the irony, and its normal methods. It is, we notice, accomplished, full of surprises, and admirably adapted to the task of shocking the reader for his moral good. For a great part of the time, moreover, it functions as it is intended to. When Swift is satirizing bad lawyers, bad doctors, bad politicians and *id genus omne*, he is driven by a genuine humanity, and by a conviction that people ought not to act in this way, and need not act so. His tone of savage indignation is justified by the content, and relates directly to normal ideals of justice, honesty, kindness.

On looking closely, however, we find that his irony is by no means directed only against things which can be morally changed. Sometimes it is deflected, and turned upon states of mind which might, or might not, be alterable. Consider, for example, the Laputans. These people never, we are told, enjoy a moment's peace of mind, 'and their disturbances proceed from causes which very little affect the rest of mortals'. They are preoccupied with fears of cosmic disasters, and apprehensions that the world will come to an end. The ironic treatment pre-supposes that Swift is analysing a moral flaw, but it seems doubtful whether such fears can be regarded wholly a matter of culpable weakness, and even more doubtful whether ridicule could hope to effect a cure. The problem exists in a hinterland between the moral and the psychological, between sin and sickness. The Laputans are temperamentally prone to worry : and worry is not usually regarded, except by the most austerely stoical, as simply a moral weakness.

This dubious usage points the way to the real metamorphosis, which occurs when the irony is deflected again, and turned against states of mind, or existence, which cannot be changed at all. The irony intended to 'wonderfully mend the world' transmutes itself into a savage exploration of the world's essential unmendability. It is turned against certain limitations, or defects (as Swift sees them), in the human predicament that are, by the nature of things, inevitable. When this happens, Swift seems to generate his fiercest intensity. The restless energy behind the style

F

becomes a masochistic probing of wounds. The experience of reading him is peculiarly disturbing at such moments; and it is then that his tone of savage indignation deepens into that *disgust* which Mr. T. S. Eliot has called his distinctive characteristic.

In the first two books of *Gulliver* alterations of perspective usually precipitate this type of irony. The Lilliputians are ridiculous not only because they are immoral, but because they are small. The life of their court is as meaningless as it is unpleasant : their intrigues and battles a game, which Gulliver can manipulate like a child playing with toys, and as easily grow tired of. Gulliver himself becomes ridiculous when he is placed beside the Brobdingnagians; whose contempt for him, once again, is not wholly, or even primarily, a moral matter. The King, after hearing Gulliver prattling about his 'beloved England', comments 'how contemptible a thing was human grandeur, which could be mimicked by such diminutive insects', and continues : 'Yet I dare engage, these creatures have their titles and distinctions of honour; they contrive little nests and burrows, that they call houses and cities; they make a figure in dress and equipage; they love, they fight, they dispute, they cheat, they betray.'

The force, here, is in 'mimicked', 'diminutive insects', 'creatures', 'little'. The smallness of Gulliver and his kind makes anything they do equally contemptible, their loves as much as their battles, their construction of houses and cities as much as their destructiveness. The survey is Olympian; and the human setting, seen from this height, becomes, irrespective of moral evaluation, a tale of little meaning though the words are strong.

Likewise, the hugeness of the Brobdingnagians makes them potentially horrible. The sight of a huge cancer fills Gulliver with revulsion, as, too, does the sight of giant flies who 'would sometimes alight on my victuals, and leave their loathsome excrement or spawn behind'.

What do these alterations in perspective suggest? We are made to feel that perhaps all beauty or value is relative, and in the last resort of little worth. To be proud of human achievement is as absurd as to be proud of our sins. The insignificance of men in space suggests an inevitable parallel in time. Perhaps men really *are* no more than ants, playing out their fleeting tragi-comedy to an uninterested or scornful void. The irony, now, is an awareness of possible cosmic insignificance. It is exploring a wound which no amount of moral reformation would be able to heal.

In Book IV of *Gulliver* the irony completes its transformation, and is turned upon human nature itself. Swift's intensity and disgust are nowhere more striking than here.[3] This is the classic interpretative crux: and Aldous Huxley's remark, that Swift 'could never forgive man for being a vertebrate mammal as well as an immortal soul' still seems to me to be the most seminal critical insight that has been offered.

The crux centres, of course, upon what we make of Swift's relationship to Gulliver. How far is Gulliver a satiric device, and how far (if at all), does he come to be a spokesman for Swift himself? The answer seems to me to be by no means clear. If we accept Gulliver as Swift's spokesman, we end in a state of despair. On this showing, it would seem that Swift has openly abandoned his positives, and that when he avows that he has 'now done with all such visionary schemes' as trying to reform the Yahoos 'for ever', he has passed from ironic exaggeration to sober truth. Few readers will be willing to take this view, especially when they reflect upon the dangers in store for those who identify themselves with Gulliver too readily. And yet, if we reject this, what is the alternative view to be? Swift leads us very skilfully to follow Gulliver step by step. If at some point we depart from his view of himself we have to depart also from the Houyhnhnms: who seem, however, to be an incarnation of Swift's actual positives, and the very standard against which the Yahoos are tried and found wanting. What happens in Book IV is that Gulliver is converted gradually to an admiration of the Houyhnhnms, and then to an acceptance of their judgements upon himself and his kind. The result of this enlightenment is that he comes to realize also the unattainability of such an ideal for himself. He sinks into bitterness and misanthropy, and ends, as a result of his contact with the ideal, far more unpleasant and unconstructive than he was before. At some stage, it seems, he has taken the wrong turning: but where has the mistake occurred?

The construction of the Book is of great interest. Gulliver first of all comes across the Yahoos, and is instantly repelled by them. 'Upon the whole, I never beheld in all my travels so disagreeable an animal, or one against which I naturally conceived so strong an antipathy.' Soon after this, he encounters the noble horses, and is equally strongly impressed, this time in their favour. Almost at once, he starts to discover between himself and the Yahoos an appalling resemblance: 'my horror and astonishment are not to be described, when I observed, in this abominable animal, a perfect human figure.' At this stage, it is the physical resemblance which disturbs him. But later, as he falls under the influence of the Houyhnhnms, he comes also to accept a moral resemblance. And this is at the core of the satire.

The cleverness of Swift's technique is that at first the horses are only sketched in. They are clean, kindly, rational, but apart from seeing them through Gulliver's eyes we learn little in detail about them. Gulliver is first 'amazed to see . . . in brute beasts . . . behaviour . . . so orderly and rational, so acute and judicious'. But almost at once he finds that they regard *him* as the 'brute beast', and with somewhat more justice 'For they looked upon it as a prodigy, that a brute animal should discover such marks of a rational creature'. From this moment, the Houyhnhnms start to insinuate into Gulliver's mind a vision of himself that becomes increasingly more repellent. They begin by rejecting his claim to be truly rational, speaking of 'those appearances of reason' in him, and deciding that he has been taught to 'imitate' a 'rational creature'. When they compare him with the Yahoos, Gulliver at first objects, acknowledging 'some resemblance', but insisting that he cannot account for 'their degenerate and brutal nature'. The Houyhnhnms will have none of this, however, deciding that if Gulliver does differ, he differs for the worse. 'He said, I differed indeed from other Yahoos, being much more cleanly, and not altogether so deformed; but in point of real advantage, he thought I differed for the worse.' The reason for this judgement – a reason which Gulliver himself comes to accept – is that his 'appearance of reason' is a fraud; and that what seems reason in him is no more than a faculty which makes him *lower* than the Yahoos. '. . . when a creature pretending to reason, could be capable of such enormities, he dreaded, lest the corruption of that faculty, might be worse than brutality itself. He seemed therefore confident, that instead of reason, we were only possessed of some quality fitted to increase our natural vices.'

Up to this point, the reader might feel fairly confident that he sees what is happening. The Houyhnhnms really are ideal, and Gulliver's conversion to their point of view is the lesson we should be learning. The contemptuous view of mankind formed by the Houyhnhnms is the main satiric charge. The view that man *is* a Yahoo and cannot become a Houyhnhnm is satiric exaggeration : near enough to the truth to shake us, but not intended to be taken literally. We shall be 'betrayed' if we identify ourselves with Gulliver at the points where the horses scorn him, but safe enough if we accept his conversion at their hands.

This, I fancy, is what many readers are led to feel : and to my mind, in so leading them, Swift sets his most subtle trap of all. The real shock comes in the middle of Chapter VIII, when Gulliver turns, at long last, to give us a more detailed description of the horses. We have already been aware, perhaps, of certain limitations in them : they have a limited vocabulary, limited interests, and an attitude to life that seems wholly functional. But Gulliver has explained all these limitations as virtues, and persuaded us to see them as a sign of grace. No doubt, we feel, these horses *are* noble savages of some kind, and their simplicity a condition and a reward of natural harmony. It remains for the fuller account to show us two further truths about the horses : the first, that they are not human at all, so that their way of life is wholly irrelevant as a human ideal; and the second, that their supposedly rational way of life is so dull and impoverished that we should not wish to emulate them even if we could.

Their society, for instance, is stoic in appearance. They accept such inevitable calamities as death calmly; they eat, sleep and exercise wisely : they believe in universal benevolence as an ideal, and accordingly have no personal ties or attachments. The family is effectually abolished : marriage is arranged by friends as 'one of the necessary actions in a reasonable being'; husband and wife like one another, and their children, just as much and as little as they like everyone else. Sex is accepted as normal, but only for the purpose of procreation. Like all other instincts, it is regarded as entirely functional, and has no relevance beyond the begetting of a standard number of offspring. They have no curiosity : their language, their arts and their sciences are purely functional, and restricted to the bare necessities of harmonious social existence. Life is lived 'without jealousy, fondness, quarrelling or discontent'; and it is lived in tribal isolation, since they are 'cut off from all commerce with other nations'.

This impoverished and devitalized society is the one which Gulliver uncritically accepts as an ideal, and on the strength of which he sinks into a most negative and unedifying misanthropy. And yet, so plausibly does Swift offer this as the ideal of Reason and Nature which his own age believed in, so cunningly does he lead us to think that this is the positive against which a satiric account of the Yahoos is functioning, that the trick is hard to detect. Even the fact that Gulliver is in an escapist frame of mind is not immediately apparent, unless we are on the alert.[4] We see at once, it is true, that the Houyhnhnms are not *like* men : that physically Gulliver might be a monkey but is nothing like a horse, and that this physical placing is linked with a moral one. Yet we assume that this placing is only one more satiric technique : and it is with a distinct shock that we realize that it exists at a more fundamental level than any *moral* amendment on the part of a man could resolve. The Houyhnhnms are literally not human : they are inaccessible to Gulliver not because they are morally superior, but because they are physically non-existent. They are mental abstractions disguised as animals : but they are no more animals, really, than the medieval angels were, and nothing like any human possibility, bad or good.

The horses have, in fact, no passions at all. Their 'virtue' is not a triumph over impulse and temptation, but a total immunity from these things – and an immunity which is also, by its very nature, an absence of life and vitality. They have no compulsive sexual impulses, no sensuous pleasures, no capacity for any degree of human love. They have no wishes and fears, and scarcely any ideas. If they are incapable of human bestiality they are even less capable of human glory or sublimity; and it is only because Swift prevents us from thinking of humanity as anything other than a real or potential Yahoo that this is not at once immediately apparent.

What is the true force of Book iv, then? Swift seems to my mind, to have posed, in new form, and with appalling consequences, the old riddle of man's place as the microcosm. Instead of relating him to the angels and the beasts, he relates him to the Houyhnhnms and the Yahoos. The Houyhnhnm is as non-bodily and abstract, in its essential nature, as an angel, the Yahoo a beast seen in its most disgusting lights. As for man, represented by Gulliver, he is left in a disastrous microcosmic vacuum. Instead of having his own distinctive place, he has to *be* one or the other of the extremes. Swift drives a wedge between the intellectual and the emotional, makes one good, the other evil, and pushes them further apart, as moral opposites, than any except the most extreme Puritans have usually done. The result is the kind of tormenting and bitter dilemma which always lies in wait for those who do this and, to quote Huxley again (a writer temperamentally very similar to Swift himself), who cannot 'forgive man for being a vertebrate mammal as well as an immortal soul'. The ideal is unattainable, the vicious alternative inescapable, and both are so unattractive that one is at a loss to decide which one dislikes the more.

Once again, then, the irony intended for moral satire has undergone a metamorphosis : and starting as an attempt to improve man, ends by writing him off as incurable.

But how far did Swift intend this to be so? This is the question which now becomes relevant, and the answer cannot, I think, be a straightforward one. My own feeling is that we are faced with a split between conscious intention and emotional conviction, of a kind which modern criticism has familiarized us with in Milton. Perhaps Swift really did intend a simple moral purpose, and was not consciously betraying his reader into despair. And yet, the unpleasantness of the Yahoos is realized so powerfully, and any supposed alternative is so palpably non-existent, that he must have been to some degree aware of his dilemma. He must have known that men do, for better or worse, have bodily desires, and that the Houyhnhnms were therefore an impossible ideal. He must have known, too, being a man, that Houyhnhnms were both very limited and very unattractive. And in identifying Reason and Nature with them, he must have been aware that he was betraying his own positives and those of his age: leaving the Yahoos in triumphant possession of all the reality and the life, and removing the possibility of any human escape by way of Reason or Nature from their predicament.

As a satire, *Gulliver* can work normally only if we can accept the Houyhnhnms as a desirable human possibility: and this, I do not for a moment believe Swift thought we could. The very energy of the style is masochistic – a tormenting awareness of its own impotence to do, or change, anything. Swift is publicly torturing both himself and the species to which he belongs.[5] The irony, then, intended for moral reformation, has undergone a more or less conscious metamorphosis; and the total effect of Book IV, as Dr. Leavis has insisted, is largely negative.

There are, nevertheless, before this is finally asserted, one or two compensating factors to notice. The first, often surprisingly overlooked, is that Swift cannot really have supposed his readers to be Yahoos, if only because Yahoos could not have responded at all to *Gulliver's Travels*. The deliberate obtuseness with which Gulliver prattles of his 'beloved England' will register only with a reader much less obtuse. The reader must not only be betrayed but see that he has been betrayed: and in order for this to happen he must have more intelligence and more moral sense than a Yahoo. Swift knew, in any case, that his readers *were* Augustan gentlemen with ideals of human decency that he had in common with them, and that however much a case against them could be both thought and felt, the ultimate *fact* of Augustan civilization – a fact embodied in his own style as much as anywhere – was not to be denied. *Gulliver's Travels* might leave us, then, with a wholly negative attitude, but the very fact of its being written at all is positive proof that Swift's own total attitude was not negative.

This may seem commonplace: but it leads on to another consideration, equally important, which most commentators upon *Gulliver* seem oddly afraid of: namely that Swift, writing for gentlemen, intended to give pleasure by what he wrote. When Gulliver says of the Yahoos (his readers), 'I wrote for their amendment, and not their approbation', there is a general readiness to accept this at its face value, and to credit Swift with a similar sternness. Sooner or later most writers about *Gulliver* hit upon the word 'exuberance', and then pause doubtfully, wondering whether, if Swift is so moral and so misanthropic as we think, such a word can have any place in describing him. Yet 'exuberant' he certainly is, even in Book IV of *Gulliver*. The 'vive la bagatelle', the flamboyant virtuosity of *A Tale of a Tub* is less central, but it is still to be detected, in the zest with which Gulliver describes bad lawyers, for example, and in the fantastic turns and contortions of the irony. Clearly, Swift enjoyed his control of irony: enjoyed its flexibility, its complex destructiveness, his own easy mastery of it. Clearly, too, he expects his readers to enjoy it. The irony is not *only* a battle, but a game: a civilized game, at that, since irony is by its very nature civilized, presupposing both intelligence, and at least some type of moral awareness. The 'war' is a battle of wits: and if one confesses (as the present writer does) to finding *Gulliver* immensely enjoyable, need one think that Swift would really, irony apart, have been surprised or annoyed by such a reaction?

On a final balance, I fancy that we have to compromise: agreeing that *Gulliver* ends by destroying all its supposed positives, but deducing, from the exuberance of the style and the fact that it was written at all, that Swift did not really end in Gulliver's position. He was, at heart, humane, and his savage indignation against cruelty and hypocrisy in the straightforwardly satiric parts reflects a real moral concern. He was, also, iconoclastic, and disillusioned about the ultimate dignity of man at a deep level: and when his irony undergoes the type of metamorphosis that has been discussed here, it is as disturbing and uprooted as any we can find. But he always, at the same time, enjoyed the technique of irony itself, both as an intellectual game, and as a guarantee of at least some civilized reality. Very often, even at the most intense moments, we may feel that pleasure in the intellectual destructiveness of the wit is of more importance to him than the moral purpose, or the misanthropy, that is its supposed *raison d'être*. Irony, by its very nature, instructs by *pleasing*: and to ignore the pleasure, and its civilized implications, is inevitably to oversimplify, and falsify the total effect.

> SOURCE: *Essays and Studies 1958* (1959) pp. 53–67; since reprinted as a chapter in *The Crazy Fabric* (1967).

NOTES

1. Basil Willey, *The Eighteenth-Century Background* (1946) chap. VI.
2. F. R. Leavis, *The Irony Of Swift* (available in *The Common Pursuit*, 1952); A. E. Case, *Four Essays on 'Gulliver Travels'* (1945); J. M. Murry, *Jonathan Swift* (1953), chaps 21 and 22; John Lawlor, 'Radical Satire and the Realistic Novel', *Essays And Studies* (1955); D. W. Jefferson, 'An Approach to Swift', *Pelican Guide to English Literature: From Dryden to Johnson* (1957).
3. That striking *tour-de-force, A Modest Proposal,* springs to mind as an exception. There, too, as Dr. Leavis has argued in his fine essay, the effect is almost wholly negative and destructive. The force of the irony is so savage that it robs its supposed positives of any power of asserting themselves. The ghastly imagery of the market and the slaughter-house ceases to sound like satiric exaggeration, and appals us with the sense of actuality. Man, we feel, really *is* as brutal and sordid as this. Theories that he might be otherwise are merely an added torment, so energetically is his inhumanity realized, so impotent is the theoretic norm in the face of this reality.

A necessary conflict seems, too, to be exposed between our ideals of humanity and rational behaviour, and the actual motives of competition and self-interest which move society. Society can no more really be expected to change for the better than Yahoos can be expected to turn into Houyhnhnms. The law of love is absolutely incompatible with things as they are.
4. e.g. '. . . For, in such a solitude as I desired, I could at least enjoy

my own thoughts, and reflect with delight on the virtues of those inimitable Houyhnhnms, without any opportunity of degenerating into the vices and corruptions of my own species.' (Book IV, chap. XI.)

5. We might feel, today, that in exploring the dangers of dissociating reason from emotion, and calling the one good, the other bad, Swift really did hit on the central weakness of his age : that Book IV is still valid, in fact, as a satire upon Augustanism itself. The Augustans, at their most characteristic, disapproved of strong emotions as necessarily disruptive, subordinated even those emotions they could not exile to the stern control of 'Right Reason', and found no place for 'feeling' in their search for 'truth'. This attitude, we might decide, is doomed to failure by the actual nature of man – and Swift, by driving reason and emotion to opposite poles (with the result that man can live happily by neither) reveals just *how* impossible it is.

If we take this view, we might see Book IV as a counterpart, on the negative side, to the sort of criticism of the 'Age of Reason' that Blake was later to offer, very positively, in *The Marriage of Heaven and Hell*. Such a view, however, is very paradoxical, since Swift can certainly not have intended anything of the kind, and would have been temperamentally very averse to accepting Blake's 'solution'. We might, then, see Swift's *impasse* as evidence that could be used in a critique of Augustanism. But we can be sure that Swift himself would not have agreed with such a critique, even had such a possibility occurred to him.

Kathleen Williams

THE FANTASY WORLD OF
LAPUTA (1958)*

. . . The immediate effect of the first two books is of growing unease, not of acceptance of a standard, for the compromise standard has to be worked out when all the creatures are assembled
and when what at first seems to be an absolute good – the life of
the Houyhnhnms – has been shown to be a false simplification.
The world of Brobdingnag is solid and sane, but we are not yet
allowed to rest at ease in it. Our amusement and annoyance with
the Lilliputians and their antlike organization, and our approval
of the decency of unpolitical man as displayed in Gulliver, are
turned to uncertainty as we find ourselves in the shifting world
of relativity and discover that Gulliver is far from being a norm
of behavior and that according to circumstances he can be as
mean-minded and vain as a Lilliputian, and even more inhuman.
Moreover, Gulliver, we begin to see, is apt to draw very wrong
conclusions from his experiences. Even in Lilliput, where he is
seen to best advantage, he too readily accepts Lilliputian standards, and talks quite seriously of the great nobles, and of the
honors he has received in this ridiculous little state. For instance :
'I should not have dwelt so long upon this Particular, if it had
not been a Point wherein the Reputation of a great Lady is so

* 'The Fantasy World of Laputa' is our title for this extract from
the chapter 'Animal Rationis Capax' in Professor Williams's *Jonathan Swift and the Age of Compromise*. The page references in
square brackets relate to the *Prose Works of Jonathan Swift* (ed.
Herbert Davis), vol. xi. [Ed.]

nearly concerned; to say nothing of my own; although I had
the Honour to be a Nardac, which the Treasurer himself is
not; for all the World knows he is only a Clumglum, a Title inferior by one Degree, as that of a Marquess is to a Duke in England; yet I allow he preceded me in right of his Post.' [*Works*, xi,
pp. 49–50] In Brobdingnag, his reactions to the King's opinions
are quite clearly wrong, and he learns nothing from his visit except
to be ill at ease at home, fancying his friends and relatives under-
sized, and looking at them 'as if they had been Pigmies, and I a
Giant'. In a little time, he came to an understanding with his
family and friends, but his wife protested he should never go to
sea any more. She was in the right, for Gulliver's malleable character and his aptitude for enthusiastic misunderstanding were
to lead to worse and more permanent difficulty after his last voyage, when the furthest accommodation he reports is that 'I began
last Week to permit my Wife to sit at Dinner with me, at the far-
thest End of a long Table; and to answer (but with the utmost
Brevity) the few Questions I asked her.' [279] Thus the qualities necessary to a satiric mouthpiece – the inconsistency, the pal-
pable wrongheadedness and absurdity, that lack, indeed, of a
positive character, so essential if ironic comment is to be made
on any but the simplest scale – are turned with the greatest precision and economy to further purpose.

The insecurity and uncertainty of direction we feel at the end
of the 'Voyage to Brobdingnag' is heightened in Book iii. The
success of this book is not at all easy for a modern reader to gauge.
Its sharp contrast in method, with the grotesque figures of the
Laputans and the excursions into magic and immortality, certainly breaks the atmosphere of moral realism which pervades the
voyages to Lilliput, Brobdingnag, and Houyhnhnm-land; even
the rational horses belong to a world of morality, not of fantasy.
This third book, the latest written, would be, by us, the least
missed. But on the other hand the fantasy world of Laputa, in its
madness and delusion, still further shakes our wits and our confidence before the final resolution of Book iv, and the Laputan
lunacies have, after all, a moral connotation as we can see if we
remember *A Tale of a Tub*. But for us, to whom the scientific

outlook is a commonplace, it is not so easy to see the 'Voyage to Laputa' in terms of modern vice and traditional virtue, and we find it less striking than the other voyages, where moral problems are more overtly considered though their presentation is influenced by contemporary thinking. Only the episode of the Struldbrugs of Luggnagg, unencumbered as it is by topical satire, strikes us with the immediate force and the moral emphasis of the second and fourth books, for to a modern reader scientific experiment is a less acceptable example of irrelevant thinking than are the speculations of Burnet or of Thomas Vaughan. Swift's opinion of the scientific achievement of his day is, in itself, inadequate, and considered as an attack on science the third book must seem wrongheaded and unfair. But considered as what it really is, an allegorical presentation of the evils of a frivolous attitude to life, it is consistent and effective, however unjust we may consider Swift's chosen allegory to be.

For the visit to Laputa itself, and to the subject land of Balnibarbi, has a more serious intention than the topical one of ridiculing the Royal Society. The flying island, though it has a precise relationship – even as to size – with William Gilbert's dipping-needle,[1] and though it uses Gilbert's idea 'of the Earth's whole Body being but one great Magnet; and, lesser Magnets being so many Terrella's sympathising with the Whole', presents through this contemporary scientific interest a political philosophy and a comment on man's relation to nature which go beyond the merely topical : beyond particular scientific discoveries or the relation of the kingdoms of England and Ireland. The flying island, 'the King's Demesn', in its devious and sensitive oblique movements, suggests the relationship of king and country. Laputa is ultimately dependent upon Balnibarbi, its motions only allowed by the magnetic quality of the 'King's Dominions'. It is this quality which has allowed the Laputan king to establish his power over the fixed land, but there is a reciprocal dependence, for if either side pressed its power too far the result would be general ruin. The King's last resource, in case of defiance from the populace of Balnibarbi, is to let the flying island drop upon their heads, but this, though it would certainly destroy both houses and men, would at the same time damage the adamant of Laputa itself.

Of all this the People are well apprized, and understand how far to carry their Obstinacy, where their Liberty or Property is concerned. And the King, when he is highest provoked, and most determined to press a City to Rubbish, orders the Island to descend with great Gentleness, out of a Pretence of Tenderness to his People, but indeed for fear of breaking the Adamantine Bottom; in which Case it is the Opinion of all their Philosophers, that the Load-Stone could no longer hold it up, and the whole Mass would fall to the ground. [156]

As for the nobles and ministers, they are in part committed to the welfare of both lands, for while they attend at the Laputan court their estates lie on the continent below, so that they will never dare advise the King to make himself 'the most absolute Prince in the Universe' by so ruthless and desperate a course. The balance of power, and the delicate relationships which subsist between a monarch and those whom he governs, could scarcely be better represented than by conditions in Laputa and Balnibarbi, and it is typical of Swift that these relationships, though given a color of respect for human life and liberties, are seen to be really dependent upon the exact adjustment of practical necessities; the self-love of each party is carried as far as it can go without that open conflict with the self-love of others which would bring it to destruction.

Further, the relation of the greater and lesser magnets, Laputa and Balnibarbi, suggests the limited usefulness of that understanding of the laws of the universe upon which the Newtonian era so prided itself, and which is one of the main objects of Swift's satiric comment in this book. The Laputan king, for all his knowledge of cosmic circumstance, for all the ingenuity of his flying island, is yet dependent upon the firm earth beneath him for every movement Laputa can make; for all his theoretic achievement man is, in practice, dependent upon and circumscribed by other men and by laws of nature, of which he can take a certain limited advantage but which he can neither alter nor, finally, ex-

plain. The astronomers of Laputa, although they have written
'large Systems concerning the Stone' whose movements control
the course of the flying island, can give no better reason for the
inability of Laputa to rise above four miles, or to move beyond the
extent of the King's continental dominions, than the self-evident
one 'That the Magnetick Virtue does not extend beyond the
Distance of four Miles, and that the Mineral which acts upon the
Stone in the Bowels of the Earth, and in the Sea about Six
Leagues distant from the Shoar, is not diffused through the whole
Globe, but terminated with the Limits of the King's Dominions'.
[154] Their pursuit of second causes ends in inscrutable mystery,
which their confident exposition can only conceal, not clarify.
The allegory of Laputa and of Balnibarbi, 'controlled by that
which it alone controls', is indeed an epitome of the situation
more fully explored in the detailed descriptions of the inhabitants
of the flying island and of conditions on the mainland below; the
neat, generalized relationships help us to find our way in the confusion of the Academy of Projectors and the alien clarities of the
Laputan court.

The Laputans, though they are in human shape, are more
obviously allegorical creatures than any in *Gulliver's Travels.*
Their physical characteristics express their nature as do those of
the Brobdingnagians or the Yahoos, but in a different way. Their
effect is made, not through exaggeration or isolation, but through
distortion, of the physical, and though by this means much of
the force of Swift's greatest figures is lost, this is in itself part of
the meaning, since the Laputans have indeed lost their human
quality in their abnormal absorption in things remote from the
concerns of men. They make little physical effect upon us, for
their outer aspect is as unnatural, as purely emblematic, as that
of a personification like Spenser's Occasion : 'One of their Eyes
turned inward, and the other directly up to the Zenith' [143]
because they are completely absorbed in their own speculations
and in the study of the stars. Their interests are entirely abstract,
and they see nothing of the everyday practical world, ignoring the
knowledge of the senses as totally as Jack or the philosopher of
A Tale of a Tub. The Laputan is 'always so wrapped up in

Cogitation, that he is in manifest Danger of falling down every Precipice, and bouncing his Head against every Post; and in the Streets, of jostling others, or being jostled himself into the Kennel'. [144] Because they scorn the evidence of the senses, the Laputans are necessarily 'very bad Reasoners', though very positive and dogmatic ones, for the senses are 'so many Avenues to the Fort of Reason', which in them as in the mechanical operators of the spirit is wholly blocked up. These strange figures are akin not only to the mechanical operators but more closely to the spider-like world-makers. Like the author of *A Tale of a Tub*, they are less consistent than inclusive, summing up various departures from the middle way. One eye looks outward, but only to a remote world of abstractions where, in the regular motions of the heavens, mathematics and music join. One eye looks inward, to the mind where systems are spun out of a 'Native Stock', not built up from that basis of observed fact which, however faulty our senses, is yet the only material upon which our reason can work constructively and practically. Laputan thinking produces results as flimsy and useless as a cobweb – Gulliver's ill-fitting suit, the devastated countryside of Balnibarbi.

The King and his court are devoted entirely to two subjects, music and mathematics, the most abstract of sciences. There is a topical reference, in that an interest in these 'two eternal and immutable verities' and in the analogies between them serves to identify the Laputans as members of the Royal Society, but for centuries an interest in the relationship of mathematics and music had existed, so that it was by no means an exclusively contemporary concern. In the Middle Ages music, regarded as a mathematical science, had been one of the purest embodiments of unchanging law, and the Laputans with their absorption in music, mathematics, and astronomy, represent specifically the members of the Royal Society but more generally all those who believe that, by turning away from the impressions of the senses and the ordinary concerns of human nature they can ignore sublunary confusion and reach eternal truth. Swift's reference to the music of the spheres emphasizes this more general meaning; the Laputans spend hours at their instruments, preparing themselves to join in the music of the spheres, which they claim to be able to hear. Since mankind is traditionally deaf to this music because of the grossness of the senses through sin, the claim implies that the Laputans believe themselves to have escaped from such tyranny. To their impracticality is added the presumption of ignoring the inherited wisdom which sees man as a fallen creature separated, through his own fault, from the order, truth, and justice figured in the celestial harmony of the nine enfolded spheres.

The narrowness, even to inhumanity, of the Laputans is indeed stressed throughout. They have cut themselves off completely from all that is humanly creative and constructive. Even their food approaches as nearly as possible to the rarefied atmosphere in which they live, for their meat is carved into geometrical shapes and their poultry trussed up 'into the Form of Fiddles'. Nor have they any conception of physical or sensuous beauty, since they see beauty only in mathematical abstractions, and judge not by sense impressions but by an arbitrary relation of animal forms to abstract shapes existing in their minds: 'If they would, for Example, praise the Beauty of a Woman, or any other Animal, they describe it by Rhombs, Circles, Parallelograms, Ellipses, and other Geometrical Terms; or else by Words of Art drawn from Musick . . . the whole Compass of their Thoughts and Mind, being shut up within the two forementioned Sciences.' [147] But the world of human beings cannot be adequately dealt with in mathematical terms, and their wives, as a consequence, have fallen into matter, escaping whenever possible into a life altogether physical and degraded, as exaggeratedly animal as that of their husbands is exaggeratedly intellectual. The King has no interest in 'the Laws, Government, History, Religion, or Manners of the Countries' [150] Gulliver has visited, and his realm of Balnibarbi is chaotic. Gulliver 'could not discover one Ear of Corn, or Blade of Grass' [159] except in a few places, during his journeys, and our minds revert to the kingdom of Brobdingnag, the land which has been called a 'simple Utopia of abundance', where government is conducted with practical good will and a due regard for traditional wisdom, and where the King regards his task as one of promoting increase and life, making 'two Ears of Corn, or two Blades of Grass, to grow where only one grew before'. The Laputans, on the other hand, produce a world of death, and the results of their efforts are purely destructive because their aims are impossibly high and are unrelated to real conditions. Some day, they say, 'a Palace may be built in a Week, of Materials so durable as to last for ever without repairing. All the Fruits of the Earth shall come to Maturity at whatever Season we think fit to chuse, and increase an Hundred Fold more than they do at present; with innumerable other happy Proposals.' [161] In the meantime, houses are ruined, land uncultivated, and people starving, and the only result of Laputan enterprise on the prosperous estate of the old-fashioned Lord Munodi has been to destroy the mill which had long provided his family and tenants, in order to make way for one which should, on scientific principles, be better, but which somehow fails to work. Samuel Johnson sums up in similar terms the humanist sense of the Royal Society's irrelevance to true and living values :

When the philosophers of the last age were first congregated into the Royal Society, great expectations were raised of the sudden progress of useful arts; the time was supposed to be near, when engines should turn by a perpetual motion, and health be secured by the universal medicine; when learning should be facilitated by a real character, and commerce extended by ships which could reach their ports in defiance of the tempest.

But improvement is naturally slow. The Society met and parted without any visible diminution of the miseries of life. The gout and stone were still painful, the ground that was not ploughed brought no harvest, and neither oranges nor grapes would grow upon the hawthorn.[2]

That Munodi, the one successful landowner in Balnibarbi, should be a traditionalist is only to be expected; 'being not of an enterprizing Spirit, he was content to go on in the old Forms; to live in the Houses his Ancestors had built, and act as they did in every Part of Life without Innovation'. [161]

The activities of the members of the Academy of Projectors,

though they involve experiment, are yet related to the abstract
thinking of the King. For the most part, they are based on some
wrongheaded abstract conception, and are really examples of
what Pope calls reasoning downward, taking 'the High Priori
Road'; they are aspects, therefore, of the great modern heresy of
ignoring 'the old Forms' and relying on a spider-like spinning of
thought. By blending experiment and High Priori reasoning in
the Academy at Lagado, Swift is able to show scientific 'projects'
as yet another example of that whole development of thinking
which leads away from the ways of a Christian and humanist
tradition, and Pope's lines would refer as well to the mathemati-
cians of Laputa and the scientists of Lagado as they do to Hobbes,
Descartes, Spinoza, and Samuel Clarke :

> Let others creep by timid steps, and slow,
> On plain Experience lay foundations low,
> By common sense to common knowledge bred,
> And last, to Nature's Cause through Nature led.[3]

Indeed one of the projects is an exact allegorical equivalent of the
process of reasoning downward to, instead of upward from, the
foundations of plain experience : 'There was a most ingenious
Architect who had contrived a new Method for building Houses,
by beginning at the Roof, and working downwards to the Foundation; which he justified to me by the like Practice of those two
prudent Insects the Bee and the Spider.' [164] We are not told
the results of this method, but in other cases the ideas of the projectors do not well stand up to experiment; for instance, the
notion of 'plowing the Ground with Hogs to save the Charges of
Plows, Cattle, and Labour' results, 'upon Experiment', in no crop
and a great deal of trouble and expense.

The experiments and their results allow Swift to collect together various images which, as so often, express his meaning
through producing a certain atmosphere which must affect our
response to Laputa and Balnibarbi. These projects leave an impression of uselessness, dirt, ephemerality, or death; the Academi-
cians present for our inspection a spider web, a hog rooting up

acorns, a muddle of painters' colors, a dead dog. Their efforts are summed up in an illustrious member who has been given the title of 'the Universal Artist', and who has been for thirty years directing his followers in various ways of converting things into their opposites, thus turning the useful into the unusable and the vital into the atrophied. Air is made tangible and marble soft, land is sown with chaff and naked sheep are bred; and perhaps most exact of all as an epitome of the achievements of the Academy, the hooves of a living horse are being petrified. The projects of Lagado are, in fact, conducted in an atmosphere similar to that of *A Tale of a Tub*, an atmosphere of aimless activity, distorted values, and a perversion of things from their proper purpose even to the point of removing all life and meaning from them. The results produced are woolless sheep, dead dogs, horses whose living hooves are turned to stone. The mechanism of the *Tale* exists in Lagado too, in the machine which is to replace the thinking and creating mind of man and will, by pure chance, eventually produce 'Books in Philosophy, Poetry, Politicks, Law, Mathematicks and Theology'.[4] While the prevailing effect of the images we associate with Lilliput and, especially, Brobdingnag is of man and other animals as vigorous physical presences, the effect of Laputa and its subject kingdom is of a wilful abandoning of the physical and of the vital for the abstract, the mechanical, and the unproductive. The prevailing images here are not of real people and animals, even 'little odious vermin', but of ruins, mechanical constructions, men who look like allegorical figures and women who are thought of as rhomboids or parallelograms. Animals are only negatively present, as in the pathetic horses and sheep of the Academy. Even Laputa itself is a mechanical device, and the flying island expresses not only the Laputans' desertion of the common earth of reality but their conversion of the universe to a mechanism and of living to a mechanical process.

From Lagado Gulliver makes his way to Glubbdubdrib, where again he is in a world of no-meaning, of delusion and death, darker and more shadowy than Laputa. In the palace of the sorcerer who is governor of the island he has a series of singularly uninformative interviews with the ghosts of the famous dead, and

Alexander and Hannibal, who as conquerors and destroyers had little to recommend them to Swift, make particularly trivial replies. We are given a gloomy enough picture of both the ancient and the modern world, and upon this ghostly history follows the most somber episode of all, that of the Struldbrugs of Luggnagg, in which the lesson of Laputa with its naïve hopes, its misplaced ambition, and its eventual sterility is repeated with more open seriousness. A right sense of values, a proper attitude to living, is here suggested not through the handling of contemporary aims and habits of thought but through the figure of man, immortal yet still painfully recognizable, and perhaps owing some of its power and poignancy to Swift's own fear of death and, still more, of decay, of a lingering old age giving way at last to helpless lunacy. Gulliver, hearing of the immortals, cries out 'as in a Rapture', exclaiming upon the wisdom and happiness which they must have achieved. They must, he says, 'being born exempt from that universal Calamity of human Nature, have their Minds free and disingaged, without the Weight and Depression of Spirits caused by the continual Apprehension of Death', [192] and he is only too willing to tell his hearers how he would plan his life, if he were a Struldbrug, to bring the greatest possible benefit to himself and his country. In fact, of course, the immortal and aged creatures, though free from the fear of death, are yet as full of fears and wretchedness as any other men : being what we are, we will always find occasion to display those vices which as human beings we will always have, however long we may live. The Struldbrugs certainly do not keep their minds free and disengaged, and for them the prospect of endless life does not conjure up visions of endless improvement in wisdom and virtue. They regard their immortality as a 'dreadful Prospect' even as other men regard their death, and indeed they long to die as did the wretched Sibyl in Petronius's *Satyricon*, regarding with great jealousy those of their acquaintance who go 'to an Harbour of Rest, to which they themselves never can hope to arrive'. [196] Immortal man is still man, limited in his capacity for growth, sinful, fearful, dissatisfied; the somber simplicity of the passage, and indeed of the whole of the visit to Glubbdubdrib, is reminiscent of Johnson's methods rather than of Swift's, and the message is essentially similar. Gulliver, who has dreamed of being a king, a general, or a great lord, and now dreams of being a Struldbrug, has to learn the same lesson as the Prince of Abyssinia : that life is a serious, difficult, and above all a moral undertaking, that whatever excuses we may find for ourselves, however we may dream of the greatness we could have achieved under other conditions, we will realize at last that humanity is always the same, and that there is no escape from our vices and our trivialities. Gulliver says that he grew 'heartily ashamed of the pleasing Visions I had formed; and thought no Tyrant could invent a Death into which I would not run with Pleasure from such a Life,' [198] and that he would have been willing, if it had not been forbidden by the laws of Luggnagg, to send a couple of Struldbrugs to England to arm the people against that fear of death which is natural to mankind.

So the 'Voyage to Laputa', which opens among a people essentially frivolous in its refusal to face the facts of human existence, ends face to face with inescapable reality. Laputa, where the search for the clarity of abstractions involves such confusion in the living world, seems at first merely hilarious and absurd, but as confusion turns to mechanism and destruction this remoteness and unreality becomes not only ludicrous but evil, and the countries about Laputa and Balnibarbi are seen to be places of superstition, sorcery, and tyranny, of ghosts and the corpselike immortals of Luggnagg. The voyage to illusion, the escape from facts, ends in a darker reality than any Gulliver has yet encountered. Gulliver himself, in this book, becomes a part of the world of illusion and distorted values. Already in the earlier voyages the shifting, inconsistent quality which Gulliver shares with all Swift's satiric mouthpieces has been made to contribute to effects of relativity, and to suggest the hold of physical circumstances over mankind. That he is, generally, a different man in Brobdingnag and in Lilliput is made into part of Swift's presentation of human nature. In the 'Voyage to Laputa', any still surviving notion that Gulliver is a safe guide through these strange countries is ended. He ceases to have any character and, in effect, vanishes, so that for the most part the satire speaks directly to us; the 'mouthpiece' performs no real function. The transparent account of 'Tribnia, by the Natives called Langden', where 'the Bulk of the People consisted wholly of Discoverers, Witnesses, Informers, Accusers, Prosecutors, Evidences, Swearers', [175] owes nothing to Gulliver, and would be quite inconceivable from what we have known of him before; in the second voyage he had 'wished for the Tongue of Demosthenes or Cicero, that might have enabled me to celebrate the Praise of my own dear native Country in a Style equal to its Merits and Felicity'. [111] Here he is being frankly used for ironic comment, as his exaggerated enthusiasm shows; in the description of Tribnia, he is not being used at all. From time to time he is given a momentary reality, but of the most perfunctory kind; there is no attempt to endow him even with the one or two dominant characteristics that he is given elsewhere. His approval of projects, or his tendency to dream about impossible situations instead of getting on with the business of living, his dismissal of obviously desirable political reforms as 'wild impossible Chimaeras', are, quite openly, mentioned for satiric purposes of a very simple kind. The handling of Gulliver is in fact far less interesting, and his contribution is far slighter, than in any other book, probably because his function had been worked to its limits in the voyages already written, which included the 'Voyage to the Houyhnhnms'. But whether or not Swift planned it so, Gulliver's virtual lack of function, indeed of existence, in the 'Voyage to Laputa' has a certain effectiveness in contributing to the atmosphere of meaningless activity and self-deceit, leading to a shadowy despair. The gradual undermining of the comparatively solid worlds of Lilliput and Brobdingnag was achieved partly through a shift in Gulliver's position; here he merges completely into his surroundings, and serves merely to describe what he sees, so that we cannot take him seriously as an interpreter. When he reappears in Book IV, we are well prepared to find that his function will not be a simple one either of sensible comment on the vagaries of a strange country, or of admiration for a Utopia, for we have accepted him as one of the many figures in the *Travels*, expressing meaning by his relationship to them, and no more exempt than they from satiric treatment. As a completion of the processes begun in Lilliput and Brobdingnag, and as a preparation for the resolution in Houyhnhnm-land, the Laputan voyage performs its task adequately, though without the formal elegance and neatness of the other books.

S o u r c e: *Jonathan Swift and the Age of Compromise* (1958) chapter 7, pp. 164–77.

NOTES

(19 notes in the original have been incorporated into the text.)

1. Nicolson and Mohler, *Annals of Science*, vol. ii, nos. 3 and 4.
2. *Idler*, 88, *Works* (London, 1825) ii, 640.
3. *The Dunciad*, iv, 465–8.
4. *Works*, xi, 166. Swift always hated, as did Pope, any use of words that suggested the mechanical : another example in Lagado is the scheme, in the School of Language, for carrying 'Things' about to converse with, since 'Words are only Names for Things' (xi, 169), a hit at the scientific view of words as mere labels for objects. At the other extreme there is the argument from words alone, in effect just as mechanical, which irritates him in Tindal's conclusion that the 'body-politic' must be dealt with in the same way as the 'body-natural'. Upon this argument his comment is, 'What, because it is called a Body, and is a Simile, must it hold in all Circumstances!' (*Works*, ii, 94). Peter's hunting of syllables and letters is of the same mindless, mechanical nature, and several of Swift's mouthpieces parody what Locke calls using words without a signification, 'only as sounds, which usually served instead of reasons on the like occasions' (*Of Human Understanding*, iii, xi, 8).

Philip Pinkus

SIN AND SATIRE IN SWIFT (1965)

Satirists have said so often that they satirize to correct the vices
and follies of mankind that they very likely believe it. Swift seemed
to, at least on certain ceremonial occasions: 'His satire points at
no defect,/But what all mortals may correct. . . . As with a moral
view design'd/To cure the vices of mankind.' We can assume
these lines to be his own epitaph on thirty years of satirizing. Of
'the two Ends that Men propose in writing Satyr', he said in his
'Vindication of *The Beggar's Opera*', one is to please themselves
as writers, the other, and to Swift the more commendable, is 'to
mend the World as far as they are able'. This is very explicit.
On other occasions Swift has lamented that satire does not mend
a thing. It is a kind of ball that the reader bats toward his neighbour, everyone being provided with a racquet for the purpose.
'Instead of seeing a full stop put to all abuses and corruptions, at
least in this little island,' Gulliver wrote to his Cousin Sympson –
and surely this is Swift's ironic comment – '. . . behold, after
above six months warning, I cannot learn that my book hath
produced one single effect according to my intentions.' We might
dismiss his lament as petulance or modesty, but the fact remains
that Swift's satire, and satire in general, has had less effect reforming the world than had Carrie Nation and her little hatchet.
There are brilliant exceptions. Swift and a band of fellow satirists
succeeded in putting one miserable astrologer out of business. If
his *Drapier's Letters* can be called satire – which is debatable – then satire managed to overturn a policy of government.
But these exceptions point to a poor average. His greatest satires
have had no calculable success in mending the world. The Royal

Society has had a long and flourishing life, despite *Gulliver's Travels*. Economic projectors thrive, despite 'A Modest Proposal'. John Dryden, whom Swift satirized in *A Tale of a Tub*, was not visibly amended, possibly because it was published four years after he died. In general, society cherishes the same Lilliputian ends, mankind trots along the same Yahoo way, the world is still mad, Celia, Celia, still does what she used to do, as if Swift had never written.

The standard comment is that satire is the 'literary art of diminishing a subject by making it ridiculous'. This may describe the *Container*, but does not do much for the *Thing Contained*. It says virtually nothing about why people write satire, unless we are to assume it is because satirists are angry – which is a good reason, though Swift would add that there must be no personal malice. But if that were the only reason, satire would be no more than an elaborate display of temper, fine for the blood pressure but hard on the spleen. Swift offered another reason for writing satire, the simple pleasure of the writer at his work. This is very significant in an age dedicated to didacticism, where everything is supposedly measured by moral standards. It has the astonishing implication that satire is a piece of writing with the same standards and requirements as any other piece of writing. The point is sometimes forgotten, though we have the satirists themselves to blame for this with their talk of whipping and scourging and purging the vices of the world. Of course, satire is didactic. But one might argue that most works of art are didactic. It is true that in satire the moral weight is greater, that we are more aware of a judgment imposed. Having said this we are still left with the fact that the essential purpose of satire is the same as that of any other art, to impose significant form on some aspect of life.

If we accept this, and it seems very obvious, then we have no more right to expect the satirist to be historically accurate, no more right to expect Swift to give us a factual description of Dryden, for example, than Shakespeare to tell the historical truth about Richard II. The writer, in each case, uses his subject for a particular literary effect. We expect some family resemblance between the historical and literary figure – and we get some of the

impact of satire by seeing the similarity – but we settle for what
we call artistic truth. It is hardly relevant that Shadwell was not
so stupid as the MacFlecknoe portrait of him, or Swift's world as
vicious as he described it. The satirist is simply using his artistic
privilege to describe what he sees. He is imposing an artistic pattern to create the effect that he requires. In some respects the
effect gained is similar to that of tragedy : the reader is led step
by step into the heart of darkness. 'A Modest Proposal' is a systematic descent into the horror of a world where everything can
be measured exactly by the price it brings on the open market.
Gulliver's Travels is a pilgrimage that brings one face to face
with the Yahoo image of man. *A Tale of a Tub* concludes in the
most frightening of all images, a world gone mad. Unlike evil in
tragedy, evil is not destroyed in satire, it is not even embarrassed;
it triumphs over everything else. This is true of every satire. The
climactic image of *Gulliver's Travels*, for example, is the Yahoo,
who is Swift's metaphoric comment on the nature of man. We
all know that, philosophically speaking, the Yahoo is not man;
it is the brute, irrational element. But to Swift, the satirist within
the literary work, the Yahoo bears the same relation to man as
MacFlecknoe does to Shadwell. The last part of *Gulliver's Travels*
methodically develops the image of a Yahoo world. Gulliver returns to a Yahoo society. His only escape from the Yahoo is the
company of his horses. There are, of course, Don Pedros in this
world, but they are crowded out. To Gulliver, and we see this
world through Gulliver, there are only Yahoos. Mankind has
not been ridiculed into some romantic limbo, he has not been
corrected – what has been satirized cannot be corrected. Swift's
conception of the evil within man has been pointed out, dwelled
on, inflated, spilled over the whole of Gulliver's world until there
is room for little else.

This is the point of satire, to make the reader aware of the
evil within the satiric target. Therefore the satirist does not di-
minish his target; he expands it into a grotesque. The whole
movement of satire is designed to create this effect. As for the
ridicule – and there is not much ridicule in Juvenalian satire –
it provides the wit and humor to give the target distance that

we may see the evil clearly; it makes the image more contemptible. It also gives the illusion of annihilating the target, a mock victory in the eternal battle between good and evil – like hanging an effigy, a ritualistic release. But it is illusion, because evil has not been annihilated in the satiric world; it has triumphed.

For Swift, the awareness of evil in a depraved world is the only way of avoiding 'the sublime and refined Point of Felicity, called, *the Possession of being well deceived*; The Serene Peaceful State, of being a Fool among Knaves'. It lands one instead in the miserable state of being a wise man among fools. But awareness is essential to the moral struggle; it is a positive impulse against the destructive element, an affirmation of life. For Swift awareness goes much further. His satire seems to have almost a religious purpose. He presents a satiric vision of an irrational world, a vision that becomes his prelude to an act of faith. The assumption here is that there is one satiric vision, that all Swift's satires make the same comment on life. By this assumption we may take various elements of the different satires and piece them together into one unified view. Swift's view of life did change somewhat from the time he wrote *A Tale of a Tub* to the time he wrote *Gulliver's Travels*. The early satire shows a control and relative calm which implies much less disgust. But the *Tale* did end in a Bedlam sufficiently enlarged to accommodate the world, so that the difference between the two satires is only in degree. With this reservation, it is possible by describing some of the dominant images of Swift's satires to present a fairly consistent view of life – Swift's satiric image of evil. By determining the nature of the image and its purpose, we should be able to explain the nature of Swift's satire. Such an approach successfully removes the wit, the humor, the delight of Swift's writing, but something must be removed in a short paper.

In *A Tale of a Tub* Swift describes three oratorial machines, the pulpit, the ladder and the stage-itinerant; and he explains that the stage-itinerant is 'the mountebank's stage, whose orators the author determines either to the gallows [that is, the ladder], or a conventicle [the pulpit]'. It can be shown that these three machines represent all the satiric targets of *A Tale of a Tub*. They occur again in the 'Digression on Madness', as the 'greatest actions that have been performed in the world', and therefore, by Tubbian logic, completely mad. That is, in order to reach greatness and what is vulgarly called madness, the first requirement is to be a mountebank, a quack, a pretender. All the inhabitants of the Tubbian world, before they are religious enthusiasts, highwaymen, philosophers, projectors, are first of all, mountebanks. Again, such pretension is found in all satire. The satiric target is never the highwayman who is universally reviled, or the condemned murderer, or the madman officially certified and put away, but the highwayman who pretends to be a respectable statesman, the madman who pretends to divine insight, the murderer who pretends to be a great general, the Yahoo who pretends to dignity and importance. In each case it is the pretense that draws the satire. Swift developed this basic principle of satire into the elaborate image of sartorism in *A Tale of a Tub*, which derives from the theory that clothes make the man, outside is inside, body is soul, surface is essence.

Those beings, which the world calls improperly suits of clothes, are in reality the most refined species of animals; or to proceed higher . . . they are rational creatures, or men. . . . If one of them be trimmed up with a gold chain, and a red gown, and a white rod, and a great horse, it is called a Lord Mayor : if certain ermines and furs be placed in a certain position, we style them a Judge. . . .

Embroidery is sheer wit, gold fringe, agreeable conversation, gold lace, repartee. Swift has created a whole world of smooth, respectable, dignified, elegant people, performing all the gestures of a rational society, except for one trivial difference : there is a void at the centre of things. Men have become objects, suits of clothes, gold fringes, ermine wraps, staffs of office. And inside, all is empty, there is no soul, no heart, no mind.

Sartorism is the image of pretense – a society of mountebanks, a puppetshow world with a fat face pretending that it is rational and ordered. It gains its effect by unhinging the subject from the context that gave it significance, which produces an intellectual weightlessness, the body having been disengaged from the gravity of the mind. The lawyer is merely certain prescribed sounds, the colonel certain disconnected motions. It is like looking through a glass partition at people dancing, where one sees the movement of the dance without the music, or like hearing one end of a telephone conversation, or describing a football game as a gang war between twenty-two stuffed men for possession of the inflated skin of an animal. One gets the same effect in the device of the noble savage looking on the corruptions of European society, for example, the king of Brobdingnag or the master Houyhnhnm. Instead of a meaningful flow of action one sees a series of consecutive events without connection because the apparent rational order and purpose have been removed. At times, the movement might seem to take on significance, but that is a coincidence. It is a world of infinite coincidence where anything might happen, where everything is equally important and equally absurd, because it is without intellect or morality or direction.

This device of unhinging the act from its meaning is very common in satire, though frequently combined with other images of the irrational. The Low-heels and High-heels of the Lilliputians, the rope-dancing, the creeping under the stick, are variations of the same technique. Politics becomes a mad ballet, a sequence of movements inappropriate to the goal it intends and therefore without rational connection. The satiric force of sartorism is in the fact that human beings have become certain unconnected noises and movements and objects. Beyond that there is nothing.

Another aspect of sartorism is Swift's satire on language. The corruption of language is a frequent theme of his writings. He satirizes language not because of man's inability to express meaning, but because there is an absence of meaning, and worse, because the absence of meaning itself is hailed as significance. 'Words are but wind; and learning is nothing but words; ergo, learning is nothing but wind'. This is why the wise Aeolists of *A Tale of a Tub* affirmed 'the gift of BELCHING to be the noblest act of a rational creature'. By a direct line from the alimentary canal, the belch becomes the height of Aeolist eloquence. And this is divine light. Another example of the emptiness of language is its use as ceremonial. 'Most mighty Emperor of Lilliput, delight and terror of the universe, whose dominions extend five thousand blustrugs (about twelve miles in circumference) to the extremities of the globe . . . taller than the sons of men, whose feet press down to the centre), and whose head strikes against the sun', and so on. Of course, this is a comment on the absurdity of courtly ceremonials and human majesty. But the words themselves are nonsense, and yet nonsense becomes the thing itself, the power of majesty. Sometimes the words become the people, just as the clothes of sartorism become the man. The jargon of the lawyer, the doctor and the pedant, is meaningless in itself, and yet they are identified by the jargon, it is their idiom – they live and practise by it, they are the jargon. There is nothing else. In his *Compleat Collection of Genteel and Ingenious Conversation*, Swift glorifies the platitude :

The flowers of wit, fancy, wisdom, humour, and politeness, scattered in this volume, amount to one thousand seventy and four. Allowing them to every gentleman and lady thirty visiting families (not insisting upon fractions) there will want but little of an hundred polite questions, answers, replies, rejoinders, repartees, and remarks to be daily delivered fresh in every company for twelve solar months; and even this is a higher pitch of delicacy than the world insists on, or hath reason to expect.

One is obliged to use words, and for a consideration you may rent a collection in the latest fashion, such as the following :

> Lady Answerall. Pray my Lord, did you walk through the Park
>   in this Rain?
> Lord Sparkish. Yes, Madam, we were neither Sugar, nor Salt,
>   we were not afraid the Rain would melt us, He, he, he.
> Colonel. It rained, and the Sun shone at the same Time.
> Neverout. Why, then the Devil was beating his Wife behind
>   the Door with a Shoulder of Mutton.

The advantages of a marketable platitude are considerable. By a simple commercial operation a man who has no fashionable words and therefore no fashionable identity can become a man of wit. What is more, the words are easily interchangeable, and therefore the identity of the speakers is interchangeable. They can abandon their own identity and become fashionably faceless.

The emptiness of language is one of the main targets of *A Tale of a Tub*. The numerous dedications and prefaces of the *Tale*, parodying John Dryden, become the empty ceremonials, the outer shell of literature, and therefore, according to sartorism, the important part. The highest reach of the aspiring intellect in the *Tale* is a gap in the manuscript, 'Hic multa desiderantur'. In the *Tale's* conclusion, Swift makes his satire on language explicit : 'I am now trying an experiment very frequent among modern authors; which is to write upon nothing; when the subject is utterly exhausted, to let the pen still move on; by some called the ghost of wit, delighting to walk after the death of its body.' The inhabitants of Swift's irrational world have discovered the secret of talking and writing and saying nothing. They say nothing because they have nothing to say, because they do not know how to think, because they have no mind and no soul. They are sartorists, mere collections of borrowed words, empty forms, meaningless jargon. It is an image that seems to have haunted Swift's imagination : a bustling, vigorous puppet world, with no meaning beyond the words or the clothes or the gestures, only the frightening emptiness inside.

Sartorism shows the absurdity and chaos of Swift's world of unreason. But Swift has also directed his satire at reason itself, that is, man's reason, sublunary reason, as distinct from divine reason. In fact, his concern about man's pretensions to reason evoked some of the most powerful satire of all his works. His frequent use of chop-logic, his numerous attacks on philosophical systems that pretend to explain the universe, the powerfully logical constructions of a work like 'A Modest Proposal', suggest how much Swift has been obsessed by the nature of man's reason. It is a critical commonplace that once one accepts the assumption of 'A Modest Proposal', that a man's value can be determined in pounds, shillings and pence, the conclusion is inevitable that children who have no other commercial value might profitably be sent to the butcher shop. It is a completely rational construction,

G

except for the premise, and the premise is not susceptible to the usual dictates of reason; it is a matter of good and evil. There is an obvious ambiguity here. Reason, in Swift's time, is still God's gift to man, the candle of the Lord. Through right reason one may distinguish good from evil. But in 'On the Trinity' Swift has also said,

Let any Man but consider, when he hath a Controversy with another, although his Cause be ever so unjust, although the World be against him, how blinded he is by the Love of himself, to believe that right is wrong, and wrong is right, when it maketh for his own Advantage. Where is the right Use of his Reason, which he so much boasteth of, and which he would blasphemously set up to controul the Commands of the Almighty?

'Reason itself,' he added, 'is true and just, but the Reason of every particular Man is weak and wavering, perpetually swayed and turned by his Interests, his Passions, and his Vices.' 'He who hath no Faith, cannot, by the Strength of his own Reason or Endeavours, so easily resist Temptations, as the other who dependeth upon God's Assistance in the overcoming of his Frailties. . . .' 'There is no solid, firm Foundation of Virtue, but in a Conscience directed by the Principles of Religion' ('Testimony of Conscience'). Swift's attack on reason was against the growing influence of Cartesian philosophy, manifesting itself in so many aspects of society that his whole world seemed threatened. Deism was spreading. The element of mystery, the essence of the religious spirit, was being undermined. The sense of sin, man's depravity, in many respects the foundation of Christianity, was giving way to sentimentalism and the belief in man's innate goodness. The conception of reason as a means for reaching certainty, as the touchstone for truth, a reason that will accept no limits, seemed to be at the core of the scientific method of the Royal Society. Beyond this was the growing secularization of society, with man's reason and God's reason becoming more and more estranged. In his satire Swift continually fought against a reason that disengaged itself from God. He attacked Hobbes, Descartes, the Royal Society, the Deists – even the Latitudinarians' faith was too rational for Swift. His satires on learning in *A Tale of a Tub*, in *Martinus Scriblerus*, and in *Gulliver's Travels* show the madness of man's reason. But it is in the careful, orderly structure of the 'Argument Against Abolishing Christianity', and 'A Modest Proposal' that we feel the full strength of his satire. The horror of 'A Modest Proposal' is not simply in showing how to increase the national income by the sale of baby meat, but in the fact that the *persona*, the economic projector, has a clear calm, orderly mind and that he symbolizes a clear, calm, orderly society, and in the awareness that a society can actually be run smoothly and efficiently with all the ingenuity of man's God-given reason, and without a soul. It is the society of *Brave New World* and *1984* and of the Hell of *Paradise Lost*. In 'A Modest Proposal' reason has taken on a surrealistic intensity, the rational world has become a nightmare world, reason has become unreason – and from the point of view of reason itself. The treachery of man's reason concerned Swift in all his writings because it undermined the basis of his Anglican rationalism.

In this description of Swift's world, unreason takes two main forms, disorder and perverted order, the chicken with its head cut off, and the professor with his head on, the Bedlam of *A Tale of a Tub*, and the nightmare of 'A Modest Proposal'. The one has no mind and no soul, with the strange sensation of there being only an outside to things and nothing inside. Soul becomes body, people become objects – a puppet-world conversing endlessly on a disconnected telephone. The other also has no soul, but is carefully organized, logical and dedicated. Its telephone is disconnected too, but the conversations are short and to the point. Both are images of madness. That is, in Swift's satiric world man is mad whether he uses his reason or not, if he is not connected to God. Madness is the sign of man's original depravity, a depravity of the mind, and without God it shows. The point of Swift's satire is to present man isolated from his God, in the fly-blown consequences of his depravity, empty, babbling, or in sinister pursuit of the wrong things. Swift continually presses home the fact of man's depravity. Whatever small pittance of reason man has, the master Houyhnhnm points out, is used to aggravate man's natural corruptions, and to acquire new ones which nature had not given him. Even where by some miraculous means, a model of moral behaviour is provided, as in Lilliput, the result is still depravity. 'In relating these and the following laws,' Gulliver explains, 'I would only be understood to mean the original institutions, and not the most scandalous corruptions into which people are fallen by the degenerate nature of man.' That is why, in this model Lilliputian society, 'the disbelief of a Divine Providence renders a man uncapable of holding any public station'. There are many illustrations from Swift's non-satiric writings to show that for him the depravity of man is also a depravity of the mind, that reason alone is not sufficient. Kathleen Williams[1] has already done the job effectively. Fear and hope, Swift said in the 'Testimony of Conscience', not reason, are the two greatest motives of all men's actions. Man is so constituted, he said in the 'Excellency of Christianity', that virtue cannot be its own reward. Man must be rewarded if he is to be virtuous. The Houyhnhnm thought differently: 'Nature and reason were sufficient guides for a reasonable animal', as men pretended to be. But one of the intentions of *Gulliver's Travels*, Swift said in a letter to Pope, was to show that man was not a reasonable animal, like the Houyhnhnm, he was only capable of reason. Man's passions, his self-love, are the facts of man's existence, and they cannot be overcome effectively except by a reason guided by conscience, by faith in God. Even great moralists like Socrates, one of Swift's favourites, do not escape this judgment.

For such a wisdom as theirs cannot descend from above, but must be earthly, sensual, devilish; full of confusion and every evil work: Whereas the wisdom from above, is first pure, then peaceable, gentle, and easy to be intreated, full of mercy and good fruits, without partiality, and without hypocrisy.

We generally accept the view now that the Houyhnhnms, the true *animales rationales*, are not a model for man to follow. But many commentators have gone to the other extreme, suggesting that since the Houyhnhnms appear absurd they are being satirized. This is another example of forgetting that satire is a literary art, and looking on it as history or philosophy or biography. Within the literary framework of *Gulliver's Travels*, the Houyhn-hnms are obviously an ideal. If we can accept the fact that Gulli-ver is sane in loathing the Yahoos, he must be equally sane in admiring the Houyhnhnms. They are a metaphor, just as the Yahoos are a metaphor, illustrating a rational order, disarmingly simple and innocent. Their reason is intuitive – not angelic in-tuition, because theirs is obviously fallible, but the intuition of creatures uncomplicated by human passions and the general human predicament. They appear ridiculous, at times; of course they do, because they are horses acting as men. Even if their way of life were as ideal as the Utopian elements of Lilliput they would be ridiculous. Occasionally, they are also too positive in their ignorance, because even here Swift cannot miss the opportunity of showing that reason without God is fallible, that Yahoo-men who pretend to this reason are fools. We must remember, though, that the simplicity of the Houyhnhnms' life has always been a wistful dream for Swift. We get something of this simplicity in the Utopian element of the Brobdingnagians. For men of Swift's temperament it was one of the forlorn ideals lost among the shifting values of an age that made reason itself suspect. But as a satiric device, the Houyhnhnms are a positive to the Yahoo nega-tive. They are a useful stick to measure the depth of Yahoo cor-ruption, and a vivid comment on the fact that man is not a rational animal, that in his natural state he cannot live the life of reason, because he is depraved.

More than any other of his satires, *Gulliver's Travels* makes explicit the fact of man's depravity. In a general way Books I to III present the two forms of unreason – the depravity of the mind – that have been discussed above. Book I is an image of a manikin world where little creatures perform their absurdities, creatures so small that we are more aware of the actions than the humanity performing them. They have become merely external. They have almost literally lost their identity in the postures they have assumed. One of the main images of Book II is the grotesque spectacle of man's body, the grossness and weight of the flesh, soulless and mindless. The Brobdingnagian king, of course, is another matter. As suggested above, he represents the moral simplicity of the noble savage observing from his great height the devious antics of European society, so that the actions become extracted from their context – a series of gestures with the logical sequence removed. Both devices demonstrate the sartorist side of Swift's image of unreason, the madness of a world where there are only externals. This interpretation does not pretend to dispose of Books I and II. They are also images of how monstrous yet insignificant man is, a metaphoric comment on man's depravity. Book III, for the most part, is a series of projects and experiments, perverted order, the runaway flight of man's sublunary reason. The result is not so intense as in 'A Modest Proposal', but a flying brainpan on a field of excrement is a discouraging escutcheon.

The first three books of *Gulliver's Travels* give us the image of a world of unreason, in all its aspects. Book IV is the comment on this world; the Yahoo, which from the opening pages drops its dung on Gulliver, methodically becomes more and more identified with Gulliver, becomes more and more loathsome and repulsive as it is compared with the Houyhnhnms, and finally is equated with the whole of Swift's world. It is the logical conclusion to the madness of the first three books, because this is the irrational element, the thing itself, the horrible shape of man's depravity which, in Swift's satiric world, has taken possession of man and has become, in fact, indistinguishable from man. The full flood of Swift's excremental imagery is used to describe the Yahoo, and consequently, Yahoo-man. Here is the third element of Swift's imagery, the excremental, which for most of us is Swift's trademark.

Since Swift's constant concern in his satires is man's corruption from original innocence, there is no more graphic illustration than the excremental. That is why his satires are obsessed with it. It is the traditional imagery of evil, of which Swift's contemporaries were well aware. This has been demonstrated by many critics. Roland M. Frye[2] quotes a passage from Swift's cousin and biographer, Deane Swift, referring to the Yahoos as 'the deformity,

the blackness, the filthiness, and corruptio⟨…⟩
inable vices, which inflame the wrath of ⟨…⟩
of disobedience'. All Swift's references t⟨…⟩
dung, the stench, the filth of man's body, ⟨…⟩
sin. This is the climactic image of evil, the ⟨…⟩
which all of Swift's satire is pointed, the s⟨…⟩
wants his readers to see and take note. ⟨…⟩
this imagery is found in many of the se⟨…⟩
poraries. It may be argued, perhaps, that ⟨…⟩
following the same path as Swift the clergyman. But there is remarkably little of this kind of imagery in Swift's sermons. They
are carefully reasoned and restrained. As a clergyman, he is defending a post, he said in 'Thoughts on Religion' : the Anglican
rationalism to which he had given allegiance. But Swift the satirist and man is not so restrained, and consequently not so rational.
Satire does not justify the ways of God to man; it concludes in an
image of evil. Evil dominates and triumphs. It dwells on the
limitations of man's condition, the evil in all men, including Swift
himself. This image of evil haunts Swift's satire to the point of
obsession. When Gulliver turns in revulsion from the Yahoo spectacle of man, this turning may be a form of madness, but we see
the same pattern in Swift's so-called misogynist poems. In 'The
Lady's Dressing Room', Strephon perceives the filth of the divine
Celia :

> But Vengeance, goddess never sleeping,
> Soon punish'd Strephon for his peeping :
> His foul imagination links
> Each dame he sees with all her stinks;
> And, if unsavoury odours fly,
> Conceives a lady standing by.

The logic of these poems is that we should accept corruption
as the fact of our existence. But the revulsion remains. It seems
to reflect Swift's own revulsion, at all mankind, including himself, his sense of sin and unworthiness as he contemplates the
enormous cleavage between man undefiled and man in the grossness of the flesh. His own involvement in his satire is expressed

...y, though secularized, by one of his favourite writers,
...efoucauld :

...ing can give us so just a Notion of the Depravity of Mankind
...general, as an exact Knowledge of our own Corruptions in particular. If we reflect upon our Thoughts, we shall find the Seeds of
all those Vices within our own Breasts, which we condemn in others.
And if we do not act it all, yet 'tis plain we are moved to it all. For
there is no kind of ill but Self-Love offers to us to make Use of as
Occasion shall serve. And few are so Vertuous as to be above
Temptation.

Swift's own comment on his sense of sin is more passionate :
'Miserable mortals! Can we contribute to the honour and glory
of God? I could wish that expression were struck out of our
Prayer-books' ('Thoughts on Religion').

Swift frequently stresses the wretchedness of life, which he links
with man's depravity. Perhaps the most vivid example is the
Struldbrugs. The universal dream of perpetual life becomes in
the Struldbrugs one of the bitterest ironies of literature. All the infirmities of life have been congealed into one grotesque image,
Swift's satiric comment on human existence, a metaphor of night-
marish proportions to show what it means to be alive. They were
condemned, Gulliver said, without any fault of their own, to a
perpetual continuance in the world. Among the people of Luggnagg, the appetite for living was not so eager. Another familiar
example is from 'Thoughts on Religion' : 'Although reason were
intended by providence to govern our passions, yet it seems that,
in two points of the greatest moment to the being and continuance
of the world, God hath intended our passions to prevail over reason. The first is, the propagation of our species. . . . The other is,
the love of life, which, from the dictates of reason, every man
would despise, and wish it at an end, or that it never had a beginning.' Two more illustrations will suffice. 'I hate life when I
think it exposed to such accidents . . . it makes me think God did
never intend life for a blessing.' This is from the *Journal to Stella*
[Letter VII, Dec. 19, 1712]. And as an old man in 1738 he
wrote to Mrs. Whiteway that he made a habit of reading the

third chapter of Job on his birthdays, cursing the day wherein he
was born.

In dwelling on man's fallen nature Swift asserts his Christian
orthodoxy. But Swift's satire is not merely an affirmation of faith.
Man's depravity and the wretchedness of life obsess him in his
satires, not in his sermons, in his satiric world where evil is triumphant. In a world where evil dominates, the implicit question is:
why must this be so? It is the question asked by Job in the chapter that Swift supposedly read every birthday: 'Why is light
given to a man whose way is hid, and whom God hath hedged in?'
This questioning is a protest, a rebellion against God. Like Job,
Swift had two alternatives. He could either curse God and die, or
accept the fact that life is incomprehensible and turn to God in
order to endure. Like Job, Swift turned to God.

Swift's satire arises from a sense of sin and from the painful
awareness of human existence. It does not cure many vices, or
mend many worlds, but by presenting the image of man's depravity it protests the ways of God to man with all the passion of his
faith.

S o u r c e : *Bucknell Review,* xiii (1965) pp. 11–25.

NOTES

1. Kathleen Williams, *Jonathan Swift and the Age of Compromise*
(Lawrence, Kansas, 1958).
2. Roland M. Frye, 'Swift's Yahoo and the Christian Symbols for
Sin', *Journal of the History of Ideas*, xv (1954) pp. 201–17.

W. E. Yeomans

THE HOUYHNHNM AS MENIPPEAN
HORSE (1966)

Book IV of *Gulliver's Travels* has become a battleground for two
opposing armies of critics in this century. On one side are the
critics who take the traditional view of the Houyhnhnms (a view
which flourished almost unquestioned in the nineteenth century),
solemnly seeing them as ideal creatures, and on the other side
are the critics who see the Houyhnhnms as ironic. Among others,
George Sherburn, W. A. Eddy, J. Middleton Murry, A. E. Case,
Charles Peake, and Ricardo Quintana have written in terms of,
or in direct defense of, the traditional view. The battle line is not
always clearly drawn; Martin Price and W. B. Ewald seem to
hold the traditional view, but they tend to see some irony in
Swift's portrayal of the Houyhnhnms. And Quintana's later discussion of the Houyhnhnms in *Swift: an introduction* (1954)
differs in a vital way from his earlier discussion in *The Mind and
Art of Jonathan Swift* (1936; reprinted 1953). In the later book
Quintana wonders whether he should be quite so solemn about
the Houyhnhnms: 'there are moments when we have to ask ourselves whether our imaginary voyage is not becoming a parody of
itself – whether, for instance, the Utopian elements are not slyly
humorous.'

   T. O. Wedel was the first to question the traditional view of the
Houyhnhnms in our century, and many critics have followed him.
Ernest Tuveson, Kathleen Williams, and Samuel H. Monk see
the Houyhnhnms as representing an ironic ideal ill-suited to the
emulation of men; John F. Ross believes that Swift intended the
Houyhnhnms to appear ridiculous, and Samuel Kliger argues

that Swift was demonstrating the absurdity of perfectionism in terms of the Houyhnhnms. Then there are the critics, among them Irvin Ehrenpreis, Martin Kallich, and Calhoun Winton, who see the Houyhnhnms as ironic mainly because they appear to represent a deistic outlook upon life.

There are very strong arguments on both sides, and it is most unlikely that resolution of the conflict will ever come about through the breakdown of one side or the other. Fortunately there is another way to bring about resolution, and the exploration of that way is the purpose of this essay.

Northrop Frye, in *Anatomy of Criticism* makes the very important point that *Gulliver's Travels* should not be judged as a novel but as fiction written within the conventions of Menippean satire. Many of the characteristics of Menippean satire which Frye cites one can easily discover in *Gulliver's Travels* : such characteristics as the free play of intellectual fancy and the practice of dealing with mental attitudes rather than with people as such; the loosejointed, digressing narrative; the ridicule of the *philosophus gloriosus*; and the use of the dialogue for the interplay of ideas or attitudes.

In addition, *Gulliver's Travels* is in that long-standing tradition of fantastic travel tales told by a brilliant liar which have as their progenitor Lucian's *A True Story*. In fact the essential idea for Gulliver's visit to Glubbdubdrib is probably borrowed from the visit to the Isle of the Blest in Lucian's *A True Story*. Furthermore, the philosophic outlook of the Cynics can often be detected in Menippean satires including those of Lucian, who was heavily influenced by Menippus himself – a student of the Cynic Metrocles. The extreme asceticism of the Cynics, their heavy emphasis upon a simple, virtuous life, and their tendency to be scornful of commonly accepted standards of social behavior are very deeply a part of *Gulliver's Travels*.

All of these things lead to the conviction that *Gulliver's Travels* is written in a tradition which is distinctly different from that of the novel. The characters in a novel tend to be naturalistically portrayed, whereas characters in Menippean satires like *A True Story*, *Gargantua*, *Candide*, and *Gulliver's Travels* are stylized, for they are subservient devices conveying ideas, theories, or general attitudes. When tight laws of character and story plausibility are lifted, the author of a Menippean satire can more effectively carry out his main purpose – the expression of intellectual concepts. As a result we can never expect to be enchanted by 'living' characters in this form of literature; instead, we can anticipate being overwhelmed by amazing erudition, by massive catalogues of social follies, by extravagant elaborations upon professional abuses, by fantastic caricatures of certain people or certain types of people, and by other dazzling displays.

Robert C. Elliott argues very effectively against the tendency of readers to interpret *Gulliver's Travels* from a novel-oriented point of view.[1] He demonstrates that Swift pays little regard to psychological consistency, and that Lemuel Gulliver is now one type of person and now another. 'Gulliver is, in fact, an abstraction manipulated in the service of satire. To say this of the principal character of a novel would be damning, but to say it of a work written according to the conventions of Lucian's *A True Story*, *Gargantua*, *The Satyricon*, is simply to describe.'

Perhaps this battle has been won, for many critics today are willing to accept this view of Gulliver. Not all of them refrain from treating other aspects of *Gulliver's Travels* from a novel-oriented point of view, however – the Houyhnhnms, for example. And if we are to escape dead-end dissension over the Houyhnhnms, we must treat them, and the Yahoos, as Menippean characters.

Not only Gulliver, a single character, but groups of people, in addition to the Houyhnhnms, are adjustable according to satiric needs. The contrast between the original Utopian institutions of Lilliput and their state when Gulliver arrives there is extreme, and the brief paragraph which merely mentions their degeneration is adequate only for a work in which realistic character depiction is far from being a main concern. In Book III the Laputans are first depicted as introverted theoreticians of music and mathematics almost totally incapable of coping with practical affairs. Later they become the opposite – shrewd, tyrannous politicians exploiting their neighbors below with the flying island (itself an incongruous, masterful feat of practical engineering). Swift saw a chance to use the Laputans for two different satirical purposes and he did so, allowing satiric concepts to take full priority over consistent, realistic character depiction. There is no special merit in this in itself; the point is that we should allow the writer of a Menippean satire a kind of 'poetic licence' in this regard as long as it serves his main purpose well.

Like the Laputans, and like Gulliver, the Houyhnhnms are flexible agents or abstractions subservient to intellectual purposes, and, as such, they can be allowed to have two different functions to perform for Swift, functions which, at first sight, might seem to be incompatible. They have a solemn function to perform (which critics holding the traditional view of the Houyhnhnms understand very well), and they also have a burlesque or comic function to perform (which critics who see the Houyhnhnms as ironic creatures understand very well).

If we study the solemn function of the Houyhnhnms in relation to *Gulliver's Travels* as a whole, we find that there is much that coaches us towards acceptance of the Houyhnhnms' ascetic Utopia. The excellence of Houyhnhnm reasoning is based strictly upon a supreme comprehension of virtue and morality and clear perceptions about simple practicality, rather than brilliant ratiocination or any kind of dazzling sophistication. Their kind of reasoning is 'recommended' in each book of *Gulliver's Travels*. In Book I the original and Utopian institutions of Lilliput have many points in common with Houyhnhnm institutions. In Book II the learning of the Brobdingnagians consists 'only in Morality, History, Poetry, and Mathematicks, wherein they must be allowed to excel'.[2] Like the Houyhnhnms they are ignorant of abstract theory and lead simple, practical lives.

We find the same practical, unadventurous outlook in Lord Munodi in Book III, and cannot fail to notice how superior the outlook is made to appear when contrasted with the adventurous, experimental chaos of Lagado and the metaphysical void of Laputa. In Book III we learn not only to love the simple, practical view of life, but to despise all abstract thought and all technical innovation which necessity is not the mother of. Book III as a whole represents the extreme pole of rejection (i.e. a way of life most objectionable because it is the worst conceivable) in *Gulliver's Travels*, just as the Houyhnhnms represent the extreme pole of acceptance (i.e. a way of life most acceptable because it is the best conceivable), even though Swift personally might not have gone all the way with these extremes. An author may often find that his fiction, especially satiric fiction, requires extremes of conflict which he himself would not hold to in everyday life.

Thirty years ago it would not have been necessary to affirm that Swift's depiction of the Houyhnhnms contains much that is to be regarded solemnly as Utopian, but so many critics of our day have seen them as anti-Utopian, that counter-arguments are necessary.

The descriptions throughout *Gulliver's Travels* of the corruption and misery brought about by proud, ambitious leaders, unfaithful or luxury-mad wives, doting parents, greedy entrepreneurs, unscrupulous professional men, etc. who are governed by ruling passions, lead the reader towards an acceptance of the ascetic but harmonious world of the Houyhnhnms ruled by reason. The Struldbrugs prompt us to reject a desire for an earthly immortality and prepare us for an acceptance of the Houyhnhnms' serene attitude towards death. Such serenity may be impossible for men, but it is the ideal way – the extreme pole of acceptance – rather than an attainable goal.

Gulliver's description of the delightful, and wise, parlour-conversation of the Houyhnhnms is amusing and, in some ways, suggests burlesque. And yet the situation has its solemn side too. The pleasant harmony of their conversation and the complete absence of all rigid ceremony seems an excellent demonstration of certain principles and suggestions to be found in those essays by Swift entitled *On Good Manners and Good Breeding* and *Hints Towards an Essay on Conversation*.

'Temperance, Industry, Exercise, and Cleanliness' are things that Swift himself respected just as much as the Houyhnhnms do. And Gulliver's Houyhnhnm master thinks it monstrous to give 'the Females a different Kind of Education from the Males, except in some Articles of Domestic Management; whereby, as he truly observed, one Half of our Natives were good for nothing but bringing Children into the World : And to trust the Care of their Children to such useless Animals, he said, was yet a greater Instance of Brutality' [*GT*, p. 253]. Behind these solemn lines there is an equally solemn Swift, for we find a similar attitude towards female education, not only in the Utopian section of Book 1, but also in Swift's unfinished essay entitled *Of the Education of Ladies*.

In the face of all this can there be any doubt that Swift intended the Houyhnhnms to represent, at least in part, solemn models of behaviour truly worthy of the emulation of men?

The purpose of the solemn function of the Houyhnhnms is the portrayal of the good life towards which all men would tend to move if they consulted reason more and passion less. The Houyhnhnm idea is impossible for men to achieve and rightly so, for ideals give permanent direction to men, not attainable, and therefore temporary, goals.

In using the Menippean satire form to convey Utopian concepts Swift is not really departing from the tradition, for Utopian stories in general owe a big debt to Menippean satire, especially to Lucian's *A True Story*; Sir Thomas More's *Utopia*, for example, adopts the form of the satiric, fantastic travel tale and adapts it to a much more solemn purpose.

Those who agree that positive Utopian ideals are depicted through the Houyhnhnms, but who reject any comic interpretation of the Houyhnhnms, are probably applying principles which are appropriate to the novel. But since *Gulliver's Travels* is a Menippean satire, its characters are subservient to its Utopian and satirical ideas rather than to any rigid principles of consistent character portrayal. Granted this, it should not be difficult to allow a combination of solemn and comic functions in the Houyhnhnms. The satirical purpose of the comic function of the Houyhnhnms, more like burlesque than any other type of comedy, is to assault pride in men by means of shock, humiliation, insult, embarrassment, invective, and, most devastating of all, the laughter which inevitably accompanies good burlesque.

The entire burlesque hinges very delicately upon pure shapes –

the man-shape as compared with the horse-shape. In Houyhn-hnmland the usual man–horse relationships are inverted satirically, and the satire is further accentuated by making the horse-over-man superiority of Houyhnhnmland far greater than the man-over-horse superiority of Europe. The Houyhnhnms' comments upon Gulliver's 'inferior' man-shape, for example, are burlesque remarks, and should not be read in any sense solemnly; it would be all too easy to demolish this aspect of Houyhnhnm wisdom and superiority.

When Gulliver first meets the Houyhnhnms, the man-shape image is subjected to humiliation as Gulliver is forced to neigh like a horse in order to be understood, instead of using his 'barbarous English'. But the satire goes far beyond humiliation and embarrassment into the realm of shock when we learn that Gulliver makes his shoes and covers his boat with the man-shaped Yahoo hides instead of horse-hide.

Not only are Yahoo skins used in place of horse skins, but the man-shaped creatures take over all the duties assigned to horses in Europe. The sight of several man-shaped Yahoos pulling a sledge while the horse-shaped creatures sit with dignity in carriages and wield a masterful whip, is pure burlesque. The Houyhnhnms are not at all models of behavior in these scenes, they function here only as agents of burlesque attack upon man's pride.

Burlesque elements and solemn elements are sometimes subtly interlaced in Book IV, and at other times whole sections are given over to one or the other. The latter half of chapter 9 and the latter half of chapter 8 are given over to solemn praise of the noble Houyhnhnm race, and the burlesque side all but disappears. But Gulliver's diatribe-description of Europe in chapters 5 and 6, bitter as it is, is almost exclusively shocking burlesque – an insulting caricature of a whole race. Caricatures of individuals and groups are very much a part of Menippean satire, and they abound in the works of Lucian and Rabelais. The scene, already cited, where Gulliver listens in awe to the wise parlour-conversation of a group of Houyhnhnms sitting on their haunches, is an excellent example of the way the solemn and the burlesque ele-

ments can work together. The Houyhnhnms are truly admirable
in this scene even though the sight of horses outdoing a man in
the parlour is both humorous and humiliating.

The main shock of Book iv is the burlesque equation between
man and Yahoo which underlies the last three chapters. We begin to build towards this burlesque equation early in Book iv
when Gulliver and a Yahoo are placed side by side and the
similarities noted. Then, after Gulliver's diatribe-description of
Europe, the Houyhnhnm master describes, almost point for
point, similar peculiar practices among the Yahoos. Finally, when
Gulliver is sexually attacked by a female Yahoo, the burlesque
equation between man and Yahoo is complete, and the burlesque
(as opposed to the solemn) superiority of horse-shaped creatures
over man-shaped creatures is fixed for ever in Gulliver's mind.
Thereafter Gulliver has only contempt for those with man-shaped
bodies, no matter how good they are.

When I thought of my Family, my Friends, my Countrymen, or
human Race in general, I considered them as they really were,
Yahoos in Shape and Disposition, perhaps a little more civilized,
and qualified with the Gift of Speech, but making no other Use of
Reason than to improve and multiply those Vices, whereof their
Brethren in this Country had only the Share that Nature allotted
them [*GT*, p. 262].

When passages such as this are treated as though they were part
of a naturalistic novel instead of a Menippean satire, there tends
to be excessive concern about Gulliver's madness and his grossly
unfair, oversimplified portrait of the human race. Gulliver here
is merely the vehicle for an extravagant burlesque attack which
takes up almost all of the three climactic concluding chapters and
which is continued in 'A Letter From Capt. Gulliver to His
Cousin Sympson'.

When Gulliver sees his own form reflected in a lake or foun-
tain, he turns away in 'horror and detestation', perhaps to
practise the 'Gait and Gesture' of a horse, and feels greatly
complimented if someone tells him he trots like a horse. Plainly,
all solemnity has departed here, and we are being 'needled' by

Swift. Sometimes the needle goes very deep; for example, when Gulliver is about to leave Houyhnhnmland, he is overcome with gratitude because his Houyhnhnm master not only allows him to kiss his hoof, but brings it up to Gulliver's mouth.

The frequently repeated judgement of this last episode, that the Houyhnhnm is guilty of pride here, is true as a solemn view of the matter. But this comic episode is one hundred per cent burlesque, and solemn views of it are out of place. It is also often argued that the kind and generous Don Pedro is as good morally as the Houyhnhnms, and many have argued that he is much better. Once again the argument is beside the point, for we are dealing with a burlesque satirical attack. The vital factor is the fact that Don Pedro is man-shaped and not horse-shaped. We are supposed to be shocked, embarrassed, humiliated, and in-sulted as we realize that even the cleanest and most virtuous of our kind give off bad odors and seem grossly inferior when com-pared with the magnificence of those who are horse-shaped. Looking at them solemnly, we can see a big difference between Don Pedro and a Yahoo, but we are supposed to go along with a burlesque satire which is based upon the fantasy that any man returning from Houyhnhnmland would find all man-shaped creatures hideous and all horse-shaped creatures beautiful, and to find ourselves properly chastened and pride-purged by the mockery of it all.

The combination of solemn and burlesque elements in Book IV, far from being incompatible, support and reinforce each other. Even in the most laughable Houyhnhnm situation the other side of these creatures, their solemn side, is there to haunt us and accentuate the satire, for we recognize that the superiority of the Houyhnhnms is not always a burlesque superiority. Con-versely, the burlesque side of the Houyhnhnms prevents their solemn side from becoming oppressively solemn at any time.

Critics, in this novel-oriented age, tend to think that the Houyhnhnms must fulfil one role or another, but not several roles. Swift, with satiric ideas and Utopian concepts uppermost in his mind, allowed his characters to be altogether subservient to his intellectual purposes – and had much Menippean precedent behind him. Because of this, the Houyhnhnms are sometimes solemn models of the good life, sometimes vehicles for satiric burlesque attack, and sometimes a combination of both.

If Book IV, as well as the other books of *Gulliver's Travels*, is studied for what it is – Menippean satire – we will recognize that its unity and strength are based upon an intellectual vision of morality and technology, and that its characters are idea-spectrums rather than likenesses of flesh and blood. We will also recognize that there is much truth on both sides of the Houyhnhnm debate, and that these truths are not incompatible, even though they sometimes appear to be.

S O U R C E : *College English*, XXVII (1966) pp. 449–54.

NOTES

1. *The Power of Satire* (Princeton, 1960) p. 200.
2. *The Prose Works of Jonathan Swift*, ed. H. Davis, *Gulliver's Travels*, XI (1941) p. 120.

M. M. Kelsall

ITERUM HOUYHNHNM: SWIFT'S SEXTUMVIRATE AND THE HORSES (1969)

There has been little support for the argument that Swift's horses represented for him an ideal of conduct which he believed to be humanly possible. Pedro de Mendez is a more sympathetic figure than Gulliver's austere Houyhnhnm master. The admiration of Gulliver, a fallible *homme moyen sensuel*, for the horses is suspect. Even if the horses are ideal, their virtues are super-human. There is, moreover, something about them that savours of the ridiculous.[1] Although in his picture of undegenerate Lilliput, in Brobdingnag and in Houyhnhnmland Swift betrays a tendency to exhibit 'Utopian' societies, his wit and irony make it difficult to judge if he is in earnest. However, there is one ideal picture in the *Travels* which even the most sophisticated critic would find difficult to read ironically, and it can tell us much about Swift's attitude to the horses. On the island of the sorcerers Gulliver summoned up the spirits of the mighty dead. He recorded tersely: 'I had the Honour to have much Conversation with *Brutus*; and was told that his Ancestor *Junius, Socrates, Epaminondas, Cato* the Younger, Sir *Thomas More* and himself, were perpetually together: A *Sextumvirate*, to which all the Ages of the World cannot add a Seventh.' [III, 7]

What was it that led Swift both to select these six men as his especial heroes, and to place them 'perpetually together' as if they shared some qualities in common? Can it be argued that their virtues are the same as those of the Houyhnhnms? If so, was Gulliver in Swift's view right to propose the horses as a model fit for imitation ?

That Swift's selection of the six was not entirely arbitrary may be shown by their appearance in company elsewhere in his works, and there are some hints of the virtues they embody. In a work typical of Swift in its moral polarity, the list *Of Mean and Great Figures Made by Several Persons*, among the great appear

Socrates, the whole last Day of his Life, and particularly from the Time he took the Poison to the Moment he expired.

Epaminondas when the Persian Ambassador came to his House and found him in the midst of Poverty.

Cato of Utica, when he provided for the Safety of his Friends and had determined to dy.

Sir Tho More during his Imprisonment, and at his Execution.

We are asked to admire three things: virtuous poverty (which to adopt the terminology of the Augustans, is part of true simplicity of life), benevolent (masculine) friendship, rational and tranquil death. That Swift was not arbitrary but was content rather to deal in traditional commonplaces, is further supported by the appearance in the list of complementary support from, for instance, Cincinnatus (virtuous poverty), Regulus (patriotic fearlessness at death), or Scipio refusing the beautiful captive (temperance).

Lucius Junius and Marcus Junius Brutus, who do not appear here, nonetheless clearly fit into the picture, for both were austere opponents of tyranny, men of patriotic and rational principles, unafraid of death. It is Marcus Junius' legendary contemptuous refusal of pardon and security from Octavian which is singled out for special praise by Swift in another work on mean and great figures, *The Contest and Dissensions in Athens and Rome* [ch. 3], thus linking him with Socrates, More or Regulus. Socrates, Epaminondas and Cato may be found enjoying each other's company in the Dedication of *A Tale of a Tub*, and appropriately so, for Epaminondas was for Swift 'a great imitator of Socrates',[2] and

Cato, in the most famous action of his life, his death, as Plutarch
tells, resolved to die after twice reading the *Phaedo*. Sir Thomas
More's stand in the face of kingly tyranny is an important theme
in Swift's *Concerning that Universal Hatred which Prevails
Against the Clergy*. The austerity, benevolence and tranquil
death of the man 'of the greatest virtue this kingdom ever produced' needs no emphasis. Finally, in a sermon balanced and
traditional, *Upon the Excellency of Christianity*, Socrates and
Cato are united as the two Ancients in whom the most celebrated
of Ancient virtues, fortitude and temperance, 'arrived at the
greatest height', their virtue engendered not by philosophical
sects, but by the 'good natural dispositions' of their minds. In Man
'the Perfection of Nature' (the meaning of the word Houyhnhnm) is to be like Cato and Socrates.

Beyond this point one must move from evidence to critical suggestion. To write in detail about the six would be to write a good
deal of the history of Western civilisation. It is precisely for this
reason, however, that they are important : because of the *general-
ity* of the qualities that they share in common. The rational virtue
of the sextumvirate (and the horses) was a commonplace. That
one important characteristic of Swift's heroes, their public virtue,
leading them either to tyrannicide or heroic martyrdom, cannot
be paralleled among the horses, only indicates that like Cicero's
Cato we are *tamquam in republica Platonis, et non in faece Ro-
muli* [*Ad Att.*, ii, i]. The horses, however, like the citizens of
the Republic (or Utopia) are complete patriots, for the individual will is the social will, and at least Gulliver warned that should
they be invaded, 'Their Prudence, Unanimity, Unacquainted-
ness with Fear, and their Love of their Country would amply
supply all Defects in the military Art' [ch. 12]. Fortunately
the Houyhnhnms do not need to demonstrate their patriotism.
That they are one community, however, is clear. Moreover, like
the sextumvirate, it can scarcely be denied that they possess fortitude and practise temperance and benevolence. It remains to be
determined whether the heroes and the horses would have understood the same things by these virtues.

In choosing his sextumvirate Swift was once again paying tribute to the Ancients. Five of them are historically so, and what is More if not the English Socrates, for both were men of simple lives, men of wit, creators of ideal societies, martyrs to tyranny? Similarly the social basis of the community of horses is Ancient. It has recently been argued that the 'Lycurgus' of Plutarch is a 'source' of the fourth voyage.[3] To come closer to the sextumvirate, *The Republic* of Plato and the *Utopia* of More (both influenced by Spartan ideals) have long been in the field. This is too narrow a basis, however. One might equally add republican Rome as idealised by the poets and historians. Lucius Junius Brutus established that republic, Marcus Junius Brutus assassinated Caesar to try to preserve it, Cato Uticensis became its embodiment, and the most famous tragedy of the English Augustan age, Addison's *Cato*, accepts that identification which had been a Roman commonplace.[4]

The land of the horses, like pristine republican Rome, is a society uncorrupted by that luxury, which coming after the conquest of Carthage and Greece brought riches and artistic culture to Rome, and debauched her – *saevior armis luxuria/incubuit victumque ulciscitur orbem* [Juvenal, vi, 292–3]. Gulliver knew the story, for it is the basis of his adverse comment on the Augustan age in the chapter following his vision of the sextumvirate. Like pristine Rome the land of the horses is a simple agricultural society. They inhabit the plainest of dwellings. Their diet is Pythagorean in its simplicity. They are strong of limb, but impoverished in culture, chaste, virtuous, austere. A fit inhabitant of Houyhnhnmland would be Cincinnatus the ploughman Dictator, a patriot with three acres, or Horace's stoical and temperate Ofellus, a poor tenant farmer held up to the rich as an example of virtue and wisdom. The ideal was a Roman and English commonplace. *Agricultura proxima Sapientiae* was Cicero's dictum quoted by Pope with approval to Peterborough [letter, 24 August 1732]. *Aude, hospes, contemnere opes* was Evander's advice to Aeneas taking him into his simple dwelling on the site of Rome [*Aen.*, viii, 364]. The words reduced Fénelon to tears, and roused Dryden translating Virgil 'to contemn the world'. That the austere and agricultural society of the horses has no use for money, drives no trade, builds no ships, would not have disturbed even the moderate Epicurean Horace. Neither Swift nor Pope gave much support to capitalistic merchant traders. Virgil, in praising the heroes of Rome in the sixth book of the *Aeneid*, mentions no artists by name. English primitivism outruns even the Roman when Swift's hero, Cato Uticensis, is introduced in the ninth of Lyttelton's *Dialogues of the Dead* [1760–5] inveighing against Augustan corruption and proclaiming, 'I would much rather have seen Rome under Fabricius and Curius, and her other honest old consuls *who could not read*' (my italics). One might add the historical propaganda of Livy or Tacitus (with his virtuous barbarians), Varro's *Rerum Rusticarum* or Virgil's *Georgics*. In England Mandeville would not have been provoked to write *The Fable of the Bees* [1714–29] had not the primitivistic tradition been well established. Add pristine Rome to Sparta, combine *The Republic* with *Utopia*, trace their influence through European history, and there is a 'receipt' for finding the 'source' of Houyhnhnmland.

Between them the heroes combine these traditional ideals, and there is nothing in their fortitude, temperance or public-spirited benevolence to suggest that they would not have found life among the horses congenial. Socrates, for instance, in his sweetness and wit is a more attractive figure than Gulliver's master, but his life was one of poverty, perhaps of extreme poverty, certainly one of austerity and simplicity, and it was his boast as Diogenes Laertius tells [II, 25], 'How much there is I do not need.' His temperance not only gave him fortitude as a soldier, but also traditionally preserved his health from the plague in Athens. Similarly, in Houyhnhnmland Gulliver enjoyed 'perfect Health of Body', and with this, in the philosophical tradition of *mens sana in corpore sano*, 'perfect . . . Tranquility of Mind' [ch. 10]. It was Socrates' tranquillity of mind which was admired by Swift at his death, his 'unruffled temper . . . unchanging mien, and the same cast of countenance in every condition of life' praised by Cicero [*De Off.*, I, xxvi, 90], and which could only come to one who realised how much there was he did not need. Temperance and fortitude were concomitant qualities, for the ideal of combining soundness of mind and body meant more than combining a first in Greats with a blue at cricket. Epaminondas hardened his body by exercise that he might be able to achieve that kind of greatness he reached in his last moments when retaining the spearhead in his side until the battle was won, he expired, *Satis, inquit, vixi, invictus enim morior* [Cornelius Nepos, *Epam.*, 9, 3]. (The horses too are strenuous athletes and celebrate their games Pindarically.) From Roper's *Life* Swift would have learnt of More's cheerfulness in privation in the Tower, which came only because More had accustomed himself to privation. Cato, in Addison's tragedy, is praised :

> While good, and just, and anxious for his friends,
> He's still severely bent against himself;
> Renouncing sleep, and rest, and food, and ease,
> He strives with thirst and hunger, toil and heat;
> And when his fortune sets before him all
> The pomps and pleasures that his soul can wish,
> His rigid virue will accept of none.   (1, iv, 52–8)

Nor, in choosing his heroes, had Swift gone to extremes. Unlike Poussin, for instance, he does not choose Diogenes throwing away his cup as the extreme example of temperance, or the life according to Nature.

If one accepts the argument that what Swift calls temperance might be glossed 'austerity', and what he calls fortitude we might call 'heroism' – are not the simple virtues of the horses mild compared with some of the acts of Swift's heroes? Further, although one may perceive in the heroes benevolent friendship and love of mankind, can one see any appreciable yielding in them to those human passions, the absence of which in the horses is supposed to render them beyond humanity? The horses' conception of matrimony, for example, is supposedly a little frigid. Their attitude to death is too tranquil to be true. However, the final heroic image of Socrates handed down to posterity is that of the benevolent philosopher discoursing cheerfully to his sorrowing companions while that embarrassing figure of low comedy, his wife, and that encumbrance to the divine flow of philosophic wisdom, his child, are swiftly removed from the stage. Sir Thomas More's second wife, apparently, is equally funny (Roper treats her appeals to Thomas in the Tower in the spirit of Noah's wife), and although, as is proper, the Christian hero has more love in him than the pagan, he precipitates the probable ruin of his family on a point of conscience over which he had equivocated to the utmost stretch of his wit. Lucius Junius Brutus had a short and bloody way with his sons. Addison's Cato *rejoices* over the death of a son in battle [IV, iv]. Such tragic situations cannot arise among the horses, but if we can admire Socrates when his family is led away, and if Swift admired Brutus and Cato, there seems no good reason why the horses should be beyond humanity merely because of their practice of birth control (for instance), or the adoption of children.

Moreover, in their determination that reason shall dominate the emotions and the flesh, Swift's heroes can be more extreme than the horses. There are no flagellant whips nor hair shirts in Houyhnhnmland. Sir Thomas More hated the Yahoo in himself more than the rationality of the horses suggested even to the sick mind of Gulliver. Lucius Junius Brutus set himself to watch the punishment he had decreed for his sons; to demonstrate to her husband her constancy of mind Marcus Brutus' wife could think of no better way to impress him than a self-inflicted wound. Antiquity can produce few more terrifying stories than Plutarch's agonising account of Cato's determined philosophical discussions with his friends on the night (admired by Swift) he had determined to rip out his bowels – this is the rank pride of Stoicism, the *atrocem animum Catonis*. There is nothing in Houyhnhnmland to match this.

Finally, a few general parallels. The dinner-time symposia of the horses are not un-Socratic. If the inflexibility of their minds is reminiscent rather of the 'rigid virtue' of a Cato than of a More or Socrates, nevertheless the Greek philosopher is singled out for special praise by the horses in chapter 8. They admire him as one who did not value mere knowledge of others' conjectures but taught instead practical virtue. This is Socrates the moral utilitarian of Xenophon who believed that beauty is use and use

beauty [*Memorabilia*, III, viii, 4–10], and although the horses
are scarcely capable of a fine Socratic irony, the teaching that
virtue is knowledge would have been appreciated by creatures
who are virtuous because they are rational. Like all Swift's sextumvirate they are committed to what they believe to be truth,
which is one and unqualifiable – thus of Epaminondas it was
told that he would not lie even in jest [Cornelius Nepos, *Epam.*,
3, 1], and the horses have no word for a lie, only a Platonic conception of the thing that is not. This imposes certain limitations
upon their imagination, but most of Swift's heroes were not imaginative men, and Socrates, if only as Plato's mouthpiece, banished poets from his most utilitarian of ideal societies. Ultimately
all Swift's heroes, because their virtue is rigid, show themselves
to be inflexible men, and because they commit themselves un-
swervingly to that one truth which they believe to be morally
right, like the horses they set standards beyond the practice of
most men.

Swift's play of wit and irony has perhaps too much obscured
that basic inflexibility and idealism of his mind which could lead
him to select Cato and Socrates as examples of a common standard, which leads to that extreme commitment to the one standard of the State-established Church which underlies his attacks
both savage and gross on nonconformity (and neither in *The
Republic* nor *Utopia* nor the land of the horses is much tolerance
extended to individual eccentricity), and which provokes the extreme patriotic idealism leading to the distorted moralistic pat-
terning of his historical writing (the politics of his day divided
between a small group of patrician patriots on the one hand, and
the ravening mouths of selfish faction on the other). So too there
is the extreme cultural idealism of his admiration for the Ancients,
which polarises literature between the sweetness and light of
Greece and Rome, and the venom of the Moderns. If reason and
Nature (in the commonplace) are the same, then there is only
one truth which is the perfection of Nature. The man who cannot
see this is a fool; the man who sees but will not obey is a knave.
Hence anger, or despair.

Swift is in many ways close to the author of *The Republic*.

Plato had seen the philosopher who should have been king put to death by fools and knaves. If it is going outside the sextumvirate to mention *The Republic*, at least the principal speaker in that dialogue passes by the name of Socrates, and in its idealism and its pessimism it can throw much light on Gulliver's fourth voyage. In its ideal picture of the Guardians *The Republic* depicts a race of men morally of basically the same breed as the horses (Platonic metaphysics we may omit as certainly not Socratic) and individually of the same mould as Swift's heroes. *If Gulliver is mistaken in his admiration, he is mistaken in good company.* To catalogue the moral qualities of the Guardians is to write a recapitulatory coda to what has already been argued. Here again we find that patriotism which places the happiness of the whole community above private interest, again a life of the utmost simplicity (carried Platonically to the extreme of communism), again the same belief that universal benevolence and friendship are superior to the narrow cares of family (again pushed by Plato to an extreme). Like the horses and the sextumvirate the Guardians are trained in youth to harden the body as well as the mind, being physical as well as mental athletes, men possessed of 'high spirit and quickness and strength' [II, 376]. When the time comes to leave the world they quit it with composure, for their minds are not troubled by pain or pleasure, fear or desire : 'Such a one is most of all sufficient unto himself for a good life and is distinguished from other men in having least need of anybody else' [III, 387]. The Guardian is free from the frenzy of sexual pleasure, free from the luxury both Socrates and Plato despised. Finally, Plato (or Socrates) has his Yahoos, those creatures who 'feast like cattle, grazing and copulating, ever greedy for more of these delights; and in their greed kicking and butting one another with horns and hooves of iron they slay one another in sateless avidity' [IX, 586]. 'You describe in quite oracular style, Socrates,' rejoins Glaucon in words worthy of Gulliver, 'the life of the multitude.' But what is really being described, in the work as a whole, is rather the life of the most uncommon of men, the man who has perfected his nature.

The horses represent an ideal, therefore, which is completely

traditional. It may be paralleled not only in the ideal community
of Plato (and of More), but also in the actual lives of the sextumvirate whether their ideals were Socratic, Stoical, or Christian. It is not tied to any creed (or source), but something which
the heroes owed to that 'good natural disposition' which led them
morally to strive for perfection. (What relation this *'natural* disposition' may possess to Christianity need not concern us, for nowhere is *Gulliver's Travels* explicitly concerned with Christian
idealism.) That Swift believed this *rational* ideal to be obtain-
able, however, is witnessed not only by his admiration for the sextumvirate, but may be supported by that famous definition of
man as *animal rationis capax* [letter to Pope, 29 September
1725]. So much has been written about it that one hesitates to
suggest, in the light of this argument, that it means just what it
says. Man is not a rational species, but men *are capable* of rationality. If a man is capable of travelling from Dublin to London
some men may do so. Swift did not write 'incapable'.

What of the objections to the Houyhnhnm ideal summarised
at the beginning of this argument? That Gulliver is emotionally
'unstable' on his return to the world does not invalidate the moral
excellence of the horses. It is perfectly clear that Gulliver is not
behaving in the least rationally. His master does not react to him
as he does to his wife. Gulliver may get the message wrong. That
does not mean it was the wrong message. As for that charming
Yahoo *rationis capax*, Pedro de Mendez, he may represent *normal* human behaviour, and is thus preferable to Gulliver, but
should one honour and admire him as a man as great as Socrates,
Cato or More? If we long to be perfect then we must aim high.

There remains the final objection that the horses are ridiculous. This cannot be so facilely evaded. At least Plato's *Republic*
was inhabited by men, but can a society of *horses* really be taken
seriously? Perhaps the answer lies with Democritus and Hera-
clitus. The true philosopher must either laugh or weep. *The Republic* is a work not untouched by pessimism. We are told that
the man 'returning from divine contemplations to the petty miseries of men cuts a sorry figure and appears most ridiculous' in this
world [VII, 517]. The philosopher is all too likely to perish 'as a

man fallen among wild beasts'. Reckoning this up he hopes at
best to remain quiet and free from wickedness 'standing aside
under the shelter of a wall in a storm of dust and sleet' [VI, 496].
Lucius Junius Brutus was forced to play the fool to survive at
the court of the Tarquins; Marcus Junius Brutus, having failed
to preserve Rome from tyranny, killed himself; so too did Cato
Uticensis; Socrates and More were both martyred. Not one of the
sextumvirate met a peaceful end. To these 'all the Ages of the
World cannot add a Seventh'. History can show only a handful
of men rationally virtuous. History did not lend to Plato one
philosopher king. Can one imagine a society giving back an image
only of Socrates or Epaminondas? To do so is to behave *tamquam in republica Platonis*. Hence the society of *horses*. There
should be no mistake. The thing is utterly ridiculous. The more
ridiculous it becomes, the blacker the pessimism.

S O U R C E : *Essays in Criticism*, XIX (1969) pp. 35–45.

NOTES

1. There is a convenient summary, with references, of recent
approaches to Swift by J. L. Clifford, 'The Eighteenth Century',
MLQ, XXVI (1965) 111–34 (pp. 126–30). For another approach
to the sextumvirate see J. C. Maxwell, 'Demigods and Pick-
pockets. . . .', *Scrutiny*, XI (1942–3) 34–9.
2. *A Discourse to Prove the Antiquity of the English Tongue*, in
Prose Works, ed. H. Davis, IV, 234. The work is jocular, but the
reader is expected to recognise Epaminondas by the description.
3. W. H. Halewood, 'Plutarch in Houyhnhnmland : A Neglected
Source of Gulliver's Fourth Voyage', *PQ*, XLIV (1965) 185–94.
4. See my 'The Meaning of Addison's *Cato*', *RES*, XVII (1966)
149–62. The evidence presented there supports the argument advanced here.

Claude Rawson

'FROM ORDER AND CRUELTY:
A READING OF SWIFT (WITH SOME
COMMENTS ON POPE AND JOHNSON)'
(1970)

Swift's satire often suggests an impasse, a blocking of escape
routes and saving possibilities. This feeling presses on the reader
for reasons which do not necessarily follow from the satiric topic
as such, from the specific wickedness Swift is castigating, or any
outright assertion that the wickedness is incurable. Incurability is
certainly often implied, and the sense of an impasse is (by a paradox which is only apparent) related to a complementary vision
of unending paths of vicious self-complication, bottomless spirals
of human perversity. This is less a matter of Swift's official ideo-
logical views than of mental atmosphere and ironic manipulation : that is, of a more informal, yet very active, interplay between deliberate attacking purposes (and tactics), and certain
tense spontaneities of self-expression. My concern is with the
stylistic results of this interplay, though I do not pretend that the
deliberate purposes can be clearly distinguished from the more
shadowy ones. It may be that in Swift such dividing lines *need*
to be unclear. I begin with Swift's most frequently discussed
passage, the mock-argument

that in most Corporeal Beings, which have fallen under my Cog-
nizance, the *Outside* hath been infinitely preferable to the *In* :
Whereof I have been farther convinced from some late Experiments. Last Week I saw a Woman *flay'd*, and you will hardly believe,
how much it altered her Person for the worse. Yesterday I ordered

the Carcass of a *Beau* to be stript in my Presence; when we were all
amazed to find so many unsuspected Faults under one Suit of
Cloaths : Then I laid open his *Brain*, his *Heart*, and his *Spleen*;
But, I plainly perceived at every Operation, that the farther we pro-
ceeded, we found the Defects encrease upon us in Number and
Bulk : from all which, I justly formed this Conclusion to my self;
That ... He that can with *Epicurus* content his Ideas with the *Films*
and *Images* that fly off upon his Senses from the *Superficies* of
Things; Such a Man truly wise, creams off Nature, leaving the
Sower and the Dregs, for Philosophy and Reason to lap up. This
is the sublime and refined Point of Felicity, called, *the Possession of
being well deceived*; The Serene Peaceful State of being a Fool
among Knaves. (*Tale of a Tub*, ix.)[1]

Here, the example of the flayed woman supports an argument
similar to that of *A Beautiful Young Nymph Going to Bed* :
whores can look horrible when their finery is stripped off, conventional celebrations of female beauty gloss over some ugly facts,
the *Outside* looks better than the *In* and creates inappropriate
complacencies. The flayed woman is portrayed in less detail,
and seems physically less shocking, than the nymph of the poem,
with her artificial hair, eyes and teeth, and her 'Shankers, Issues,
running Sores'. But she is, in a sense, more 'gratuitous'. In the
poem, however horrible the details, the main proposition is sustained by them in a manner essentially straightforward, formulaic, and indeed conventional.[2] The account is a nightmare
fantastication, but it is also simply a *donnée* : the poem asks us to
imagine such a woman, and the point is made. The nymph is
entirely subordinated to obvious formulaic purposes, even though
'subordination', in another sense, ill describes the vitality of the
grotesquerie.

The flayed woman (and stripped beau), on the other hand,
are momentary intensities which do not merely *serve* the argument they are meant to illustrate, but actually *spill over* it. They
take us suddenly, and with devastating brevity, outside the expectations of the immediate logic, into a surprising and 'cruel'
domain of fantasy. 'Cruel' is here used in something like Artaud's
sense, as lying outside or beyond ordinary moral motivations, and

Swift's brevity is essential to the effect. For this brevity, and the astringent blandness of the language, arrest the play of fantasy sufficiently to prevent it from developing into a moral allegory in its own right. The point is important, because brevity is not a necessary condition of a literature of cruelty in the modern sense, of Sade, Jarry and post-Artaud dramatists, of Breton's *humour noir* and allied literary explorations of the 'gratuitous'. When Breton placed Swift at the head of his anthology, as *véritable initiateur* of a black humour emancipated from the 'degrading influence' of satire and moralising,[3] he told a real truth, for Swift has (I believe) a temperamental tendency in this direction. But the tendency is powerfully held in check by conscious moral purposes which harness it to their own use. Hence his gratuitous cruelties are usually brief eruptions, only as long (so to speak) as the Super-Ego takes to catch up, and any extensive development of a grim joke normally dovetails into a fully-fledged moral demonstration or argument, as in the *Beautiful Young Nymph* or the *Modest Proposal*. Brief quasi-cannibalistic frissons in *Gulliver* (Gulliver using the skins of Yahoos for making clothes or sails, *GT*, IV, 3, 10) are more gratuitous than the *Modest Proposal*, as the flayed woman is more gratuitous than the *Beautiful Young Nymph*. The *Gulliver* passages are extremely minor comic assaults on our 'healthy' sensibilities, lacking the intensity of the passage from the *Tale*; but in one paradoxical sense they also are more unsettling than the more extended use of the cannibal image, precisely because in the *Proposal* the image is the direct sustaining principle of a moral argument. To this extent Breton seems off the mark when he follows his Swift section (which includes a substantial portion of the *Proposal*) with an elaborate cannibal extravaganza from Sade.

This is not to say that the briefer passages have no moral implication (nor that the extended ones lack the power to shock, or have no local and subsidiary intensities of their own). Presumably the clothes of Yahoo-skin are also a reminder of the animality of man, while the flayed woman purports to illustrate the notion that appearances are more agreeable than reality. But it would take a perverse reader to feel that these moral implications provide

H

the dominant effect. The gruesomeness of the flayed woman is so shockingly and absurdly *over*-appropriate to the ostensible logic as to be, by any normal standards, *in*appropriate. Critics who recognise this sometimes sentimentalise the issue by arguing that the flayed woman overspills the immediate moral not into an amoral gratuitousness, but into a different and more powerful moral significance : that she represents, for example, Swift's pained protest at this treatment of whores. This seems as wrong as William Burroughs's notion that the *Modest Proposal* is 'a tract against Capital Punishment'.[4] I doubt Swift's opposition to either oppression, and if anything the allusion to flaying bears comparison with this sudden *redirection* of the cannibal irony in the *Modest Proposal* :

Neither indeed can I deny, that if the same Use were made of several plump young girls in this Town, who, without one single Groat to their Fortunes, cannot stir Abroad without a Chair, and appear at the *Play-house*, and *Assemblies* in foreign Fineries, which they never will pay for; the Kingdom would not be the worse.

In both cases the black joke suggests, if not literal endorsement of the hideous punishment, a distinct animus against the victim. The presence of this animus indicates that the irony is not, after all, gratuitous in the strictest Gide-ian sense. No human act can be entirely gratuitous (that is, absolutely motiveless), as Gide himself admitted :[5] it can only be disconnected from its normal *external* functions, in this case the moral implications expected of the satire. If in both cases the animus is transferred suddenly away from the official paths of the formula (truth vs. delusion; eating people is wrong), yet still carries a redirected moral charge (against whores, or foolish girls whose vanity is crippling Ireland's economy), there is an explosive overplus in the sheer wilful sud-denness of the act of redirection as such. A haze of *extra* hostility hangs in the air, unaccounted for, dissolving the satire's clean logic into murkier and more unpredictable precisions, spreading uneasiness into areas of feeling difficult to rationalise, and diffi-cult for the reader to escape. Part of Swift's answer to the dilemma posed for the satirist by his own belief that '*Satyr is a sort of* Glass, *wherein Beholders do generally discover every body's Face but their own'* [*Battle of the Books*, Preface] is thus to counter, by a strategy of unease, the reader's natural tendency to exclude himself from the explicit condemnation: his escape into 'Serene Peaceful States' is blocked off even when he is innocent of the specific charge.

Often in such cases, moreover, the irony is manipulated in such a way as to suggest that the reader cannot be wholly unimplicated even in the specific charge. It is not only through unexpectedness or diversionary violence that the flayed woman and stripped beau spill over the logical frame. They also have an absurd tendency to generalise or extend the guilt to the rest of mankind, through a tangle of implications which act in irrational defiance of any mere logic. If the argument had been overridingly concerned to demonstrate that appearances can be fraudulent, superficial views inadequate, and vanity misplaced, the notion that people look ugly when stripped of their clothes or cosmetics would have been a sufficient, and a logically disciplined, support to it. To specify whores and beaux would be a perfectly legitimate singling out of social types who trade disreputably on appearances, and are otherwise open to moral censure. These didactic reasonings, and the larger-scale exposure of mad 'moderns', obviously remain present. But, in the wording as it stands, they are also, characteristically, subverted; as though the several wires crossed, making an explosive short-circuit. Flayed or dissected bodies hardly produce the most morally persuasive evidence of the delusiveness of appearances; nor do they as such prove a moral turpitude. If a whore's body alters for the worse when flayed, or a beau's innards look unsavoury when laid open, so would anyone else's, and the fact does not obviously demonstrate anybody's wickedness. The images, which begin as specific tokens of guilt aimed at certain human types, teasingly turn into general signs of the human condition. The images' strong charge of undifferentiated blame is thus left to play over undefined turpitudes attributable to the whole of mankind. The beau's innards recall an earlier statement by the *Tale*'s 'author', about having 'dissected the Carcass of *Humane Nature*, and read many useful Lectures upon the several Parts, both *Containing* and *Contained*; till at last it *smelt* so strong, I could preserve it no longer' (*Tale*, v).

The passage parodies Wotton and others,[6] but, as often with Swiftian parody, transcends its immediate object. And the imagery's characteristic oscillation between moral turpitude and bodily corruption irrationally suggests a damaging equivalence between the two, placing on '*Humane Nature*' a freewheeling load of moral guilt which is inescapable and which yet attaches itself to faults outside the moral domain.

For if satire that is 'levelled at all' (i.e. 'general' rather than 'personal') 'is never resented for an offence by any, since every individual Person makes bold to understand it of others, and very wisely removes his particular Part of the Burthen upon the shoulders of the World, which are broad enough, and able to bear it' (*Tale*, Preface), this is only likely to be true of a 'general' satire of *specific* vices. Where the aggression turns indistinct, and overspills the area of specifiable moral guilt, no opportunity is given for complacent self-exculpation on a specific front, and the reader becomes implicated. Instead of permitting the individual to shift his load onto the world's shoulders, Swift forces the reader to carry the world's load on *his*. The result, second time round, is that even the specific charges begin to stick : we become identified with whores, beaux, moderns. We cannot shrug this off by saying that it is Swift's 'author' who is speaking and not Swift. The intensities are Swift's, and depend on the blandness and even friendliness of the 'author'. The 'author' is saying in effect *hypocrite lecteur, mon semblable, mon frère*, and saying it kindly and welcomingly; but it is Swift who is making him say it, and the reader must decide whether he likes the thought of such a brother.

The cumulative sense of impasse (all mankind becoming implicated in the attack, the attack surviving any dismissal of specific charges, the curious re-validation of these charges by that fact, the miscellaneous blocking of the reader's escape-routes) depends, then, on energies which exceed the legitimate logical implications of the discourse. These energies cannot be accounted for by a mere retranslation of the mock-logic into its non-ironic 'equivalent', and part of their force depends on the violation of whatever consequential quality exists either in the hack's zany reasoning or its sober didactic counterpart. The carefully and extensively prepared polarity between the mad values of the modern hack, and the sanity of the non-singular, traditionalist, rational, unsuperficial man of sense, may seem for a while, in the Digression on Madness, solid and definite enough to provide at least limited reassurance against the more unsettling stylistic tremors. The reassurance is undermined but perhaps not eliminated by the flayed woman and stripped beau. But in the final sentence of the paragraph, the bad and good cease to function in lines that are parallel and opposite : the lines collapse, and cross. The comforting opposition is brought to a head, and then shattered, against the whole direction of the argument, by the suggestion that the alternative to being a fool is to be not a wise man but a knave.

Critics often assume some form of 'diametrical opposition' between putative and real authors at this point. Either Swift's voice suddenly erupts, nakedly, from the other's vacuous chatter, or at best 'fools' and 'knaves' have simultaneously one clear value for Swift and an opposite one for his 'author'. I suggest that the relationship is at all times more elusive, and that the rigidities of mask-criticism (even in its more sophisticated forms) tend to compartmentalise what needs to remain a more fluid and indistinct interaction. (The theoretically clear opposition, in the preceding part of the Digression, between mad and sane, or bad and good, is a different thing : a temporary build-up, created for demolition.) The notion that in the 'Fool among Knaves' we suddenly hear Swift's own voice makes a kind of sense : but it runs the danger of suggesting quite improperly both that we have not actively been hearing this voice throughout, and that we now hear nothing else. In actual fact, the phrase trades simultaneously on our feeling that the sudden intensity comes straight from Swift, and on our reluctance to identify Swift even momentarily with an 'author' whom the work as a whole relentlessly ridicules. The paradox of that 'author' is that he has enormous vitality, a 'presence' almost as insistent as Swift's, without having much definable *identity* as a 'character'. He needs to be distinguished from Swift, but hardly as a separate and autonomous being. He is an ebullient embodiment of many of Swift's dislikes, but the ebullience is Swift's, and the 'author' remains an amorphous mass of disreputable energies, whose vitality belongs less to any independent status (whether as clear-cut allegory or full-fledged personality) than to an endlessly opportunistic subservience to the satirist's needs. Unduly simplifying or systematic speculation as to when Swift is talking and when his 'persona', or about their 'diametrically opposite' meanings if both are talking at once, often turns masks into persons, and induces in some critics the most absurd expectations of coherently developed characterisation. Thus W. B. Ewald's classic work on *The Masks of Jonathan Swift* (p. 39, n. 73) footnotes its discussion of the fools–knaves passage with the astonishing statement that 'The author's interest in observing and performing anatomical dissections is a characteristic which remains undeveloped in the *Tale* and which does not fit very convincingly the sort of *persona* Swift has set up' (though there actually *is*, if one wants it, 'consistency' in the fact that the 'author' is the sort of fool who performs experiments to discover the obvious!).

It is, of course, true that the 'author' uses 'fool' as a term of praise, as Cibber in the *Dunciad* praises Dulness. The Digression on Madness is a 'praise of folly', and the 'author' proudly declares himself 'a Person, whose Imaginations are hard-mouth'd, and exceedingly disposed to run away with his *Reason*'. The *Tale* presents, in its way, quite as much of an upside-down world as Pope's poem, but relies much less systematically on any single or dominant *verbal* formula. I do not mean that the *Dunciad* lacks that rudimentary two-way traffic between terms of praise and blame which we see in the *Tale* when, for example, the 'author' praises his 'Fool' as 'a Man truly wise', although it may be true that even at this level the *Tale*'s ironic postures are more teasingly unstable (indeed the 'author' seems not only to be scrambling simple valuations of wisdom and folly, but also perverting the 'true' paradox that 'folly is wisdom'). But the poem's mockexaltation of fools rests essentially on a few strongly signposted terms (*dunce, dull,* etc.), which advertise the main ironic formula, and guarantee its fundamental predictability. When we feel uneasy or embarrassed in the *Dunciad,* it is because the main irony is *too* consistently sustained, rather than not enough. When Cibber praises Dulness (whose good old cause I yet defend', 'O! ever gracious . . .' 1, 165, 173, etc), we may feel that Pope's blame-by-praise becomes awkward, not because the formula threatens to slip, but because it strains belief through overdoing. The implausibility may be no greater in itself than the hack's celebration of 'Serene Peaceful States'. But Cibber's praise has the slow unemphatic stateliness of a rooted conviction, while the hack's occurs in a context full of redirections, 'Fool' being disturbed by 'Knaves', as indeed the paragraph's happy style is disturbed throughout by alien intensities (flayed woman, beau's innards). Cibber at such moments fails to take off into the freer air of Pope's satiric fantasy, and solidifies instead into an improbably oversimplified 'character'. His heavy consistency embarrasses differently from the 'inconsistencies' of Swift's hack, who, being in a sense no character at all, obeys no laws but those of his creator's anarchic inventiveness. The embarrassments in Pope are rare, but damaging. They are unintended, and disturb that poise and certainty of tone essential to Pope's verse. In Swift's satiric ambience, embarrassment is radical : it is a moral rather than an aesthetic thing, and is the due response to the rough edges and subversions of a style whose whole nature it is to undermine certainties, including the certainties it consciously proclaims.

Such blurred and shocking interchange (rather than sharp ironic opposition) between speaker and satirist is not confined to unruly works like the *Tale.* It occurs even in the *Modest Proposal,* that most astringent and tautly formulaic of Swift's writings. When the proposer uses the famous phrase, 'a Child, *just dropt from its Dam*', a shock occurs because the style has hitherto given no unmistakeable indication of its potential nastiness. Swift means the phrase to erupt in all its cruel violence, yet it is formally spoken by the proposer, and we are not to suppose *him* to be a violent, or an unkind, man. Is the nasty phrase 'inconsistent' with his character? In a way, yes. On the other hand, part of Swift's irony is that prevailing values are so inhumane, that a gentle and moderate man will take all the horror for granted. If he can sincerely assert his humanity while advocating monstrous schemes, may he not also be expected to use a nasty phrase calmly and innocently? In which case, the usage might be 'consistent' with his character, thus indicating 'diametrical' opposition between him and Swift. But inhumane propaganda which claims, or believes itself, to be humane (say that of a 'sincere' defender of apartheid), does not use inhumane language; and we should have to imagine the speaker as incredibly insensitive to English usage, if he really wanted himself and his scheme to seem as humane as he believed they were. Such discussion of the 'character' and his 'consistency' leads to deserts of circularity. But the problem hardly poses itself in the reading (as it poses itself, down to the question of insensitivity to usage, over Cibber's praise of Dulness), and what becomes apparent is the irrelevance, rather than the truth or untruth, of the terms. The violent phrase is not an 'inconsistency' but a dislocation, among other dislocations. It has nothing to say about character, but breaks up a formula (the formula of a calm, kindly advocacy of horrible deeds), within a style which both includes such formulas and is given to breaking them up. Thus, when (in contrast to the *Dunciad*'s blame-by-praise, where it is easy to translate one set of terms into its opposite) Swift's speakers praise fools, or proclaim their humanity in brutal language, our reaction is to oscillate nervously between speaker and satirist. If we bring this oscillation into the open by asking (as critics are always asking) whether a bad speaker is using bad terms in a good sense, or whether Swift himself is making some form of explosive intervention, we find no meaningful answer. But there is a sense in which it is a meaningful *question*, for it brings into the open an uncertainty which is essential to the style.

The uncertainty is most strikingly illustrated in the Digression's 'Knaves'. For it is this electrifying term, with all its appearance of simplifying finality, which most resists tidy-minded schematisms of parallel-and-opposite valuation, and the rest. If

'Fool' was good to the 'author' and bad to Swift, are 'Knaves' bad
to the 'author' and good to Swift? Does the sentence's impact
really reside in our feeling that 'Knave' is the fool's word for a
quality Swift would name more pleasantly? If so, which quality?
The answer is deliberately indistinct. Perhaps the 'Knaves' are
those 'Betters' who, in the Preface to the *Battle of the Books*, are
said to threaten the serenity of fools (the Preface too is 'of the
Author', though an 'author' at that moment more similar than
opposite to Swift). But if this points to a partial explanation, it
does so *ex post facto*, and is not experienced in the reading. To the
extent that we are, in context, permitted to escape the suggestion
that the world is absolutely divided into fools and knaves, we
confront alternatives that are elusive, unclear. If we do not take
'Knaves' as Swift's word, literally meant, we cannot simply dismiss it as coming from the 'author' and to be therefore translat-
able into something less damaging. We cannot be sure of the
nature of any saving alternative, and may even uneasily suspect
that we are in a fool's 'Serene Peaceful State' for imagining that
such alternatives exist. The style's aggressive indistinctness thus
leaves damaging possibilities in the air, without pinning Swift
down to an assertion definite enough to be open to rebuttal. And
so it seems more appropriate to note the imprisoning rhetorical
effect of 'Fool among Knaves' than to determine too precisely
who means what by those words. A rhetorical turn which wittily
blocks off any respectable alternative to being a fool, is reinforced
by those either-way uncertainties which the whole style induces
in the reader. The reader is thus poised between the guilt of being
merely human, and an exculpation which is as doubtful as the
charges are unclear. The apparent definiteness of the epigram,
and the reader's cloudy insecurity, mirror and complete each
other in an overriding effect of impasse.

. . . Pope's usual way with damaging generalisations is to turn
quickly to particulars, which are more amenable to the sort of
enclosed definition which lets the rest of humanity out. 'Characters' overwhelm their universalising contexts. In the *Epistle
to Cobham*, the generalising lip-service to human nature's
'puzzling Contraries' [1. 124] is even greater than in *To a Lady*:

>   Our depths who fathoms, or our shallow finds,
>   Quick whirls, and shifting eddies, of our minds? (ll. 29 30).

The corresponding stress on triumphs of individual categorisation is also greater. The 'ruling passion' seems a convenient formula less because it is a particularly good means to psychological insights than because of the pleasures of conclusive definition which it yields:

>   Search then the Ruling Passion : There, alone,
>   The Wild are constant, and the Cunning known. (ll. 174 ff.)

The satisfactions are largely aesthetic. The lengthy portrait of Wharton which follows this couplet is full of vivid debating triumphs:

>   This clue once found, unravels all the rest,
>   The prospect clears, and Wharton stands confest.
>
>   .   .   .   .
>
>   Ask you why Wharton broke thro' ev'ry rule?
>   'Twas all for fear the Knaves should call him Fool.
>   Nature well known, no prodigies remain,
>   Comets are regular, and Wharton plain.

If the concept of a 'ruling passion' is something whose dialectical completeness imprisons the satiric victim, and if Pope's play of paradox and antithesis reinforces this imprisonment, there is nevertheless in the poem a feeling not of imprisonment but of release. 'The prospect clears': such manifest delights of the controlling intellect have at least as much vitality as the turpitudes of Wharton and the rest. Contrast the very different finality of Swift's famous mot about Wharton's father, where the witty energy is entirely devoted to closing-in on the victim, and where the astringency of the prose-rhythms makes Pope's verse seem almost jaunty: 'He is a Presbyterian in Politics, and an Atheist in Religion; but he chuseth at present to whore with a Papist.'[7]

This astringency is revealing. It is often found where Swift practises what we may call couplet-rhetoric, that style in both verse and prose whose qualities of balance, antithesis, and pointedness mirror (ironically or not) Augustan ideals of coherence, regularity and decorous interchange, as well as paradoxes of enclosed self-contradiction. He seldom wrote heroic couplets, perhaps resisting the almost institutionalised sense of order which the form seemingly aspires to proclaim, and preferring more informal verse styles. His more exuberant effects, unlike Pope's, occur in more open-ended or unpredictable styles, and the patternings of a pointed or epigrammatic manner frequently freeze in his hands to a slow harsh deliberateness. The fact that such patternings occur mostly in his prose may have something to do with the greater amplitude of the medium, which makes possible longer, slower units of sense. But there is no Popeian buoyancy in Johnson's verse, and plenty in Fielding's prose, as the following passage shows :

Master Blifil fell very short of his companion in the amiable quality of mercy; but so he greatly exceeded him in one of a much higher kind, namely, in justice : in which he followed both the precepts and example of Thwackum and Square; for though they would both make frequent use of the word mercy, yet it was plain that in reality Square held it to be inconsistent with the rule of right; and Thwackum was for doing justice, and leaving mercy to Heaven. The two gentlemen did indeed somewhat differ in opinion concerning the objects of this sublime virtue; by which Thwackum would probably have destroyed one half of mankind, and Square the other half. (*Tom Jones*, III, x)

This may recall some of the passages from Pope's *Epistle to a Lady* : balance, contrast, a tremendous display of powers of summation, an obvious delight in the feats of style which so memorably and satisfyingly categorise some unsavoury facts. There is, too, the confident authorial presence, a decorous and gentlemanly self-projection, simplified but enormously alive, free of the vulnerabilities of undue intimacy with the reader or undue closeness to the material, yet proclaiming an assured and reassuring moral

control. The categorisations point to a kind of vicious closed
system, but unlike Swift's imprisoning paradoxes and like those
of Pope, they deal with single persons or types, rather than with
mankind or at least with wide and damagingly undefined portions of it. Moreover, the kind of exuberance found in Fielding as
in Pope turns the closed systems into authorial triumphs of definition, instead of allowing them to generate an oppressive feeling of impasse. When Swift is exuberant on Fielding's or Pope's
scale, he does not produce a finality towards which the preceding
rhetoric has been visibly tending, but assaults us with sudden
shocks of *re*definition, turning us into knaves if we refuse to be
fools. Fielding, like Pope, rounds his paradoxes to a conclusiveness which, being both prepared-for and specific, limits their
applicability and creates a feeling of release. If the buoyant brevi-
ties of Pope's couplets are absent in Fielding's passage, the amplitude of the prose medium in his case permits versatilities of
elaboration, of weaving and interweaving, which are their
counterpart in exuberant definition.

Prose, then, does not in itself make couplet-rhetoric astringent.
Here, however, is Gulliver on prime ministers : '. . . he never tells
a *Truth*, but with an Intent that you should take it for a *Lye*; nor
a *Lye*, but with a Design that you should take it for a *Truth* . . .'
(*GT*, IV, 6) and on the causes of war :

Sometimes one Prince quarrelleth with another, for fear the other
should quarrel with him. Sometimes a War is entered upon, because
the Enemy is too *strong*, and sometimes because he is too *weak*.
Sometimes our Neighbours *want* the *Things* which we *have*, or *have*
the Things which we want . . . (*GT*, IV, 5)

These passages create little 'anti-systems', absurdly self-consistent
worlds of perverse motivation, whose complete disconnection
from humane and rational purposes gives them an air of unreality, of disembodied vacancy. (The vision is partly a satiric
counterpart to Johnson's tragic sense of man, shunning 'fancied
ills' and chasing 'airy good'.) Such satiric systematisations are
not uncommon in Augustan literature, and Pope's *Moral Essays*
also occasionally turn excesses of vice and irrationality into para-

doxical pseudo-systems. Pope does not, however, allow them to take on so much crazy autonomy, but often refers them to an all-embracing ruling passion. Because Swift deliberately withholds explanations at this level, we have to fall back on some absolute notion of the ingrained perversity of the human species, which alone can account for such ghoulishly self-sustaining perversity.

Above all, where the epigrammatic summations of Pope or Fielding suggest that vicious matters have been 'placed' or disposed of, there is here a sense of being weighed down. The categorisations are witty and precise, but the voice is flat and rasping, not buoyant with those righteous energies with which Pope and Fielding can outmatch the most viciously animated turpitudes. I suggest that this astringency is Swift's rather than Gulliver's, so far as we bother to disentangle them. This is not (once again) to say that Gulliver and Swift are identical, but that the feeling seems to come from behind the Gulliver who is speaking. Within a page of the last passage, in the same conversation or series of conversations, Gulliver gives this, not astringent but high-spirited, account of human war:

I could not forbear shaking my Head and smiling a little at his Ignorance. And, being no Stranger to the Art of War, I gave him a Description of Cannons, Culverins, Muskets, Carabines, Pistols, Bullets, Powder, Swords, Bayonets, Sieges, Retreats, Attacks, Undermines, Countermines, Bombardments, Seafights; Ships sunk with a Thousand Men; twenty Thousand killed on each Side; dying Groans, Limbs flying in the Air: Smoak, Noise, Confusion, trampling to Death under Horses Feet: Flight, Pursuit, Victory; Fields strewed with Carcases left for Food to Dogs, and Wolves, and Birds of Prey; Plundering, Stripping, Ravishing, Burning and Destroying. And, to set forth the Valour of my own dear Countrymen, I assured him, that I had seen them blow up a Hundred Enemies at once in a Siege, and as many in a Ship; and beheld the dead Bodies drop down in Pieces from the Clouds, to the great Diversion of all the Spectators. (*GT*, IV, 5)

The note of animated pleasure is at odds with the preceding astringency, and with the notion (see especially the *later* stress on this, IV, VII) that he was in these conversations already disen-

chanted with humanity : but there is a very similar, complacently
delighted, account of war given to the King of Brobdingnag
before Gulliver's disenchantment [II, 7]. The method of the
Travels, putatively written ofter the disenchantment, is often to
have Gulliver present himself partly as he was at the relevant moment in the past, and not merely as he might now see himself, so
that in both chapters [II, 7 and IV, 5] twin-notes of affection and
dislike might be felt to mingle or alternate. Unless we are prepared
to regard Gulliver as a very sophisticated ironist or rhetorician
(let alone a highly-developed Jamesian consciousness) – and
some readers are – we must feel that the alternations are modulations of Swift's ironic voice. Even if we deny Gulliver's pleasure
in the list about war, we cannot deny the list's comic exuberance,
and its difference from the dry epigrams of a moment before.
However we describe Gulliver's attitude at this time, the shift
cannot be attributed to any significant variation in his feelings,
just as the inordinate and chaotic cataloguing cannot be accounted
for as a subtly motivated departure from Gulliver's earlier an-
nouncement in IV, 5 that he is only reporting 'the Substance'
(and an ordered summary at that) of these conversations. The
modulations in the *actual* atmosphere as we read emphasise again
the abstractedness of any separation of Swift from his speaker
(even where that speaker, unlike the *Tale*'s, has a name, wife,
family and other tokens of identity). Swift's most expansive satiric
energies kindle not at those sharp and witty summations which
would have delighted Fielding or Pope, but at the humour of
Gulliver's anarchic submission to an evil whose chaotic vitality
has not been subdued to epigrammatic definition. At the mental
level at which we, as readers, respond to such transitions, we are
face to face with Swift's inner fluctuations, without intermediar-
ies. Big men, little men, Gulliver and the rational horses, become
so many circus animals, deserting. The encounter is, of course,
unofficial : we do not admit it to ourselves, as distinct from experiencing it, and no suggestion arises of Swift's conscious design.
When Swift participates harshly in Gulliver's tart epigrams there
is no formal difficulty in imagining that the two converge, almost
officially. But when the tartness unpredictably gives way to Gulli-

ver's unruly exuberance (whether Gulliver is felt *at that instant* to hate war or to relish it is not a problem which occurs to us in the reading, as distinct from knowing Swift hates it, and sensing the exuberance), Swift's participation is unofficial and closer, a variant form of that mirror-relationship I have already suggested between an unruly and right-minded Swift who wrote the *Tale*, and the *Tale*'s unruly but mad and wicked 'author'.

These identities establish themselves in that very charged penumbra where the satirist's personality overwhelms his own fictions, in a huge self-consciousness. It is no coincidence, from this point of view, that Swift's *Tale* is both a pre-enactment and an advance parody of Sterne; nor that the self-irony, at once self-mocking and self-displaying, of Sterne, or Byron, or Norman Mailer (whose *Advertisements for Myself*, for example, use every trick that the *Tale* satirically *ab*used, digressions, self-interruptions and solipsisms, solipsistic reminders of digression or solipsism, etc.) sometimes develops from Swift or shares formal elements with his work. The major formal difference is that Swift's 'authors' (the hack, the proposer, Gulliver) are predominantly satirised figures, officially Swift's complete antithesis most of the time, whereas the speakers or narrators of the later writers are either identical with their creators (as in many of Mailer's *Advertisements*), or projections and facets, hardly massively dissociated. The satiric plots and formulae which guarantee this dissociation in Swift may be thought of as immense protective assertions of the Super-Ego, part of the same process which sees to it that potentially 'gratuitous' effects of any length are in fact more or less subdued within frameworks of moral allegory. Because Swift's person is not *openly* permitted to take the slightest part in the affair, his self-mockery (for example) is denied all the luxuries of coy self-analysis available to the later writers. (Where he does, however, speak through voices which are direct self-projections, as in *Cadenus and Vanessa* or the *Verses on the Death*, a tendency to such luxuries becomes evident.) The fact that Swift's presence remains felt despite the formal self-dissociation creates between the reader and Swift an either/or relation whose very indefiniteness entails more, not less, intimacy. In that whirlpool of indefiniteness, where any tendency to categorise is arrested, individual character becomes fluid and indefinite, as in Sterne, despite the un-Sterne-like (but rather nominal and cardboard) firmness of 'characters' like the modest proposer, or like Gulliver in his more self-consistent interludes. There is a relation between this and Swift's readiness in some moods to think of the human mind as prone to bottomless spirals of self-complication. An implication that hovers over both is that human behaviour is too unpredictable to be usefully classified in rounded conceptions of 'personality', as 'in (or out of) character'. Despite its strong moral point of reference, Swift's self-implicating sense of our anarchic tortuosity is close in conception to some of those visions of complexity which in our time are often embodied in the extraordinarily recurrent image of a spiral (and its relations, vortex, whirlpool, winding stair, endless ladder, vicious circle), with all its suggestions of perpetual movement and interpenetrating flux. We think of the Yeats of *Blood and the Moon*, who charged the image with a direct and passionate self-commitment, and with splendours and miseries which Swift would shrink from as too grandiloquent,

> I declare this tower is my symbol; I declare
> This winding, gyring, spiring treadmill of a stair is my ancestral
> stair;
> That Goldsmith and the Dean, Berkeley and Burke have tra-
> velled there.
> Swift beating on his breast in sibylline frenzy blind
> Because the heart in his blood-sodden breast had dragged him
> down into mankind,

but whose inclusion of Swift represents no mean insight; of 'those endless stairs from the buried gaming rooms of the unconscious to the tower of the brain' in Mailer;[8] of the dialectical psychologies of Sartre or R. D. Laing.

A reflection of this on a more or less conscious, or 'rhetorical', plane are those familiar fluidities of style : the irony seldom docile to any simple (upside-down or other) scheme; 'masks' and allegories seldom operating in an unruffled point by point correspondence with their straight non-fictional message, or with sustained consistency to their own fictional selves; stylistic procedures at odds with one another, or deliberately out of focus with the main feeling of the narrative; contradictory implications on matters of substance. The effect is to preclude the comforts of definiteness, while blocking off retreats into woolly evasion, so that both the pleasures of knowing where one stands, and those of a vagueness which might tell us that we need not know, are denied.

Pope's writing, by contrast, depends on a decorous clarity of relationship (with the reader and subject), without the active and radical ambiguity we find in Swift. Pope's speakers (outside the *Dunciad*) are usually not enemies, from whom he must signpost his dissociation, but rhetorically simplified projections of himself (as urbane Horatian commentator, righteously angry satirist, proud priest of the muses). The somewhat depersonalised postures are traditional and 'public', secure within their rhetorical traditions (and so not subject to unpredictable immediacies), and they permit certain grandeurs of self-expression precisely because the more intimate self recedes from view. Urbane or passionate hauteurs ('Scriblers or Peers, alike are *Mob* to me', 'I must be proud to see/Men not afraid of God, afraid of me')[9] can then occur without opening the poet to easy charges of crude vanity. The 'masks' of Pope may thus be thought of as melting the poet's personality in a conventional or public role, but also as a release for certain acts of authorial presence. The finalities of the couplet form serve Pope in a similar way. They formally sanction a degree of definiteness which might otherwise seem open to charges of arrogance or glibness. The clearly patterned artifice hardly engulfs Pope. He moves within it with so much vitality and such an assurance of colloquial rhythm, that a powerfully dominating presence is always felt. But it remains a simplified presence, and Swift is in many ways paradoxically closer to his parodied enemies than is Pope to his own rhetorical selves.

But if couplets help Pope to formalise his presence, and to free it from certain inhibiting vulnerabilities, the effect is largely personal to Pope, and not primarily a cultural property of the form. Couplets do not, in Johnson, guarantee to suppress vulnerability, nor create triumphs of self-confidence; and their prose-counter-parts do not in Swift (as they do in Fielding) attenuate the close intimacy of the satirist's presence. The balanced orderliness of couplet-rhetoric need not, even in Pope, reflect a serenity of out-look, nor a civilisation which is confident, stable and in harmony with itself. The *Dunciad*, like the *Tale* and *Gulliver*, envisages cherished ideals not only under threat, but actually collapsing. The absurd moral universes which are locked away in the neat satiric patternings of both Swift and Pope often show 'order' parodying itself in its nasty uncreative antithesis. Each vicious 'anti-system' seems the ironic expression not of an Augustan or-der, but of a 'rage for order' gone sour. Pope's later style (at least) suggests no easy dependence on stabilities visibly and pub-licly achieved, but (like Swift's) highly personal encroachments on chaos.

Pope's way with chaos, however, is to keep his distance. He is temperamentally one of those for whom categorisation and wit offer satisfactions which as such reduce chaos, or keep it at bay : not only aesthetic satisfactions as, once labelled by 'ruling pas-sions', the 'prospect clears', but the comforting moral solidity of a decisive summation, however damaging or pessimistic. A style had to be forged for this, since the enemy to be mastered was subtle and resilient enough to expose the smallest verbal evasion or complacency. Pope's rhetoric suggests not denial but *contain-ment* of powerful and subtle forces, and thrives on an excited decisiveness. If his lapses lead to complacency and patness, his strengths are those of a thrilling and masterful vision, in which delicate perceptions and massive urgencies of feeling marvel-lously cohere. Swift's rhetoric is no less masterful, but its whole nature is to suggest forces which cannot be contained, thus tend-ing away from categorisation. This is often evident at moments of clinching finality, and nowhere more clearly than in the phrase about the 'Fool among Knaves'. The clear and uncompromising lines of the completed epigram imply, as we saw, that 'knaves and fools divide the world'. But the surprise of this implication, its violation of the general run of the preceding argument, and our impulse to discount something (we do not know what, nor how much) because the words are formally spoken by the mad 'author' cause a blur of uncertainty to play over the cheeky patness of the phraseology. Categorisation yields to unresolved doubts. The clinching phrase, subverting its own finality, becomes disorderly and inconclusive. If it is also a self-assertion, buoyant with the satirist's masterful grasp over his material, it is not, in Pope's manner, part of a steady rhetoric of definition, but seems a dazzling momentary victory wrested from chaos. Of course, the playing for sudden dazzling victories, and to some extent the chaos itself, are also a rhetoric, though not (like Pope's) self-announced and openly visible as such. It is important to Pope's manner that he should seem to stand clear-sightedly on top of his material; and essential to Swift's to appear, as the phrase from *Lord Jim* puts it, in the destructive element immersed.

This is evident not merely in the mechanics of verbal style, narrowly conceived. Whole allegorical sequences, whose straightforward message has Swift's full endorsement, dissolve in a self-undercutting inconsistency, or explode in violence. The most unsettling thing about the Academy of Lagado, and especially its School of Political Projectors, is not the allegorical *substance*, but the Swiftian manoeuvres which force change of focus in the midst of an apparent moral certainty. The projectors are associated not only with predictably silly and repugnant programmes, but, by an astonishing redirection in III, 6, also with 'good' schemes ('of teaching Ministers to consult the publick Good', etc.), some of which in turn dissolve into an Ubu-like absurdity (like the zanily beneficent 'cruelty' of eliminating political dissension by a redistribution of the mixed brains of opponents, lobotomised in couples for the purpose), and thence back to crude totalitarian horrors. Or consider this initially straightforward allegory from Section IV of the *Tale*: '. . . whoever went to take him by the Hand in the way of Salutation, *Peter* with much Grace, like a well educated Spaniel, would present them with his *Foot* . . .' This is one of several Swiftian jokes about the papal ceremony, and the passage so far is adequately accounted for in Wotton's gloss, which Swift prints in a note: *'Neither does his arrogant way of requiring men to kiss his Slipper, escape Reflexion'.* The passage then continues : '. . . and if they refused his Civility, then he would raise it as high as their Chops, and give them a damn'd Kick on the Mouth, which hath ever since been call'd a *Salute.'* This development is outside the scope of Wotton's comment, outside the clean outlines of the allegory. It is not, as with the school of projectors, a redirection of the allegory, but an over-spilling. One may argue it into the allegorical scheme by saying (accurately enough) that it represents the authoritarian brutality of the Roman Church. But the real force of the passage is to explode the emphasis away from the domain of allegorical correspondence as such.

The sudden violence is only one of several means of subversion, capping other subversions inherent in the context. Swift's appropriation, here and throughout the *Tale*, of Wotton's hostile exegesis, is not merely a means of explaining the allegory. Various piquancies of attack and of mocking self-exhibition, which lie outside the mere purposes of allegorical translation, are at work : the bravura of exploiting an enemy's attack for the serious illumination of one's own work; the tendency of this trick, while explaining the text, to mock it as requiring such solemn annotation, and from such a source; all the conventional seasoning of mock-scholarship, and so on. These effects combine with the fact that the allegory, like everything else, is spoken by the crazy 'author', and that it is an allegory which parodies allegories. The straightforward import of the story of the three brothers is thus not only undercut, but fragmented by a host of competing energies. Swift's real commitment to the direct import or core (the potted history of the Church) and to the primary satiric implications (the 'Abuses in Religion') becomes complicated by huge and distracting pressures : of self-mockery, of self-concealment, of tortuous and exuberant self-display. To say that this self-mockery simply subverts the allegory, or satirises allegories in general, would be too crude, not only because part of the allegory somehow survives straight, but also because that diffusive spikiness injected by Swift is an attacking thing, *adding* to the satire's total fund of aggression and reinforcing the allegory's attack by that fact. But there is certainly, in practice, an exposure of the limits of the allegory to express all that Swift wants, to a degree which far exceeds the superficial and routine self-deflations of 'self-conscious narrative'.

The centre cannot hold. These unharnessed centrifugal energies of the form, its huge disruptive egotism, mirror the satirist's conscious vision of man's self-absorbed mental restlessness endlessly spiralling away from the rule of sense and virtue. The satirist is reflected in that mirror, 'satirised' beyond all his rhetorical reaches, yet *aptly* implicated, since his attack, so deeply rooted (as we saw) in a *psychological* diagnosis, extends to all mankind. Johnson was to take that vision a step away from moral censure, but largely by means of compassion and a rueful self-tolerance rather than by any radical reappraisal of moral standards. It is only much later that one hears of a 'human condition', psychologically determined, but without God and without attribution of sin. Nevertheless, the vicious spirals, and those related energies (of sudden violence, or of deliquescence) which overspill their official (didactic or discursive) purposes, have the further point in common with black humour and the cult of the 'gratuitous' that their world is no longer secure in its values. When straightforward categorisable vice has dissolved into the unpredictabilities of the *Tale*'s freewheeling madness (the vice/madness equation is commonplace, but the *Tale* is surely something special), the most cherished finalities no longer seem to solve anything. A conclusiveness where, 'Nature well known, no prodigies remain,/Comets are regular, and Wharton plain', yields to conclusions 'where nothing is concluded'. Swift and Johnson clung, of course, with an urgency often authoritarian and sometimes close to despair, to their faith in a traditional morality, to their Anglican piety and Augustan ideals of order. They had no consciously formulated sense that traditional values cannot any longer apply. This partly explains the tendency of Swift's 'gratuitous' effects to dovetail into a moral argument, especially if they are protracted; and it doubtless has something to do with Swift's and Johnson's stylistic attachment to the perspicuous finalities of couplet-rhetoric, Swift's in some of his prose, John-

son's in prose and verse. But Johnson's laboured, eloquent sadness in this mode, and Swift's imprisoning harshness, also tell
their story. So, I believe, does the corresponding tendency of
Swift's prose to kindle to a ferocious vitality in proportion as
(in much of the *Tale*, and in Gulliver's list about war) its subject
grows anarchic. The radical difference from Pope lies here, for
all Swift's conscious closeness to Pope's outlook, and for all the
likelihood that he would have given Breton and the other modern
theorists a most comfortless home in his *Tale*. The matter transcends official themes, and outward feelings, as it transcends mere
couplets. Cultural disorder for cultural disorder, the Academy
of Lagado's relatively lighthearted or low-pitched inconsequence
(not to mention the *Tale*'s seems more disturbing that the *Dunciad*'s Fourth Book, Miltonic Darkness and all. This is perhaps
part of what Leavis meant about Pope being more 'positive'
than Swift, and if so it leads me to an exactly opposite valuation
of the two men. For if Pope's positives, even in defeat (when the
massive heroic ruin of the *Dunciad* proclaims the world that has
been lost), are vividly adequate to the crisis as Pope recreates it
in all brilliant truthfulness, they do not measure up to the evoked
quality of deepest malaise with which Swift *relives* that crisis.
Swift's writing exists at a level where no act of containment, however complete and resourceful, can in the end be validated, its
subject being, not Augustan culture, but the nature of man. And
the matter of Swift's vitality in anarchic contexts is not wholly
accounted for by Leavis's notion (in what is, despite its hostility,
the most acute general discussion of Swift ever written) that Swift
is most creatively alive in 'rejection and negation'. The slow harsh
epigrams negate and reject just as much, and when it comes to
Yahoos having 'all the life', we may wonder whether (as in the
Tale) Swift is not most profoundly in his element not merely as a
scourge of anarchy, but as its *mimic*; participating inwardly, as
well as protesting at those limitless escalations of folly and vice,
those feverish spirals of self-complication. As the satire finally
devolves from the third on to the first person, from world to
gentle reader and back to the satirist, we could do worse than
entertain the thought that Swift, in that place where all the lad-

ders (and the spirals) start, was and sensed that he was, in all rebellious recalcitrance, himself Yahoo.

SOURCE: *Essays in Criticism,* xx (1970) pp. 24–35; 42–56.

NOTES

(7 notes in the original are here omitted.)

1. All quotations of Swift's prose are from Herbert Davis's edition, and of Swift's verse from Harold Williams's; Pope quotations use the Twickenham text and lineation; Johnson quotations are from the Yale Edition, except for *Rasselas,* where R. W. Chapman's text, Oxford, 1927, is used.

2. See Irvin Ehrenpreis, *The Personality of Jonathan Swift* (London, 1958) pp. 43 ff.

3. André Breton, *Anthologie d l'humour noir,* new ed. (Paris, 1966) pp. 25, 17.

4. *Naked Lunch,* Introduction (New York, 1959) p. xxi. I find it hard to accept suggestions that this is not what the passage means.

5. See G. W. Ireland, *Gide* (Edinburgh and London, 1963) pp. 46–50.

6. *Tale of a Tub,* ed. A. C. Guthkelch and D. Nichol Smith, 2nd ed. (Oxford, 1958) p. 123 n.; Ronald Paulson, *Theme and Structure in Swift's Tale of a Tub* (New Haven, 1960) pp. 53 ff.

7. *A Short Character of . . . Thomas Earl of Wharton,* in *The Examiner,* etc., ed. Davis, p. 179.

8. *An American Dream,* ch. II (London, 1965) p. 47; see also *Advertisements for Myself* (London, 1961) pp. 429, 430.

9. *The First Satire of the Second Book of Horace Imitated,* l. 140; *Epilogue to the Satires,* II, 208–9.

SELECT BIBLIOGRAPHY

BIBLIOGRAPHIES

(Studies mentioned in the Introduction are not listed.)

The Cambridge Bibliography of English Literature, volume 5, ed. George Watson (1957) brought Swift studies up to 1954. See also, Louis A. Landa and J. E. Tobin, *Jonathan Swift: A List of Critical Studies from 1895 to 1945* (1945): Claire Lamont's checklist in A. N. Jeffares' *Fair Liberty was all his Cry* (1967) for the years 1945–65; and the continuing bibliography in *Philological Quarterly*. For evaluative comment, Donald H. Berwick's *The Reputation of Jonathan Swift 1781–1882* (1941), Milton Voigt's *Swift and the Twentieth Century* (1964), and A. N. Jeffares' introduction in *Swift: Modern Judgements* (1968).

CRITICAL ESSAYS

John B. Moore, 'The Role of Gulliver', *Modern Philology*, xxv (1928) pp. 469–80. Sees Gulliver as a character: 'as much an individual, almost, as Parson Adams or Squire Western'.

D. Nichol Smith, 'Jonathan Swift: Some Observations', *Essays by Divers Hands*, xiv (1935) pp. 41–8. An elegant discussion of the Yahoos as part of Swift's 'greatest sermon on humility'.

Marjorie Nicolson and Nora M. Mohler, 'The Scientific Background of Swift's "Voyage to Laputa"', *Annals of Science*, ii (1937), reprinted in *Science and Imagination* (Oxford University Press, 1956) and in Jeffares' *Fair Liberty*.

Louis A. Landa, 'Jonathan Swift', *English Institute Essays, 1946* (Columbia University Press, 1947) pp. 20–40. Contra Shaftesbury, the anti-Hobbists, the Stoics and the Deists, Swift sees man as 'a frail and sinful being in need of redemption'.

Ricardo Quintana, 'Situational Satire: A Commentary on the Method of Swift', *University of Toronto Quarterly*, XVII (1948) pp. 130–6. The earliest of that select body of good essays on Swift's technique.

Edward Stone, 'Swift and the Horses: Misanthropy or Comedy?', *Modern Language Quarterly*, x (1949) pp. 367–76. A reminder that Swift's contemporaries thought *Gulliver* comic.

Henry W. Sams, 'Swift's Satire of the Second Person', *ELH*, XXVI (1959) pp. 36–44.

Charles Peake, 'Swift and the Passions', *Modern Language Review*, LV (1960) pp. 169–80. Swift believed in the passions as well as reason but the Horses are not ironical: they humble 'man's pride in his rationality by presenting a genuine *animal rationale*'.

R. S. Crane, 'The Houyhnhnms, the Yahoos, and the History of Ideas', in *Reason and the Imagination*, ed. J. A. Mazzeo (Columbia University Press, 1962) pp. 231–53. An important challenge to the critical methods of Wedel, Ehrenpreis and others.

Irvin Ehrenpreis, 'The Meaning of Gulliver's Last Voyage', *Review of English Literature*, III (1962) pp. 18–38; to some extent a qualification of his earlier view in 'The Origins of *Gulliver's Travels*', *PMLA*, LXXII (1957). But still, 'We fail to approach the Brobdingnagians, and we suppose we can be Houyhnhnms'.

C. J. Rawson, the title essay in *Gulliver and the Gentle Reader: Studies in Swift and our Time* (Routledge, 1973).

Peter Steele, 'Terminal Days among the Houyhnhnms', *Southern Review*, IV (Adelaide, 1971) pp. 227–35. A close study of 'truth' in the final chapter: when Gulliver tries to bring events 'into some kind of moral compass, he is at his most absurd'.

BOOKS AND ANTHOLOGIES

W. B. C. Watkins, *Perilous Balance* (Princeton University Press, 1939).

Martin Price, *Swift's Rhetorical Art* (Yale University Press, 1953).

Robert C. Elliott, *The Power of Satire* (Princeton University Press, 1960), contains a brilliant chapter on Swift's Menippean satire.

Milton P. Foster, ed., *A Casebook on Gulliver among the Houyhn-hnms* (Crowell, New York, 1961), contains the text of Book IV, a good bibliography, and a comprehensive selection of essays up to 1960 including John B. Moore, Edward Stone, R. M. Frye, S. H. Monk, George Sherburn and Charles Peake.

Edward W. Rosenheim, *Swift and the Satirist's Art* (University of Chicago Press, 1963).

Ernest Tuveson, *Swift: A Collection of Critical Essays* (*Twentieth Century Views*, Prentice-Hall, Inc., 1964), includes Quintana on 'Situational Satire', N. O. Brown and Joseph Horrell.

A. Norman Jeffares, *Fair Liberty was all his Cry* (Macmillan, 1967), includes essays by F. R. Leavis, K. M. Williams, Orwell, Yeats, Ehrenpreis's 'Origins', Nicolson and Mohler's 'Scientific Background' and a bibliography, 1945–65, by Claire Lamont.

Brian Vickers, ed., *The World of Jonathan Swift* (Blackwell, 1968), includes mostly new essays. Pat Rogers on 'Swift and the Idea of Authority', Ehrenpreis on 'Swift and the Comedy of Evil', Angus Ross on 'The Social Circumstances of Certain Remote Nations' and Vickers' essay on Swift and More are all important and rigorous.

C. J. Rawson, ed., *Focus: Swift* (Sphere Books 1971), contains a useful essay by Charles Peake, 'The Coherence of *Gulliver's Travels*' and Rawson's 'The Character of Swift's Satire'.

NOTES ON CONTRIBUTORS

The late R. S. CRANE, an editor of *Philological Quarterly*, author of *The Languages of Criticism and the Structure of Poetry* (1953) and *The Idea of the Humanities and Other Essays* (1967), was Distinguished Service Professor at the University of Chicago.

The late HERBERT DAVIS, whose editorial work covered Pope and Congreve in addition to Swift, was Emeritus Professor of Bibliography at Oxford after his retirement in 1960. He taught at many universities including Leeds, Cologne, Toronto and Cornell, and was for ten years President of Smith College.

A. E. DYSON, Senior Lecturer at the University of East Anglia, is co-editor of *The Critical Quarterly*, and author of *The Crazy Fabric* (1967), *The Inimitable Dickens* (1970) and *Between Two Worlds: Aspects of Literary Form* (1971). He also edited the 'Modern Judgements' volume on Dickens and the *Bleak House* volume in this Casebook series, of which he is the General Editor.

SIR CHARLES FIRTH (1857–1936) was for twenty years Regius Professor of Modern History at Oxford. A trustee of the National Portrait Gallery, and a keen lobbyist for English studies at Oxford, he was author of *Oliver Cromwell* (1900), *Cromwell's Army* (1902) and *The Last Years of the Protectorate* (1909).

RICHARD GRAVIL co-edited the Casebook on *Wordsworth: The Prelude* (1972) in this series. He has taught at the University of Victoria, B.C., and was in Tokyo when this book was compiled. He is now with the British Council in Tanzania.

MALCOLM KELSALL is Lecturer in English at the University of Reading. He has published several essays on eighteenth-century literature and the classics, and edited a number of works including

Otway's *Venice Preserved*, Congreve's *Love for Love* (1969) and a new edition of *The Playboy of the Western World*.

PHILIP PINKUS, author of *Grub Street Stripped Bare* (1968), is a Professor of English at the University of British Columbia. He has published essays on the genre of satire as practised by Swift, Mandeville and Peacock, and is now writing a study of the Nature of Satire in Augustan England.

CLAUDE RAWSON is Senior Lecturer in English at the University of Warwick. He is the author of *Fielding* in the Profiles in Literature series, and has published many essays on literature of the eighteenth and twentieth centuries.

The late JOHN F. ROSS, author of *Swift and Defoe: A Study in Relationship* (1941) and editor of the Holt *Gulliver's Travels*, was Professor of English at the University of California, Los Angeles.

THEODORE O. WEDEL, at the time of his death in 1970 was Canon and Warden Emeritus of Washington Cathedral; he was formerly a Professor of English at Yale and Carleton College, and President of the House of Deputies in the Episcopal Church. He wrote several religious works including *The Pulpit Rediscovers Theology*.

KATHLEEN WILLIAMS, a graduate of University College, Swansea, and of Rice University, Texas, is Professor of English at the University of California, Riverside. Her publications include *Spenser's World of Glass: 'The Faerie Queene'* (1966), *Jonathan Swift* in the 'Profiles in Literature Series' (1968) and *Swift: the Critical Heritage* (1970).

W. E. YEOMANS, a published poet, is Associate Professor of English at the University of British Columbia, and author of essays on Yeats and Dylan Thomas.

INDEX